Starting with Tuscany

Giovanna Peel

BIRCH TREE
PUBLISHING

Birch Tree Publishing Ltd.
P.O. Box 761, Station Q, Toronto, Ontario M4T 2N5, Canada
www.birchtreepublishing.com

CANADIAN CATALOGUING IN PUBLICATION DATA
Peel, Giovanna
Starting with Tuscany
ISBN 0-9685862-0-1
1. Italy - Description and Travel.
2. Peel, Giovanna - Journeys - Italy.
3. Peel, Giovanna - Childhood and youth. I. Title
DG738.794.P43A3 1999   945.092   C99-932139-0

Starting with Tuscany is published in paperback edition and is
available from Hushion House Limited, Toronto, Canada

Set in 10pt Garamond ITC Book BT
Cover background from a detail of
'The Agony in the Garden' by Sandro Botticelli.
Cover design and text illustrations by Giovanna Peel.
Printed in Canada by Transcontinental Printing Inc.

To my Mother

Acknowledgements

When one sets out to write a book, three ingredients are required. First, an unshakable if naïve belief that one has the talent and imagination to make the white page come alive with people, situations and landscapes of locale and mind. Second, the stamina and perseverance to spend hours in isolation and doubt in search of the sometime elusive right phrase or proper word. Third, the encouragement of family and friends without which few books would be written. It is to those in the third category that I would like to address my gratitude, for without their support I would have lacked the faith in myself to undertake the task.

     My thanks go to my husband, Adrian Peel, who was on my side from the very beginning. To my son, Timothy Peel, for believing that his mother is worth cultivating—if for no other reason that I am the only one he has. To my editor, Erika Krolman, for her patience and thoroughness. To my friends, Ruth Colombo, Judy Rutledge, Marion Gartler, Luciana Benzi and Olena Kassian for reading the book while it was still in its underwear and telling me that they loved it, whether they did or not. To my publishers at Birch Tree for trusting their reputation on my writing. Last, but not least, to Elizabeth Hill without whose support this book would never have seen the light of day.

G.M.P.
Toronto, 1999

CONTENTS

Benedicta

I feel good enough about myself now to risk a visit to Italy. Probably not much remains of what I remember, but a visit is in order for the purpose of stencilling my childhood memories onto what Italy has become, and to see how they fit.

Italy has changed in thirty years, as I have; and the chemistry between me and the country of my birth must also have mutated. I know it will be a new territory made up of slightly more exotic cuisine, diluted dialects, more crowds, busier people and other international curses.

Even memory is a slippery thing. It changes with time. Facts acquire the outlines of icons, and reality imperceptibly loses its definition and is replaced by poetry. The sharp edges of facts get duller until they become more acceptable and easier to live with. I don't know anymore how much of my history is what I wish it to be. So I am prepared for a series of surprises.

In fact they have already started. I make a call to a Benedictine abbey in the Chianti hills, which surround Siena, and reach a multilingual friar with an unidentifiable accent who asks me to fax my request. A fax machine in an abbey?

"And what about the cells?" I ask.

"Of course," he says, "single or double?"

"Three singles," I say, wondering, had I requested a double, would he have asked me if I was married? And would he then have asked, to a person of which sex? It feels as if I have reached an international hotel adorned by a sprinkling of religion, a sort of Benedictine theme park, equipped with a cloister suitably mediaeval, a covered well at its centre, the miniature replica of which would be available in the gift shop.

But when I ring a pensione in Florence, the lady at the other end of the phone brings me back to the Tuscany I know. Unmannered, unvarnished, brutally direct. When I ask under what category her pensione is listed—one, two or three stars—she answers archly.

"For your information, we have just been awarded the Medal of the Order of Labour for having been in business for fifty years, and should you have any concern for your safety, you ought to know that we are situated one floor above a retired chief of police."

How can you top that? I apologize abjectly and ask her to give me the honour of staying at her pensione. If there is any irony in my tone, she seems blissfully unaware of it.

When I phone Venice, I find impersonal courtesy and a different accent. I almost don't want to go to Venice, but I have promised two friends, a Canadian and an American, neither of whom know Italian, that I would accompany them to Venice since it is a stop de rigueur for visitors on a sampling tour of the country.

Having lived in Italy for the first twenty-seven years of my life, I feel I am an expert on it. The reason I would much rather avoid Venice is that, because of excessive tourism, it seems to have become a kind of Disneyland on the lagoon legitimized by authentic garbage.

I will spend two weeks with my companions, one in Italy, the other in Provence. I already worry about attempting to translate not only the language, but a whole culture to people with little or no previous contact with it. I don't know what Italy has become while I wasn't looking all these years.

A week-long visit to Italy is short, but long enough to fulfil the expectations tourists have of that country, which are that it is romantic and charming. On the other hand, I fear my insight into my native culture and my inability to keep silent about the love-hate relationship that tends to develop between difficult affinities. I don't want to spoil my friends' holiday with memories of a land I left in bitterness and resentment. I now regret my impulsive promise to go with them on a journey that will be of a very personal nature for me, since there will certainly be times I will wish I were alone.

Luckily, I am joining my companions in Provence, an area about which I have no personal feelings, only curiosity. The travel there will cushion me before the plunge into emotional territory. I am not normally one to dive into anything.

The days before I leave are bedlam. I wonder if it must always be so before a departure. Surely some things can be taken care of by someone else. When I look at the number of chores I have to attend before I leave, I feel dizzy—the idea that, if I eliminated half of them, the world would not collapse from neglect doesn't seem to occur to me; I am conceited enough to believe that I am at the centre of a whirlwind of vital last-minute decisions.

And then there are the goodbyes to my husband, my son, my friends. I have read that in certain parts of Indonesia goodbyes do not exist. When the people leaving have finished talking to the ones who are staying, they simply stand up and go. I wish it were so here. I hate the awkwardness of these conversations that cannot light on any meaningful topic because all that has to be said has already been said, and then repeated again and again: feed the dog, water the plants, pay the credit card bills.

Then, suddenly, the announcement that the plane is ready to be loaded comes and one must utter noises of regret.

So here I am in a line of resigned-looking people inching towards the aeroplane which roars menacingly at the end of the covered walk. I never like to look too closely at a plane when I am ready to embark because it always looks awfully patched. Not only am I afraid of flying, but I also find the seats horribly small. It isn't as if the aeroplane designers don't know that the seats are uncomfortable; they must because first class is built for normal people. Perhaps it is assumed that poverty results in smaller bodies. Economy-class folks like me are punished with discomfort for having trespassed onto rich people's body sizes.

The woman next to me holds a sleeping infant. The baby's little hand is moving as if grabbing something, I would like to put my finger into that hand but I am afraid to wake her up. The way I like babies on long plane trips is, like this one, beatifically asleep.

On the screen in front of us a blond who looks as if

she has just stepped out of a girlie magazine tells us that in case of a crash we can wear those dainty little life-savers and blow a little whistle. This reminds me of those short films that used to train children to take refuge under their desks in case of nuclear warfare. Repetition must breed numbness, for the futility of these instructions seems to escape the crew's notice. But maybe it is only a mantra for soothing scared passengers like me.

When we touch down at Orly Airport in Paris, the fact that the passengers cheer makes me feel better about my own relief. I am not the only coward. Aeroplanes might be the fastest way to travel, but I remain a steadfast fan of trains. And it is by train—one of those *Grande Vitesse* metal bullets—that, after a blur from airport to station by taxi that might have been Paris, I embark on a rhythmical journey towards Provence.

It already feels so foreign.

The language rolls along like an unravelling land-scape, and every time they call me *Madame* I feel they are putting me on. None of the North American casualness here, everybody is formal and well dressed. In my denim skirt and T-shirt I feel like a barbarian.

The rapid turnover of passengers speaks of the smallness of the land. The villages, joined by short, narrow roads, zip by the window like a string of postcards. Sometimes the train slackens its headlong rush and I am able to take in some details: the Charcuterie, the Restaurant au Deux Oies, the potted geraniums around the miniature station, the Mesdames and Messieurs, a Quatorze Juillet of bedsheets hanging up to dry. Then, with a lurch forward, the blurring poppy fields again. The roofs here are pointed and of various colours, like in a fairy-tale landscape. They will flatten and become uniformly terracotta red as we approach Italy.

I observe the subtle interactions of passengers. I know

it all so well. I used to travel by train the same way young people in Canada go to a mall. A train is still a meeting place full of allure. The quick glance at the passports presented to the inspector, a look at the magazine being read, the names and addresses dangling from the luggage tags in the overhead storage. And then the snatches of conversation from the compartment next door and the change in dynamic with the disappearance of one passenger and the appearance of another. An intimate living room on wheels.

I am immodestly proud of being able to sustain a conversation in several languages, as if it was a gift of a superior brain, instead of a simple matter of training. Still I like to be able to flex my foreign-language muscles, jumping in and out of different cultures like a Berlitz chameleon.

In moments of quiet I look out the window. I see a cyclist resting on one foot at a crossing, and then look into the interior of a house—the family sitting around the table having a meal—and fantasize about the lives behind those fleeting images. The expressionless familiarity with which people look at the train tells me that while we, the voyagers, peek into a moment in their lives, they see nothing but a ribbon of train windows. Travelling on a train is also seeing without being seen.

I sink into a sensual, rhythmical, way of thinking in tune with the cadence of the movement, a sort of poetic trance. It was always so, my best thoughts spring from motion, be it water, fire or other lullabies.

An African girl of extraordinary beauty opens the compartment door and picks the seat opposite me. Suddenly there is a new energy, both men and women look at her with rude intensity, a mixture of admiration and absorbed wonder. While she is trying to fit her suitcase on the storage shelf above, two gentlemen leap to their feet to help her. She thanks them with a condescending little smile that gives nothing more than is strictly necessary. She sits down languidly, draping herself across the seat as if her bones were made of pure cartilage, crossing her legs with no concern for such trifles as the availability of space. I make myself smaller in my seat to let her expatiate.

She is dressed in casual, expensive nothings that leave her navel peaking out for air, just above her belt. A small circle of blue star-shaped tattoos surrounds her navel. On her ears she has twenty-four—I count them—earrings, and on her nails is laquer the colour of an iridescent snail's track.

The old worship of beauty hits me again, as if thirty years of cultivating common sense had not made a dent in me. The puritanical idea that physical appearance doesn't matter has always been as foreign to us Europeans as the other rather bizarre notion that everybody is beautiful in his own way. Ah, the decency of Canada! It wasn't until I came to Canada that I started to relax about my appearance. But then, when beauty, or a lack of it, lived with us daily, I knew the difference between beautiful and ugly, and never bought that kind of piousness. My mother must have known it too, because in her war against me she made sure that I understood my place in life. My sister Lieta was beautiful and I was not. Period.

But even then not being a beauty never bothered me so much.

That is, not until that bathroom at 35 Fanelli Street. After that I knew that being born beautiful was like having won the lottery without even having bothered to buy the ticket.

I had planned not to start recounting my memories until I got to Italy. It seems premature, in this train speeding towards Provence, to remember an episode of my childhood that has nothing to do with this fugue of manicured Gallic villages. I might have to let memory run its own irrational, inscrutable path. Right now, I feel it wouldn't be right to let this glorious African beauty give the rest of us plain mortals such a gift of herself, without responding with an adequate epiphany of my own.

So I remember Benedicta.

❦

Let me start at the beginning. In Florence, just after the Second World War—the one we usually referred to as "the War"—I was no more than nine or ten when we lived at 31 Fanelli Street, above the wine cellars. The back of the five or six tenements making up our neighbourhood over-looked a row of very large terraces, which were, in effect, the roofs of the wine cellars. We children practically lived on these terraces, because playing there was safer than playing in the street, and it was easy enough for us to lift up the wire fences separating the terraces so that we could happily trespass on one another's territory. All the fences were easy to cross except the one at the very end, its bottom having been nailed firmly to the terrace floor. That one belonged to a family that didn't consider it appropriate to mingle with the rest of us.

We hardly ever saw the members of this family. Signor Falchi, his stick of a wife, and their two cringing children, who attended—incredible oddity—a private school. When we occasionally met them in the street, we ex-changed stingy salutations consisting of no more than a "morning" or "night," which, given the open-theatre character of our neighbourhood, almost amounted to an insult. Rumours that Signor Falchi had been a fascist big-shot in the city of Volterra where he was said to have lived earlier were unverifiable given the impenetrable wall surrounding the family.

Since his apartment was at the end of the row of tenements and his terrace abutted against other buildings, his privacy had to be defended on only one side, the side of us barbarians. He had gone to great lengths to ensure such privacy: he had stretched a piece of canvas over the wire fence, so that we couldn't see into his domain. It was an unnecessary precaution because nobody seemed willing to play with his children or wanted to trespass on his jealously guarded property. There was no doubt in anybody's mind, that Signor Falchi was not quite right in the head. What with dressing him- self with funny baggy pants gathered below the knees and smoking a pipe instead of the regular stinking cigarettes every other man was sucking on, he looked like a caricature of an Englishman.

Like most children my age, I lived in an innocent frenzy of self-absorption, a fact not acceptable to the rest of my family, particularly my mother. I had daily rows with her, probably because I refused to help her with her chores. I say probably, because I don't really recall what the scenes were about, only that my mother, as a final assault, used to tell me that I was as evil as I was ugly.

Not a delicate way of putting it, but then, before the Freudian Era everybody spoke in biblical magniloquence to children. The problem was, I half believed my mother, and I had come to think that I was a plain little rat with the heart of a weasel. In retrospect, I ask myself why I thought so, since when I look at pictures from that time, I see that I was no different from anybody else. We all had that scared look of the underprivileged, rooted in a black-and-white world, against a frozen backdrop of pretentious gentility provided by the photographer. In fact I had a cute, slightly pathetic little face. But family mythologies are hard to crack. Two thousand miles and thirty years haven"t quite succeeded in lifting me out of the box in which I had been placed. Now it doesn't matter that much anymore; getting older has superseded lack of looks as a reason for undesirability. Even then, it didn't matter much because I was recognized as having other qualities. My life strategies had to rest on my brain, such as it was. It was comforting to be in my niche, while the beautiful people outside engaged in their struggle for supremacy. I had declared peace on myself, and beauty elicited only admiration in me. And although I would have welcomed being the gift to the world Benedicta was, I never really knew what I was missing. Not, that is, until that episode on 35 Fanelli Street.

Benedicta was about fourteen years old at the time, just beginning to show signs of becoming a woman but still lingering on the outer edge of childhood. She lived on the top floor at 35 Fanelli Street, just above the Falchis. From our terrace, I could look up and see her at the window, combing her long hair in the sun, like a Rapunzel waiting to be rescued by the knight. Women from the surrounding tenements would stop in mid carpet spanking to look at that ambassador from an alien universe. Benedicta, however, had been spared the usual envy and malevolence bestowed on creatures gran- ted an embarrassment of gifts. She had had the foresight to be stricken with polio as a baby. One arm, withered and useless, hung from her shoulder like a broken wing. Benedicta took care of it though, never letting go of it, always holding it with the other hand, even when she played hopscotch or ran. The result was a tall, willowy figure always wrapped in herself, contained within her own embrace, with her hair billowing around her like a multicoloured flag. Her beauty was exceptional enough for her arm to be of no consequence. All her life Benedicta had walked in a cloud of admiration and compassion, safe in her innocence. When we were in her company, we simply basked in the reflected glory of her extraordinariness, competing with each other in doing things for her.

Being four years older then me, she had never really been my friend but she was gracious and kind to me in a Virgin Mary sort of way, and sometimes she let me carry her bag up to her apartment. She never asked me in, though; in fact I don't think she ever asked anybody in. She was in many ways isolated by her beauty. I don't quite remember all the details of her beauty, I know she had dappled green eyes with high, arched eyebrows, suggestive of Botticelli's Venus. Her nose must have been appropriately small. As for her mouth, I recall her eye teeth being a bit protuberant. We liked to make her laugh to see those little fangs appear. She laughed easily and often; she had no reason not to.

Signor Falchi lived two floors below Benedicta.

Aside from Signor Falchi, none of us in the neighborhood had bathtubs. On a Sunday morning we would take the galvanized zinc tub from the nail on the terrace, fill it with hot water and have what passed for a bath. All the family washed in the same water, starting with the smallest and going up to the biggest. This way the water stayed warm longer. Within the logic of scarcity, it made sense: bigger body, more dirt; smaller body, less dirt. To Signor Falchi, who was said to have been an administrator of sorts in both Africa and America, the idea of surviving without a proper bathtub must have seemed unbearable and barbaric. He created a structure on his terrace that to the rest of us looked pretty outlandish. He had made a cubic bathroom out of a camouflage tent stretched over a frame of scaffolding. The canvas cube wasn't an unpleasant sight and certainly didn't disturb anybody's aesthetic sense, since the terraces were no more than places to hang the washing and a cemetery of toys and discarded ideas.

But it was all strange enough to attract the attention of people who saw, in the desire of a person to have a proper bath, a condemnation of their own ways. Our cleaning habits were not that perfect; therefore, a condemnation was easy to deduce from his behaviour, which was really, no more than slightly odd. And because Signor Falchi was meek, people felt free to speculate at will about his mysterious past without fear of retaliation.

We were all quite curious about his life, but I doubt that anybody was more curious than me. As a child, I was pathologically nosy. Whenever I was taken to a house where I had never been before, I would invariably ask to go to the bathroom to see what I could find there. A thirst for knowledge, one might say. In fact I didn't feel I knew the people we were visiting until I had given their bathroom a thorough search. Once inside that most intimate of people's rooms, I would open all the closets and cupboards, inspect their laundry basket, and sniff their perfumes voluptuously. Knowledge requires investigation.

So, given who I was, I would have no peace until I saw what, beside the bathtub, was inside that cube of canvas on Signor Falchi's terrace. I chose my moment with great care: two o'clock in the afternoon, when the whole of Italy falls into a couple of hours of blissful coma.

I easily lifted the three or four wire fences that separated my terrace from the one adjacent to the one of Signor Falchi. I paused, making sure nobody was seeing me, and then climbed over the last fence, sticking my toes in the mesh of the wires. It was difficult and quite painful, but I made it to the other side. Once on Signor Falchi's terrace, I felt a bit dizzy with danger. If discovered, it wouldn't be Signor Falchi I would fear, but my mother. The strangeness of the place, all neat and perfectly clean, with potted plants in ordered blooms and no scattering of toys, made me wary and uneasy. In two cages yellow and green canaries hopped about, and in another a giant rabbit was living a life of continuous munching.

I gingerly approached a corner of his "bathroom" where the canvas hadn't quite closed properly. At first I saw nothing, because of the strong sunlight outside. Then, gradually, my eyes adjusted to the gloom and I was able to see inside. I expected nothing more than a bathtub in the middle of the room, but I gasped and almost gave my presence away when I saw, not only a bathtub—the tall old fashioned type, poised high on lion's feet—but also sitting regally in the water-filled tub, none other than Benedicta. She was looking at herself with great interest, as if inspecting an unopened package of promising gifts. I was no more than a few feet from her and had almost stopped breathing for fear of being detected. Her eyes were wet, her eyelashes were bunched up into delicate little brushes giving her the tearful appearance of an abandoned orphan. Small foamy clouds caressed her body whenever the water had neglected to reclaim them. She was made of white marble except for her pink nipples floating wetly in and out of the water. Her breasts were heavy and round, the one on the side of her useless arm slightly lower. Her hair was all around her in a cascade of many colours: red, copper, black, brown and orange, in ringlets, waves and falls. There was no end to the abundance of her mane. And at the side of the bathtub washing her, was Signor Falchi. He did so with infinite tenderness and compassion, with the care and concentration of a jeweller setting a precious stone.

They were facing me, both looking at Benedicta, both absorbed in her presence to the point of hypnosis. At first he was partly hidden by the bathtub, and it wasn't until he came around to wash her withered arm that I saw that he was wearing only a pair of oversized underpants, that covered him from his armpits to his knees. His thick glasses were tied around the back of his bald head with a string. His nearsightedness made his eyes look like two capers peering out of two bottle bottoms.

His reverence for the girl gave his movements a mincing, almost effeminate character, a motherhood of sorts. There was in his movements the kind of slow motion veneration found in the rites of an ancient religion.

Signor Falchi was washing every secret of Benedicta's body. Under her armpits, between her every finger, tenderly and carefully behind her ears, each pink toe of her feet. He made her stand up and, holding her wilted arm to keep her from her usual wrapping of herself with her other arm, proceeded to wash her little patch of pubic hair, stopping out of delicacy at the door of her privacy. Then he turned her around and washed her young girl's buttocks, with circular hieratic motions. When he circled around her belly button in a slightly jocose fashion, he blinked his capers at her with a myopic look of childish conspiracy.

Meanwhile, Benedicta followed every movement of his hands with an intent, serene look, turning dutifully one way and the other to comply with his gentle prodding. There was not the least bit of shyness in her demeanour, no uncertainty or reluctance, and no coquetry. Her innocence was matched only by his own. These two creatures were engaged in a rite of such purity and innocence that I felt myself transformed into a voyeur looking into that enclosed bathroom of Eden.

I couldn't have put it into words then, but I was witnessing the spiritual and emotional power of beauty, the delicacy with which we treat a thing of beauty, the ease with which we give into and indulge the perfection of forms.

I left Signor Falchi's tent as if being exiled from a place where I had really never been. I wished I hadn't seen how one's mere presence could elicit a universe of welcomes. I wished I possessed the currency to buy that kind of worship, that maternal tenderness. For the first time in my life, I wished I were beautiful.

The Cannibal

At the station in Avignon I see my two companions, Violet and Clara. I can't miss them since they stand out from the rest of the crowd, one in sober clothes, dark glasses and a squashed hat, as if she were incognito; the other in a kind of discount store pyjama, the colour of a young tomato, and dripping plastic jewellery. To the eyes of a European these are tourist uniforms. If we don't get mugged, it will be a miracle. I am of two minds about meeting them—I was starting to feel European again.

With them is a fast-talking, eager little man, who apparently has been instrumental in finding us a suitable place to stay in the hills of Provence. After the required noises of introduction, he whisks us around to the car rental place where we go through the bureaucratic routine of renting a car, which Clara will drive.

We are to follow Monsieur Corby, who drives speedily around the walls of the city before we are able to take a look at anything. I desperately want to stop for a while in this papal city but the situation is out of my hands. Violet has made all the arrangements for France and takes her seat next to Monsieur Corby, while I ride with Clara in the rented car. I console myself with the promise that I will come back to Avignon later.

We seem to be driving forever—out of Avignon, on to Carpentras, past Île sur Sorgue, through immaculate vineyards, olive groves and huddling villages. I feel a blanket of tiredness fall over me. Though I haven't slept in the past 24 hours, I manage to stay awake because I am fascinated by the countryside—I have never before been in the south of France.

But I must have dozed off, because I open my eyes to an overhead sun flashing through a grove of pine and chestnut trees. We have left the open road and are driving slowly into a private area, with walls on each side of us and a few dogs barking in the thick of the trees—a sure sign of jealously defended privacy.

We stop at the gate and Monsieur Corby jumps out and rings a bell. While he talks into the intercom, he looks at us rather proudly. He has reason: the place looks forbiddingly luxurious. The gate opens and a magnificent villa of flesh-coloured stone appears before us. The eaves are covered in wisteria and the path to the entrance is dotted with bushes of lavender and roses. We pass under a majestic arch in rusticated stone and a breathtaking view of the distant village and Vaucluse valley gradually unfolds through an opening in the oleanders, as if arranged by a florist. I lean forward excitedly at the marvellous sight, hardly believing our good luck. I want to jump out of the car and explore the grounds, but the arch is slowly left behind while we drive past it. I think maybe we are driving around it to reach the garage, but the garage is also passed by without stopping. The car continues along the gravel path until it stops in front of what appears to be a small hut. I think that this must be where we are to put our car and I worry about not being able to drag the little wheels of my suitcase back to the villa because of the gravel path, when I hear Monsieur Corby saying, *"Voilà. Jolie, n'est-ce pas?"*

He is actually pointing at the hut. With a gallant gesture, he stops Violet from taking her suitcase out of his car trunk, to be almost dragged to the floor by the immense weight of it. Unable to lift it, he instead drags it through the door and stops inside, waiting for the rest of us to reach him. I still naïvely think that maybe we will only be putting our suitcases here and then go to the main house.

But this is it. Months of correspondence between Violet and Monsieur Corby have produced one bedroom with two single beds and one double, an entranceway which doubles as a dining room and living room, the dimensions of which add up to those of a large closet, and a kitchen the size of a refrigerator.

"I told you it was going to be pretty," Monsieur Corby says looking around with proprietary pride. My French has become very rusty all of a sudden. I can hardly utter a few polite words of appreciation.

Monsieur Corby wastes little time with pleasantries; in a few seconds he is gone. We are left to explore our domain. We discover that one of the single beds has not been made up; the owners, Madame and Monsieur Reggiani, do not believe in using more linen than necessary. Three people, two to a large bed, one to a small one. We are three large women, each over five feet ten inches tall, and none of us terribly slim. We are all in our fifties with well-entrenched habits accumulated through our respective lifetimes and we are thrown into a place barely large enough for a teenager slumber party.

The quaint Provençal flowery prints called Souleiado are everywhere—on the kitchen table, on the walls, on the bed and on the cover of a honey pot in a dainty basket containing a note of welcome to sunny Provence. Only one of us can be in the kitchen at any one time. Since I have been designated the cook, that "one of us" will be me. I am quite an adaptable sort of person, but nothing in this kitchen is above my waistline. The kitchen counter is so low I have to bend in order to work at it. I feel like Snow White in the house of the seven dwarves.

When we meet the owners in the afternoon, I realize that the smallness of our place is not due to meanness on their part, but to the fact that Madame Reggiani barely comes up to my nipples. The Souleiado prints found everywhere tell me that she is the one who took care of the design, and thus its diminished proportions. She is a gamine ex-dancer from Normandy and makes us feel like a herd of elephants. She gives us a feudal tour of her magnificent house. It is ten times the size of our abode and the kind of house featured in decorating magazines. Madame picks at invisible imperfections, apologizing prettily for such disarray and asking my advice on this or that decorating problem. I don't know how I have given the impression that I could advise her on how to improve on such perfection, but I feel flattered. I reply with a few nonsense and abundant praise.

Her man is a muscular Italian, earthy, uneducated and handsome, who looks as if he still cannot believe that such a chic, delicious woman has deigned to share her life with him. He looks at her adoringly, hardly able to utter a few words of welcome to us. When she leaves the room to attend to her tisane-making, he tells me that she is 15 years older than he is. "But it doesn't matter," he adds.

Everybody is happily drinking wine except me. I have invented a story of an allergy to alcohol to avoid the drinker's usual insistence on offering me a glass. No moral superiority is intended, I happen to hate the taste of alcohol.

I am insecure about my French—not having spoken it for over thirty years—so I speak quickly and nervously, jumping over grammatical traps as if they were rain puddles. Every so often I try to pass the ball of conversation to Violet who is fluent in French, but no help is coming from her. Clara doesn't speak the language at all, so she sits on the sofa between Violet and me, erect and silent. At the end of the evening we return to our hut to sort out the logistics of our sleeping. We have been given extra linen so that we can all sleep in different beds. Violet snores like a Boeing 747, so Clara and I put silicon plugs in our ears. With my ears plugged I feel as if the world is going on without me, an eerie sensation of alienation.

In the morning we begin our travels through the countryside in the rented Peugeot: Clara driving, Violet in the front seat navigating, I in the back giving incorrect supplementary directions. Since the road signs are confusing and intermittent, we get lost often, ending up either in sleepy villages, where nobody seems awake enough to give us directions or in a grey-blue cloud of untended olive trees. We don't mind, though, Provence is an art history book: Manet poppies here, Van Gogh fields there, a rugged Cézanne mountain beyond the horizon.

Almost everybody speaks English or is English, since for well-to-do Britons a place in Provence or Tuscany is de rigeur. I begin to wonder if I shouldn't have gone to Yorkshire instead, where it's probably cheaper and certainly cooler. Tuscany is on my mind because I have decided that my companions should stay in Florence a little longer. I had planned to stay in Florence only one night, just long enough to change trains, but now I am of two minds about it. Florence is at best a difficult city, stony and hot, its character a mixture of proud introversion and excessive virility; it doesn't immediately captivate and makes no concessions to the prettification I find in the quaint villages of Provence. I also feel that I might be a little too emotional about my birthplace to be a proper guide. I feel safe here in Provence, and free to look at the local human fauna and criticize with abandon.

We go around to local miniature markets and buy food from stalls in quantities that must seem outlandish to the locals, since each delicacy is lovingly packaged in tiny parcels fit for our dainty madame Reggiani's aristocratic appetite. Clara has bought enough olives and asparagus to feed us for the week, and I hope that she and Violet will be the ones who eat them because I am not crazy about either.

Practically every market we visit is upholstered in Souleiado prints, or their imitation. I am sure that I shall dream that night of Souleiado prints crawling all over my body.

But during the night, not only do I not dream of Souleiado prints, I also don't sleep at all since it rains with tropical incontinence into our bedroom through three holes in the ceiling. We spend the night moving beds and playing a game of musical pots to collect the rain.

In the morning the garden is shrouded in an opal fog, the village and the hills and even the Reggiani's villa have lost their substance. I am walking in candy floss. Anything farther than the length of my arm is nothing more than a mauve silhouette. The donkey that yesterday had been braying hoarsely from the adjacent property is silent, the magpies and the crows are also silent. There is nobody around, the garden is a green orphan, loaded by this pervasive wetness, so I squish around picking dead geraniums and putting them in a wheelbarrow. I shake reclining hydrangea to set them upright again, indulging in my new rôle as gardener.

I trespass onto the property next door, feeling hidden by the fog, and survey a display of statues of baby Eros half hidden in niches carved in rusticated walls. I play chatelaine in this aesthetically literate, bourgeois, enclosed paradise—so lacquered, so refined, so different from the arrogant directness of Tuscany. I should stay here and forget about Florence.

We spend the rest of the day waiting for the sun to keep its promise, but the fog remains earthbound until evening, when the sky acquires a phosphorescent unearthly blueness.

The next morning we prepare to make our way to Carcassonne for the day. I have been told that it is worth a visit, so I have asked Madame Reggiani to supply us with a train schedule. We arrive by car in Avignon, and again I fail to see this city this time because we are preoccupied—all our attention is on trying to find a parking space for the car in the limited amount of time we have. We make to the station just in time. I ask somebody where the train for Carcassonne is and a gesture indicates the train just in front of us. We jump in and hunker down with a sight of relief. We sit and wait for the train to leave. Almost immediately we notice that the coach in front of ours is leaving, while we remain in the station. We think that maybe there are some manoeuvres the train has to undertake before we leave and so don't worry much, but after fifteen minutes we become suspicious and ask where our train is going. *"Mais à Marseille, Madame"* is the answer. "And where is the train for Carcassonne?" I ask. Apparently, it was the front half of the train, the one we saw departing 15 minutes ago and which is now happily running towards Carcassonne. We make it just in time to jump from the train before we are taken to Marseille.

We never saw Carcassonne. I convince myself that maybe it wasn't worth seeing. We decide to go back to our hut in the hills, though not before we have a consolatory meal at one of the restaurants in the city. After eating, it is almost time to leave because Clara, who has a problem with her eyes, cannot drive in the twilight, and the drive to our place is long.

On our way back we discover a Souleiado fabric supermarket. I am not joking here. There it is, a Wal-Mart of tiny prints, so thoroughly Provençal. We descend into a mini orgy of buying, which I feel is a way of compensating for having failed to see Carcassonne. I, as cheap as ever, spend all of 35 dollars.

Time is closing in on us, the week is nearly over. When it is almost time to leave, I remain behind while Violet and Clara go out for a last look at Provence. I intend to clean the hut and do some washing. The truth is I need some time to be alone. I want to paint some flowers, sit silently on the edge of the hill overlooking the village, which has remained unnamed, and write a few notes about my experience. I am not feeling too secure about Italy yet, I feel like procrastinating. I continue to check that I haven't made any scheduling mistakes and plan to call Venice one last time to make certain of our timing.

I try to read a book but I am distracted by Monsieur Reggiani who comes to repair the roof and enrich me with the story of his life. He also asks about my life in Canada. I tell him about my husband and my son, but he is better at telling than listening. He seems to have a bad case of short attention span. I start talking to him and end up addressing the geraniums. It's all right because I don't really want to talk about myself to this Lady Chatterley's lover.

Talking about my son, I am suddenly taken by a strong urge to call him, back in Canada. I leave the gentleman to his roof and walk down the road to a public phone. The perversity of the telephone system is hard to describe, but I finally get through and hear my son's young voice on the other end of the wire. His excitement at hearing me gives the day a domestic, familiar tone; his problems with girlfriends, betrayals of friends and financial catastrophes makes me feel right at home.

I realize how much I miss him. Not that I don't argue with him when I am at home. He is in a spurty growth stage where parts of him are well into adulthood, while other parts lag behind, waiting for a chance to catch up. But like my husband, he has a gentle feminine side. This is reassuring to me, for I grew up with no men and with fierce women whose feminine side was hard to find.

I realize how stressful travelling is, even in the best of conditions.

In a reflective mood I sit by the side of the road and make a mental catalogue of my state of mind.

I miss pristine, impersonal and inexpensive Canada, capable of absorbing the four corners of the world, at the same time failing to give us immigrants an identity that none of us is equipped to find for ourselves. In such a vast land people end up huddling in their own cultural niche, as if where we are didn't matter. Canada is perceived by us immigrants as a place where one lives and works, not a culture to belong to. Not at all a bad situation.

I remember when I arrived from Italy with two suitcases and a less than scant knowledge of English, which was more than the rest of the immigrants had. I had travelled on an creaky boat, so moribund that a year later it was retired. I had been with southern Italians, some of whom had never been at sea before and stayed in bed for most of the crossing, fearful that if they got up they might drown. Their children had vomited throughout the whole two weeks at sea, which had been angry all the way from Gibraltar to Halifax.

April 15 to us Italians already means late spring. That's when we arrived in Halifax to find the new Promised Land in the grip of one of the worst snowstorms to hit that city in years. I remember looking down from the side of the ship and seeing the dock workers flitting around like black rodents against the blinding whiteness of the snow. Since we were all in light clothes, the authorities had us run down the gangway so that we would not get sick from the cold. We huddled in the middle of what looked like an empty hangar waiting for our destiny, failing to under-stand what was asked of us. I had become the wretched group leader because I possessed a university degree and could speak some English. They called me "Professor" and expected me to explain to them what we were seeing. While waiting for the bureaucracy to take its course, I don't remember how many telegrams I ended up by writing, to reassure whomever was left in the Old Country that they had arrived safely.

I didn't send a telegram to my sister Lieta in Florence, thinking I would wait until I had some good news to send. The way it looked in that hangar full of lost people, I didn't feel I could trust myself to say anything positive yet. When one leaves defiantly, it had better be for a better life; otherwise one is submerged in "I told you so's."

It seemed an eternity before the authorities checked all our documents. I was the last to be processed since I had been helping everyone else go through the formalities.   I remember a customs officer, a cheery fellow, looking back at me while a colleague asked him how many of us were left.

"Just one," he said, winking at me.   "One more of them Pasta people."

I looked back to see who they were talking about, but there was nobody behind me.

I had entered a new country, and a new definition.

❦

Back in the hut I try to restore a semblance of order. When I make my bed, an immense scorpion jumps out of the blankets, its lethal tail high up above itself, repulsive and menacing.   I shudder at the thought that it has been sharing my bed for over a week.   It runs too fast for me to kill it and takes shelter under Clara's bed.   I mention it to Monsieur Reggiani, who is still up on the roof.

"Yes," he says, "we have all kinds of animals here. Scorpions, foxes, hares, wasps, God knows how busy I am trying to keep them out of the way.   And then this roof, do you know how much its repair will cost me?"

I don't want to know.   I want him to repair the roof and kill the scorpion, not necessarily in that order.   His plea for sympathy strikes no chord in me; I am rather irritated that he has managed to focus my attention on his problems rather than attending to mine.   Besides, I know I will find it hard to sleep tonight with a scorpion at large, a small gesture toward a safari to kill it would have been appreciated.   When Clara and Violet come back from their drive, I don't mention the scorpion.   Why bother their sleep?

The week has gone faster than I'd thought it would. We are almost ready to leave.   The suitcases are packed and a note of thanks, together with a small colander we have bought at an open market, has been left on the table, together with our payment, as a token of our appreciation for Madame and Monsieur Reggiani's hospitality. When I go to give the key of our hut to Monsieur Reggiani, he asks me with some urgency if I think he should plant more wisteria around the main living room window or, better yet, forsythia bushes on each side. He runs about looking for a pad for me to make a sketch of the facade with alternative bushes. I have only a few minutes to spare and ask myself why hasn't he asked me earlier, when I would have had the time to think about his design problems. Suddenly I know the wisteria and the forsythia are not the issue. He is anxious about something else, but I am not sure what. I think he feels insecure about Madame Reggiani, but doesn't know how to speak about it. I almost feel like writing a few words of encouragement, but possibly he wouldn't understand what I am on about. I want to be kind to him, but time is running out and I must go.

I see Madame Reggiani's elegant silhouette against the lit interior of her beautiful home. I approach to say goodbye. She keeps my proffered hand longer than necessary. Here, too, I feel something is being communicated, but the shortness of our stay doesn't allow for the confidences that seem to skim just below the surface. After a moment of hesitation I embrace her. She feels as insubstantial as a chihuahua.

I walk back to the hut where my companions are all set to go. I look around for the scorpion. I want to show it to Violet and Clara so that they can, in retrospect, be properly horrified. But the hut is empty and clean. It has already closed over our presence there like water over a sinking stone.

We enter the car and pass the gate with a great show of fluttering hands and au revoir. Madame and Monsieur are left behind, in their ridiculous disparity of sizes, to become smaller and smaller until they melt into the background of their grand garden.

Finally I will be able to see Avignon, if we do not get lost.

We get lost.

Violet has made some mistake with the train schedule, so we arrive with barely half an hour to spare, not enough to visit the papal palaces or the city. I leave the station on my own for a few minutes to survey the Renaissance walls, which might have seemed massive at the time they were built but now are upstaged by the surrounding buildings. Still, a city within a belt of walls feels defined and protective of its citizens; what lies outside the walls seems blurred and vague. Against one of the entrance portals, two young Gypsies play a barrel organ. Their little mongrel dog has been trained to assume a begging position by standing on its hind legs and raising its front paws. A few people stop and drop a few francs in the hat in front of the dog as the two boys grind away at their antique instrument and the little dog gets tired. Its legs start to shake, but the boys keep propping it up. I want to go and stroke the tired little animal, but there is no time, I have to leave. When I enter the station with a crowd of other passengers, I give a last look at the little dog. It is still there, obedient, shaking more strongly now.

The Grande Vitesse train is hurtling towards Nice. The Mediterranean Sea on our right is a cobalt expanse dotted with small bursts of white around the rocks just off the coast. In the distance sails bob like surfing seagulls. The edge of the continent is embroidered with small beaches, level crossings, grand little hotels and secluded coves in the sun with nude bathers waving happily at the train. The giant striped umbrellas cover nobody; word that the sun is not good for one's health has not reached these shores yet.

The sign "Nice" on the station quay hits us at the same time as a strong smell of iodine typical of the sea air. There are sailors in nineteenth-century children's clothes, laughter and wolf whistles at the beauties in minimal clothes and vendors of straw trinkets all over the station. Mini one-man bazaars on rickety wheels and retired old folks leaning on canes. Nice is the Florida of Europe.

I leave my two companions on a seat and go to the information desk to inquire about a hotel. I ask for three single rooms; after the hut in Provence we need some individual spaces. I practically salivate at the thought of a room to myself.

We are able to find a small hotel on a relatively quiet street. It has the endearingly atrocious wallpaper that the French love to plaster on all their walls and ceilings. I lie in bed reeling a bit from the train and look up to masses of faded printed roses so noisy I feel unable to rest unless I switch off the light. The room is darkened by the wooden Venetian blinds. But the bustle from the main road reaches me even in this quiet street. I am excited about the new city so I have a quick shower and go down to the tiny lobby to wait for Clara and Violet. The concierge, a man in his fifties with a Stalin moustache, is busy making espresso coffee on his wheezing machine and trying to keep his eyes on the television. When I ask him what the distant noise is about, he tells me that Nice is in the throes of jubilation over having won a soccer match, thus climbing from series C to series B. The match was against the Italians just across the border, twenty miles from here. He describes the "Macaroni" with such extravagant contempt that I can only laugh. I never tell him I am

Italian since I like the fellow. Such belief in one's own superiority deserves respect and admiration—I have never managed more than a mild embarrassment at being Italian.

"Next week, we play against the Germans," he says, and I can see that he is ready to tell me what he thinks of them. That's the Europe I remember, everyone despising everyone else. I would like to stay longer and revel in this good old-fashioned jingoism but I want to see the city, so I leave him welcoming some Genoese with the warmest of smiles. Clara and Violet want to go to the train station to change some money, but I know that the area around European train stations is never pleasant. It's where the prostitutes ply their trade and their pimps prowl. Besides, I am sure we will find money-changers throughout the main streets of the city. I want to follow my instinct and wander into smaller side streets, away from the cheering crowd.

So, in spite of my advice, we part. They towards the station, I in the direction of shops and cafes. Almost immediately I am immersed in a silent, wonderful pedestrian-only maze of elegant shops and wedding cake architecture. The apartments above the shops have balconies of wrought iron painted in all the colours of the ice cream cones sold below. The effect is that of a resort town with flair, the cafes and restaurants spilling onto the streets one next to the other in a single *al fresco* dining room. Somewhere past the tall buildings, out of sight, one senses the Mediterranean with its salty breath, but here the city is intimate, rococo, emblazoned in geraniums and oleanders, and comfortably still. The evening is cool, and for the first time since I left home, I feel as I should when travelling: free, uncommitted, open to new experiences and basking in unstructured time.

After a while, I walk reluctantly back to the hotel to share my experience of this beautiful city with my companions. Violet is somewhere inside but I meet Clara at the entrance door in a state of distress. I ask her what has happened but she doesn't seem to be able to talk about it until we find a place where she can have a glass of wine. She explains that the area around the station was taken over by throngs of people riotously celebrating the soccer victory. She and Violet found themselves surrounded by half-drunken men bumping into them at every step.

I reflect wistfully how the wrong turn in the road can lead to a completely different experience. Violet is in her room phoning her husband in Canada to remind him that today is their wedding anniversary. He has agreed to pay for our dinner as a way of atoning for his forgetfulness. I feel the tension in both of my companions and try to restore in them some kind of enthusiasm for the experience at hand. When they calm down, I take them to the place I had explored earlier, where we stroll in quietness, looking for a suitable restaurant. We find one and we take seats in the middle of the street under blue-and-coral-striped umbrella. We order an immense bouillabaisse. Slowly the domestic magic of the continuous street theatre relaxes my companions and we end the evening laughing at some of my stories. Violet pays the enormous bill. Tomorrow we leave for Italy.

In the train again. The landscape changes noticeably. After the frontier, the mountains to my left become steeper, the roofs flatter, the villages older and a little shabbier, and my response to it is suddenly more personal, more emotional. At a stop in a village, our train is parked in front of a church where a wedding is underway. While my companions sleep, I wander in the corridor, open a window over the Italian countryside and, without thinking, wave at the members of the wedding party posing for a photograph. They are all ready with their smiles plastered on their faces and dressed in their Sunday best, but when I wave they are transformed into a great mass of hands waving at me. The dressed-up children run towards me to yell *Ciao, Ciao,* and the mothers run after them smiling at me, trying to pull them back onto the church steps for the wedding photo.

To my horror, I feel the sting of tears in my eyes. If this is a taste of reactions to come, I am in trouble. Luckily Violet and Clara are asleep, unaware of my sentimentality. I have always regarded sentimentality as the most kitschy of emotions, and I am determined not to give in to tears. I haven't cried since the death of my sister, twenty years ago, and I am not going to start now over some children waving their hands at me.

The light has changed and keeps changing. The sun's rays seem stronger, the colours more bleached, almost absorbed by the sunlight. The villages seem to be asleep and solitary, the fishing boats still, resting upside down on miniature beaches. The coast here is steep and dangerous, the houses are grafted onto the rock like stone birds of prey, the road is a ribbon blasted out of a stingy mountain. Nature is not as smiling and tamed as in Provence. Although Italy has been inhabited for millennia, the land has never been an easy one. The mountains and the sea have been fighting for space and crushing against each other; the frequent earthquakes and the volcanoes are the outcome of their struggle.

I have decided that it would be a good idea to stop in Pisa for a couple of hours, to give my companions a chance to see the cathedral and the leaning tower. At the tiny station we deposit our luggage, and take a city bus to the main square.

It is the end of May and the square is full of tourists

reclining on the grass under the scant shade afforded by the buildings. There are no trees in the square, only those solitary mediaeval structures that are incongruous, almost metaphysical, in their unrelatedness. On one side of this strange square stands an enormous wall as blank and primitive as the bogus façades that are used to train firemen. It is the perimeter of the Campo Santo, the monumental cemetery. My companions look disappointed and perplexed so I leave them in the shade of the baptistery and go inside the cemetery. I do not really know why, I never visit cemeteries, even if they are monumental. This is not monumental. I find its appearance rather derelict, the white statuary is, after so many centuries, meaningless. There are nothing but weeds in the large cloister and the hot southern breeze adds a note of forlorn melancholy to these tombs of long-forgotten people. I don't feel its sacredness, only its loneliness. I walk around a bit, to get the value of the entrance fee, but I don't want to be here. I look vacantly at the monumental tomb of the mathematician Fibonacci, engage in the mandatory musing on the ephemerality of life and join my companions outside. We go together to a dirty little cafe to have an ice cream.

We want to leave this mediocre little city as soon as the first train can take us. At the station we wait briefly for a local, clanky, slow train that delivers us to Florence's ungainly station late in the afternoon.

❦

The taxi we hail to take us to our pensione, negotiates its way through streets so narrow the pedestrians have to squeeze against the walls to let us pass. But the taxi never honks and the pedestrians never curse. The driver is silent and calm. Could it be that in the thirty years I wasn't looking the Italians have gone polite on me? It is possible, since the one thing I know about my country-men is that they never do what one expects.

The pensione is just behind the Arno River in a building that bears the typically forbidding character of this austere, stony city. We ring the bell at a portal that could easily accommodate a bus. A little door cut in the bigger door opens mechanically and we enter a vast echoing entrance with no lights. I push a button and the lights come on. I know from past experience that the light is on a timer and we must reach the elevator door before we are plunged into darkness. The lighting device does not account for heavy suitcases and ignorance of the habitat. It has its own diabolical pace and punishes lingering and indecision with a slap of blackness. We don't make it to the elevator in time. We have lost Violet and her suitcase halfway through the entrance. I call to Violet to stop and I blindly retrace my steps to the button that glows in the darkness.

Finally, we are all squeezed into an elevator in which a notice says quite clearly that it cannot carry more than three passengers at a time. The size of each of us is at least twice that of any self-respecting Italian, but I take heart in the fact that the elevator is a cage rising in the centre-well between the stairs; should it stop in midair we can always yell at the passersby for help. In our slow, rickety rise we notice the polished brass sign on the retired chief of police's apartment door.

When we arrive at the fifth floor, the pensione's entrance door opens as if by magic, and Signora Norma appears in front of us and kisses each of us on both cheeks. I don't know what to think, since she was so difficult when I spoke to her on the phone from Canada. But here she is, happy to see us, saluting us as if we were family. She inquires about our trip and looks my two companions up and down, with an assessing eye that shows practice, warmth and shrewdness—not necessarily contradictory qualities. While she is talking to us, she is also busy pawing a beautiful young violinist from France on his way out, saying that at her age she is permitted to like gorgeous men unabashedly, given the regrettable fact that her husband is not well, poor soul. This mixture of the pious and the maternally lewd pleases me enormously. I feel in known territory. That's how I remember my Italians: crazy.

Signora Norma shows us her pensione with pride. Our bedroom is vast, clean and charmless, but it promises to be silent, since the windows open on an inner courtyard better described as a light-well.

"Didn't I tell you not to worry about my pensione?" Signora Norma says while opening closets and fluffing pillows.

Indeed, the place has the comforting large proportions the three of us have been missing since leaving Canada. Our room has an en suite washroom, but Signora Norma shows us another one down the hall. "Just in case you need a bit more privacy," she says. When she shows us the dining room where we are to have our breakfast, we step right into history. The room is magnificent, monumental and unadorned; it has that Tuscan essentiality that I remember so well. My Tuscany, often artistic, never merely aesthetic.

She explains to me later that the building is protected by the city's historical heritage board and cannot be changed. She is busy ironing the bedsheets in a little loggia overlooking the tiled roofs of other establishments, their windows festooned with drying laundry. I feel very happy. I love the place for its grand, unpretentious, scrupulously clean, unpretty shabbiness. I don't even mind its zigzagging, indecipherable topography due to a series of architectural afterthoughts added through the centuries.

❦

We descend upon Florence with the excitement of children entering an amusement park. This is not a new city for me, but being with my companions makes me feel like a tourist. I am almost beginning to speak Italian with an accent. Memories can come later, when I am in a more reflective mood.

Still, I know where to go and how to search for certain intimate areas of historical meaning, how to bargain in the market, what to order in a restaurant and what shopping areas to avoid because they are too expensive. It is such an odd feeling, a kind of new déja vu. The changes are not apparent in the late evening, but maybe tomorrow in the light of day I will be able to discern some. Right now though, the city is warm and, strange—her stone buildings softened by the darkness. The traffic has been banned from the historic centre and new high-intensity lights have been installed at the level of the roof eaves. The result is well-diffused lighting that glides down the facades of the Renaissance buildings, lending drama to the strong architectural details. There is no noise except that of human steps and the steady rolling of conversation; every now and then laughter or the crying of a baby punctuates the steady hum.

All the very well-known monuments are there in casual abundance, mingling with the people as if almost one of us: Michelangelo's youthful *David*, as ill proportioned as ever, Verrocchio's *David*, a truly beautiful sculpture ignored by most tourists, Cellini's *Perseus* standing under the Loggia of the Lanzi, which is falling apart because of the pollution caused by car emissions.

Signora Norma has given us the name of a trattoria where the food is supposed to be good and the prices not outrageous. We find it at the end of our street and sit in a little upper room on long benches, beside a small window carved into a wall so thick it gives the impression that the window is inside a closet. No tablecloth or flowers are on the table, and the menu is recited in broken Italian by the waitress. Most waitresses are foreign students, parked in Florence for the duration of the international studies school term. A kind of prolonged economy-class Grand Tour. We wait the customary long time that it takes for the cook to prepare what is called an "espresso" meal, which means it is cooked after it is ordered. The notion of "pre-prepared food" is just not acceptable to pernickety Italians.

I have ordered my favourites of old: a dish of tripe, a bread and black cabbage soup called *ribollita* thick enough to be eaten with a fork. As we wait, the room slowly fills up with regulars, workers from nearby work-shops whose wives are on holiday, students with enough money to eat out. The room is made of stone and stucco, the floor of polished bricks. The wood of the tables is so old it looks fossilized.

Even though my Italian is a little stilted I feel at home and I banter a bit with the owner about the food and the political minestrone that has always been part of the Italian scene. His answers are irreverent and dotted with mild sexual references to the wives and mothers of choice politicians, but the old lewd innuendos have lost their sting on me, and I feel I can answer in kind since I am accorded a certain amount of licence on account of my middle age. I don't feel threatened anymore and I am relaxed about Italian men. They have lost their power to shock me, and I have lost my power to entice them. I could almost love them again.

In the morning, even before the markets are fully awake, we stroll about while it is still cool, and I notice the changes. Some of the old statuary are under a layer of scaffolding, so is the facade of the great cathedral. In fact almost all the great monuments are under a veil; the city's marble is being eaten by a cancer caused by the pollution from cars. The cost to the municipality of repairing the monuments is staggering. Added taxes are levied on tourists, making the city very expensive to visit. But the tourists keep coming and the level of pollution remains unmanageable; each year sixty million visitors come to the Italian peninsula, doubling the population.

The Straw Market, a lovely renaissance loggia where straw goods were sold at one time, is still there and the boar fountain with its snout polished by thousands of hands still spurts a live trickle of water into thirsty mouths. Now, the Nigerians and Senegalese use the space to sell their African wares on spread-out blankets. Because most of them have no permits, they have to keep one step ahead of the police. The economic niches once occupied by the southerner are now being filled by people from developing countries. I see Filipino girls pushing children in strollers, and I have been told that a glut of Chinese restaurants have sprouted up around the city, patronized mainly by tourists in search of a bargain. In the main market, in San Lorenzo Square, the stalls are still there, a place of vociferous bargains and copies of Florentine designs made in the Orient.

But when I walk on the other side of the river, I see the old workshops where most of the Florentine wares are produced and exported to the luxury markets of the world. The artisans are in a class of their own. Intensely proud of their ability, and justifiably so, they are at same time a blasphemous, arrogant lot who have traditionally commanded so much respect that they are addressed as

"Maestro" by the rest of us common mortals. They carve wooden picture frames, make copper chandeliers, inlay coloured marble, paint parchment, beat silver, tan leather and make endless copies of originals from the past. As a child I loved to stand by the doors of the workshops looking at the ease with which an expert could create what in my hands turned out to be so difficult. The men used to throw me scraps of left-over leather or parchment, which I used to make something for my dolls.

I do not yet go to the place where I was born, I need to be alone for that. Going around the city with my two companions is not always easy. I am continuously torn between pride and embarrassment. I feel as if I am showing off a beloved but enfeebled parent. In an effort to be objective and non-nationalistic, I have emphasized the negative and neglected the positive—a preemptive attempt to dissociate myself from eventual embarrassments. I have always been proud of my lack of national pride. I find nationalism silly at best, at worst dangerous. But the Italians are behaving with grace and kindness, and I find myself trying to suppress a feeling of pride that throws me off balance. I am in a dilemma. If I like the Italians too much, I have wasted thirty years of my life in self-imposed exile; if I dislike them the way I did when I left, I will forever hate a part of myself. I cannot be expected to be neutral.

I attempt to take Clara and Violet to the unglamorous part of the city where the labourers live. It is still Florence, only a little older, a little crumblier, with streets that are tiny and crooked, the shops no more seductive than greengrocers and bakeries. There are lots of bicycles and scooters, and those miniature Fiats that appear to be made of parts left over from better cars. But my companions are not interested; used to driving cars, they find walking any distance uncomfortable, and are distracted by hunger. But eating in restaurants is not an Italian tradition, and in this part of town the women still prepare the meals three times a day, which is why the country is encumbered by four rush hours—one in the morning, two for lunch and one in the evening. After walking on for a while and feeling as though I have let them down, I finally surrender and take the two women back to the bright lights and elegant international crowd of the city centre. We are too tired to look for an inexpensive restaurant, so we stumble into one with subdued lights and starched immaculate tablecloths. When I see the waiter, dressed like a navy officer, serving food in that bizarre way, with one spoon below and another above the meat, as if to stop the meat from escaping, I know I am going to pay too much. I hate to overspend on food since, although I am a skilful enough cook to know good food from bad, I cannot call myself a gourmet. I tend to like just about anything that's put in front of me as long as it doesn't bleed. The sight of rare beef makes me sick. Also peanut butter. I can't stand anything that sticks to my palate because it reminds me of Communion wafers.

In Europe food is extraordinarily expensive and, should a restaurant's price be unusually moderate, mysterious charges like "Cover" or "Service" appear on the bill to make up for its timidity. I am on a one-hundred-dollar-a-day budget so I keep filling myself up with affordable bread.

When we finish our dinner, Clara and I feel like walking before retiring so we let Violet go to the pensione by herself. I walk with Clara down to the Academy of Fine Arts where I went to school, but when we arrive the school is dark. It looks small and dilapidated, the wear and tear of generations of students having taken their toll. We are unable to see the beauty of the inner loggia with its gypsum reproductions of classical statuary, as the academy is closed for the night. We walk among groups of students who are talking sedately about young-people's business, but nobody looks at us. It is almost midnight but there are a lot of people around and, despite Signora Norma's dire warning about marauding muggers, we feel safe and adventurous.

Upon our return to the pensione we find Signora Norma greatly upset. When we emerge from the elevator, she is there waiting for us and marches us indoors with a look that promises nothing pleasant. It seems that Violet had picked up a man on her way home, taken him upstairs, where he proceeded to belittle Signora Norma's establishment in front of her, and then went out again, with the man. I know from experience how our hostess takes any criticism about her pensione, but it seems that this is not the point. The point is that Violet has put herself in danger by going out with a man she doesn't know personally, but who is apparently well known in the neighbourhood as a sleaze. We keep trying to suggest that Violet is not a fool and must have met somebody she knew, but Signora Norma, who doesn't waste any time with verbal niceties, disagrees with us vehemently.

"Does your friend think that a man meets her and falls in love with her on the spot?" she asks and then proceeds to make comments on Violet's appearance and age that are too crude for me to translate for Clara, who by now is almost hysterical with worry. She insists that we go out and tour the local cafes to try to find Violet. It's hard for me to believe that Violet could have fallen for the sort of Italian man who believes that foreign women know nothing about romance until they taste the Latin brand. I firmly refuse to go and search for Violet, who is about sixty years old and so should be allowed to have a tryst if she desires one. I proceed to prepare myself for bed, but Clara is too upset and paces the room worrying about

Violet.

After about an hour, Violet returns. She is flushed and a bit out of breath. I tell her of our concern about her safety but she is not in the mood to talk about it. Meanwhile Clara, who until now was so upset about our friend's foray into the Florentine night, disappears into the washroom. She never talks to Violet about her apprehension, leaving me puzzled over her peculiar silence. A while later Violet feels confident enough to tell us how she thought it was a good idea to go out with the gentleman. He spoke French and was helpful in finding the pensione for her, since she was lost.

"But," she says, "he was not very nice in the end."

How he was not very nice is not mentioned. I do not press for an explanation, for it seems indiscreet, and I bid her goodnight.

This afternoon we will be leaving Florence. In the morning we go into the beautiful breakfast room to serve ourselves croissants from large willow baskets on the side table and coffee from the espresso machine. While we are eating, Signora Norma comes in to put some flowers on the tables. She speaks about her husband's heart condition and weeps openly. He has had two bypass operations and doesn't seem to have very long to live. I have spoken to her husband, an urbane gentle man with a strong Austrian accent, who loves art, particularly paintings. They have been married for over fifty years and Signora Norma for all her fierceness seems to be quite capable of deep, tender feelings. She keeps talking and tending to her flowers while tears roll down her nose. I quietly translate her words to my companions. I extend a few useless words of sympathy, but it is difficult to reach her in the fortress of her sorrow.

Signora Norma leaves the room still weeping. We are

about to leave when she comes back with a good-bye present of a bottle of wine for each of my companions. None for me because she knows that I don't drink wine.

I need a little time on my own before I leave Florence so I leave my companions to their own devices and walk briskly over the Ponte Vecchio to the other side of the Arno River. I know what I am looking for, but I am not sure I can find it. It is an area of small workshops whose owners are poorer than the artisans. Generic workers, who devote part of their house to a tiny industry. They are usually women who must work, but have to stay home to take care of their children. These workshops are not at street level, but three or four floors up in buildings so decrepit that they have acquired the picturesque appearance of an opera backdrop.

I am looking for the place where my mother's dressmaker lived. I remember the street but not the number. I go from one oversized entrance to the next, trying to find the one that fits my memory of it. Finally I choose one at random because it has a friendly dog roaming around, unmuzzled, and a little stone seat, carved into the thickness of the wall. It might well be it, the smell of basil and rosemary is there as it was then, and the voices of children and their mothers echoing from the landings above, gives the place the domestic background noise of my younger days. It is my first intimate moment since I have come to Italy. I let my memory take over; I have five hours before the train is to depart for Siena.

❦

The season was not established yet, as it is now at the end of May. It was early spring. I hate that time of the year. I hated it even then. Days were a string of broken promises, the sun always cheating. Dressed in the light clothes my mother insisted it was time to wear, the cold wind coming down from the mountain behind Fiesole, the Roman village that was once Florence, made me shiver.

Still one couldn't help but notice the swallows in the sky, back from Africa, and a few timid geraniums beginning to soften the sills of Florence.

With the swallows came my mother's visit to the dressmaker. She and my sister had new summer clothes made at this time of the year, which meant endless fittings. I was spared the torture because, being the youngest, I was always given my sister's discarded dresses.

Since I was five years old, too young to be left home alone, that spring morning my mother and I started out early, with bundles of fabric and the address of a new dressmaker somebody had recommended as being not only very capable but also recently widowed and therefore in need of new clients.

We walked briskly—my mother always walked briskly—past the gold merchants on the old bridge, past the silk-cord makers and the frame gilders, towards this old musty area on the left side of the river.

We walked along one of these narrow streets to a doorway opening onto a cavernous lobby as empty and dark as a church. The stairs had been polished smooth in the centre by centuries of feet, but were rougher on the sides where people did not tread. A carved grey-stone bannister was embedded in the ochre walls. The stairs had low, wide steps majestic to look at, but difficult to negotiate. On the landings of each floor were great windows with sills so high that steps had been carved into the thick walls to allow one to climb them for a peek into the garden below. On the outside of the windows great iron bars curved outwards, creating aerial cages from which one could, unseen, watch the people below. I cannot swear that nestling up there, I never spat a few cherry pits on the passerby below.

After the third floor, the stairs changed. The steps became higher and narrower, and the bannister a mere iron cord with curlicues at the ends. The windows became mere holes in the walls, without iron bars, the walls thinner and rougher.

On the top floor we stopped at a rickety door. This was where the dressmaker lived. The iron bell was attached to a pulley with a metal wire that disappeared into the bowels of the building. My mother let me pull the wire, which produced a tinny sound—muffled, distant as if from the Himalayas—and after a long while a little woman in black satin opened the door, drying her hands and apologizing for everything.

We entered a large room. Immense beams curved into the space like the ribs of a whale's belly, dark and aged, and festooned with garlands of dried vegetables and braids of garlic. There were even some pigeons on the rafters, their rainbow necks craning down to look at us with their round onyx eyes.

Four pyramidal skylights, cut into the roof, let in shafts of sunlight on the polished brick floor, like a scatter of carpets. The smell of rosemary and basil hung in the air like a veil of gentle domesticity and on a table by the door a great mound of dough rose silently.

In the middle of the room, a child of indeterminate age was propped up on pillows in an antique wheelchair, bathed in the sunlight from one of the skylights. His head was abnormally large, his body twisted on one side as if shunning the light. His eyes were empty and watery, the colour of aquamarine. On his chest a bib collected a steady stream of saliva glistening in the sun, like pale honey. My mother smiled at the boy, as she was obliged to, and then, to my horror, she pushed me towards him.

"Play with the boy," she said, "while I am busy with Signora Cecilia." And then she disappeared with the dressmaker, leaving me alone in that place of mildly surrealistic menace.

At first I was determined not to go near the boy. He frightened me with his lolling head and vacuous stare. I circled around him, looking at him from different angles, taking the measure of his presence. Finally, boredom and curiosity prompted me to ask his name. There was no response, so I told him mine. Still no response, so I went a little nearer and told him the names of my sister and my best friend, and a few naughty things about the latter, to whet his appetite for more. I also talked about my favourite games in the hope of eliciting some response, but none came.

When my mother returned from the back of the flat I was relieved.

On the way home she explained that the boy was severely retarded and could not respond to my questions. She suggested that next time I bring something to show him, for although words were too much for him, there was nothing wrong with his sight; he could probably appreciate seeing something that I could show him.

At home, I surveyed my possessions in the hope of finding something to interest him. Most of the toys I had were dolls, and since he was a boy, surely he would not like dolls. There were my books, like the *Travelling Ant* and *Pinocchio*, but I knew my mother wouldn't let them out of the house, since I had lost *The Lion and the Mouse*. Then there was my collection of printed images of saints, each with a little prayer printed on the back, which were given to my sister Lieta and me when we went to church on Sundays. The best of these belonged to Lieta, but I had a few good ones too. The following day, I took two images to show the boy.

When my mother disappeared with the dressmaker, I showed the boy the printed images. He didn't display much enthusiasm, so I put a card very near his eyes, on the bib he wore around his neck. In the beginning nothing happened. Then, slowly, he moved his hand towards the card and, looking straight at me with his watery eyes, pushed it in his mouth and, slowly and deliberately, ate it.

I was horrified and fascinated at the same time. I didn't know if he was going to vomit, or die. I was also puzzled. I licked the other image to see what it tasted like, but it tasted of nothing.

I did not mention any of this to my mother. I wanted to see if the boy would eat other, more interesting saints.

In four visits he ate St. Joseph—the father of Jesus, bald, with a beard and carpenter's tools; St. George, dressed in armour, spearing a dragon; St. Sebastian, tied to a tree, arrows sticking out of his body; and St. Lucia, holding a little dish containing her eyes, complete with lashes and eyebrows.

The boy did not hesitate to eat Jesus himself. The image where Jesus's heart is outside him and his eyes are rolled upwards like those of the epileptic boy who lived down the road.

I was left with only two images: one of St. Christopher, who protected me from being struck by a lightning bolt, and the other of a little baby Jesus who protected me from everything else. I definitely wasn't going to let him eat those.

Out of ideas, I told my sister about the boy who ate saints.

"A cannibal," my sister pronounced, "He is just a cannibal."

"But he doesn't eat live things," I retorted.

"That's because you haven't given him live things."

My sister was five years older then me and had pubic hair. So she knew.

Still, I wouldn't take what she said for granted. I had to find out if what she said was true. I started to look around for something live to test my sister's theory. I thought of Otto, the bird. No, I couldn't do that. Otto had talent. He used to hang upside down and look at me, first with one eye, then with the other. I could just see Otto being eaten up, his yellow feathers falling around like dead songs. No, not Otto.

I was very good at catching lizards with a grass noose, but it was still too early in the season. Frogs were more difficult to catch, but with the help of my friend Silvio it would have been possible, that is, had there been frogs around at this time of late spring.

That left only the kittens.

Cleopatra had given birth to a litter of five kittens about a week earlier. I had assisted Cleopatra in her last days of pregnancy. I had made a little litter of old rags and arranged them in a basket, which I put in a corner of my bedroom, and placed one of my dolls with her for company. I had been hoping that I could witness the birth of her babies but she was a stealthy animal, and managed to give birth when none of us was looking. One moment there was Cleopatra, the moment after she was joined by five tiny creatures looking blindly for her teats.

It had to be planned carefully. I knew that my mother had to be kept in the dark about it. When we were almost out in the street, I said that I had forgotten to pee, went back to my room, picked up one of the kittens and hid him under my sweater, together with a rag soaked in milk to make him feel reassured and cozy. Then I put my coat on top of the sweater and held my hand close to my body to stop the kitten from slipping away. I kept walking slightly behind my mother, which annoyed her no end.

I arrived at the dressmaker's house successfully hiding the little creature.

I waited until my mother disappeared and took the kitten out. He was asleep, his little body was a doughnut of warm fur. My hands were trembling, not out of fear or guilt, but out of obscene curiosity.

I placed the kitten on the boy's bib very close to his mouth and waited.

The boy looked at the kitten intently, almost with what amounted to an expression. He put his hand over the kitten, and slowly and gently attempted to stroke it. The kitten seemed to enjoy the experience, for he closed his eyes and sniffed the boy uncertainly and licked his mouth.

I kept watching the scene, mesmerized, half expecting the boy to eat the kitten, half knowing that he wasn't going to do it.

I don't know now if I would have taken the kitten away had the boy made a move toward eating the little creature. I like to think that I would have, but I am not so sure.

It was then that my mother came in with the dressmaker. They were horrified. The dressmaker said that I should not have given the kitten to the boy, for he might harm the little animal. She explained to me that the boy could not tell right from wrong and couldn't be given such a fragile creature to play with. She also praised my generosity and willingness to share.

My mother knew better. She yanked me and the kitten down the stairs, put the little beast in one of her gloves, and marched briskly home, all the while scolding me about my lack of responsibility and about how I never, ever thought about the consequences of my actions. I had heard it all before and I kept my mouth shut. When we arrived home, she ordered me to put the kitten back into

Cleopatra's litter.

I never saw the boy again. I never learnt his name.

A few days later, my mother drowned all the kittens. She said we couldn't keep more than one cat.

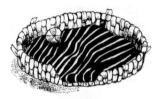

The Nun

We arrive in Siena on a market day.

At the station we are advised to take a pollicino into the city because parking is next to impossible. A pollicino is a tiny bus for about ten people, an intelligent solution to the problem of twentieth-century traffic in a twelfth-century city. Though the bus is nothing more than a sardine can on wheels, it is as big as most of the city's streets can allow.

People on the street squeeze away from the bus, flattening against the walls as they did in Florence, but don't seem to be perturbed by it. There was a time when the battle between pedestrians and drivers was an ongoing street drama, but now it seems that an armistice has been achieved, and things have dulled into the standard of reciprocal tolerance found in the rest of Europe.

Siena had lost all the battles against the ferocious Florentines, sinking slowly into a provincial slumber rescued from total oblivion only by its passionate architecture. Smaller, less elegant and more provincial than Florence, it does, however have this small-town grace; a civic countenance of proud charm, an ancient place for an ancient people. Living here must be pure archaeology. With a character of its own, its buildings look like barricades of bricks pierced by a few stingy windows; on the sills the pots of geranium advance a truce of gentleness among the factious populace. During the Palio—the Sienese horse race that pitches one quarter of the city against another—this contentiousness is displayed in all its violent colours for a week of pure insanity.

I have always loved Siena and its magnificent setting in the Chianti countryside. We walk down in the secret shade of tiny alleys towards the glory of the main piazza, the best in the world. I almost feel like applauding when I emerge from the tight network of side streets, into the curved, slanted expanse of cobblestones that makes up the floor of the piazza, polished by time and tourists, converging towards the severe shadow of the main civic tower. Hanging from some of the mediaeval balconies are the flags of the different city districts. The flags in primary colours, display symbolic animals the meanings of which have been lost over the centuries.

We sit in one of the cafes in the main piazza where my two companions make the observation that will become our constant refrain every time we sit at a cafe in the main piazza of any city: "They are robbing us." Of course, it is true.

Italians are reluctant to frequent the main piazza cafes. They are for tourists only and priced accordingly. The old cities of Italy have nothing but tourism for the revenue needed to keep them in the historical style to which the tourist likes to be accustomed. It is difficult enough to keep buildings properly functioning when they are sixty or seventy years old; when a building is over four hundred years old, keeping it fit is an ongoing battle costing millions. Of course, these little cities could become industrialized and cease to live off tourism, but then, nobody would want to see them. To pay exorbitantly for a coffee in the main piazza is really paying the ticket for an open-air museum. For the locals, there are little-known local cafes or the coffee-bar which is always a stand-up affair, as if sitting down is a luxury afforded only to people on holidays. This is rather puzzling to a tourist who is used to sitting in a cafe in other parts of the world for the price of a cup of coffee. I try to explain to Violet and Clara that we could buy a coffee and sit on the steps of a church or on the stone seats usually carved in the building's wall, but they prefer to sit in the main cafe and I can do nothing but feel responsible.

Since we have not arranged for accommodation in the city, we rent a small Peugeot and leave for the Benedictine abbey where we are expected before nightfall.

We drive into the Chianti landscape with the sun starting to slant the cypresses' shadows into long black pencil strokes on fields of young wheat. The terrain is undulating in gentle knolls all the way to the horizon. Sometimes a blue mist of olive trees is ruptured by a rift of sienna-red, long-eroded earth. At other times the field's solitude is interrupted by terracotta villas, their architecture so unpretentious they look as though they might be farms.

It is this lack of cuteness, this essentialness of form that I have missed the most in my exile from Tuscany. This uncompromising respect for the brutally practical, this abhorrence of the useless gesture and the lack of regard for the facade or patience for metaphors are what will tie me to this land, no matter how long I am away from it. At the same time it is not an easy place to come from, for it never equipped me with a script of the social graces that oil so many otherwise unpleasant encounters.

The fields have a translucent peaceful appearance that the evening light softens into an idyllic quilt. But those verdant hills have been soaked in blood, the sweetness of the countryside hides a rabid violence that began with the first wars of conquest by the steamrollers of antiquity, the Romans, who wrenched it from the Etruscans. The bloodshed continued with the Papal forces that tried to annex the proud city-states of later periods. But Italy always was and still is a hopeless country, divided into small factions at the mercy of individual allegiances rather than national ones. French, Austrian, Spanish, Dutch and other assorted mercenaries were invited by one villain or another to have a field day in a land that was weak, sunny, bountiful and disorganized. When I feel in need of an identity, I like to think of myself as Etruscan, mainly because I like those thin-lipped, hook-nosed, smiling, mysterious people who are said to come from Asia Minor. But, with so many armies having run the width and the length of the peninsula—one of the most coveted rewards of war being the rape of the women—who knows where anybody comes from? And this is a comforting thought.

When the light starts to fade into a rose-grey gauze, we start worrying about the abbey, which, like a Cheshire cat's smile, exists only in the signs that feature a white cross on a black church silhouette. Clara has her eye problem, Violet can only drive a car with an automatic shift and I cannot drive at all. We always think that past the next hill the promise of the black-and-white sign will give away to the real thing, but hills come and go and there is no sign of the Abbey. Clara is going faster now, and the magic of the hills is lost in a flurry of olive trees, cypress groves, brick villas, cypress groves, olive trees, trefoil fields. It is almost dark when we stumble upon a mediaeval wall with an impressive towered entrance astride a dry moat. The draw-bridge is permanently lowered because there are pots of aspidistras across its width. We leave the car there and enter into an enclosure reminiscent of medieval fortified enclaves, complete with a large stone cistern and kitchen gardens surrounding huddles of plain introverted buildings that withstood marauding hordes of soldiers of fortune. It looks like the background to a *Fra Angelico's Nativity*; all that is needed are a few magi and a Star of Bethlehem.

It smells of jasmine.

Above the massive entrance portal a blue-and-white ceramic lunette depicts the Virgin Mary and child. Strange how those communities of misogynous men dedicated themselves to the cult of Mary; its pagan irony never touches their "saintly" souls. Approaching the cistern, we see that it is green with algae and rotting. It has a sinister stillness barely relieved by cascades of daffodils. We walk along a majestic brick road that winds down to the abbey. The road is flanked by the black lances of the cypreses —that most Tuscan of trees. The place appears deserted. We see nobody, hear no voices and see no signs except a few, exhorting visitors to respect a place of prayer. We come to a courtyard that is surrounded by a two-storey red brick building with several doors all closed. We have no doubt that this is the abbey, but would like some reassurance.

I remember the impression I had when I called the abbey from Toronto—the feeling that I had contacted an international hotel. I now feel ironically that I am being punished for my arrogance. Not only is nobody welcoming us, but I also start to feel quite anxious about our accommodations for the night. There is no possibility of going back to Siena in the impending darkness and there seems to be nobody here to whom I can even ask a question. Feeling responsible for the welfare of my companions I gingerly go through a gate above which an unequivocal sign declares: "Strict Benedictine Cloister. Under no circumstances are people not belonging to the order allowed past this gate."

I decide that I do not read Italian. I open the gate and walk along a ledge high above the now-misty landscape and enter one door after another always asking, very loudly, for permission to enter, then entering when nobody answers. I keep advancing deep into a monastery that seems to be in a twelfth-century time warp. I finally happen on a vast refectory and all at once I face about thirty monks who sit in silence in front of their plates and individual jugs of water. The scene is so incongruous for this secular age, it is almost threatening; one of those dreams where everything is recognizable but out of context. I have such a visceral feeling of not belonging here that I want to turn and run. I am afraid of being caught trespassing not only onto their space but also into their silent male ritual. Above them in the semi-lit depth of the high ceiling a last supper painted by an unknown mediaeval painter looks more real than the one below. None of the monks looks at me, although I am sure they can't have missed my loud request for permission to enter. I look at them, trying to find a countenance suitably contrite, when behind me a voice asks if it can be of any help. Although the voice is soft, almost a whisper, I jump as if caught sinning. I foolishly ask for the person I talked to back in Canada, but realize that I never took down his name. I feel so awkward I stumble over myself, mentioning my two companions waiting for me by the closed door and how I have been unable to make any contact with anybody. The more I talk, the more I feel I must sound mundane and preoccupied by trivialities, such as finding a place to sleep for the night and worrying about losing the trust my companions have put in me.

Silently another friar appears next to the one I am talking to. He is so decrepit he seems to be two hundred years old. He doesn't deign to look at me, but hisses at the younger one. "You see what happens if we do not lock the gate?"

What happens is me, a woman in a cloister of monks. I am almost blushing in the welcome semidarkness. The younger monk asks me to wait until their dinner is finished and promises that someone will come to show us to our rooms. Feeling chastised but a little less anxious, I retrace my steps and wait with Clara and Violet in a courtyard full of crazed swallows flying around us before reaching their nests, in the dormitory's eaves.

We are tired and very hungry, not having eaten since morning. I suddenly remember having seen a few people in secular clothes, back at the entrance in what appeared to be a little restaurant. I leave Clara and Violet where they are and run back to the entrance tower to a small area with a "Closed" sign on the door. It is my day of breaking and entering; I feel I am starting to become expert at it. Inside is indeed a restaurant but today, Wednesday, is their employees' day off. I put on my last remaining charm of the day and ask if they could give us something to eat. The woman, a virago of indeterminate age, does not seem to mind being bothered in her day off. She lives there anyway, she says, fixing some hard Tuscan bread, prosciutto and a plate of salad. I feel victorious and childishly proud, and run back, afraid of missing the monks coming out of their supper. I arrive just in time to catch a very young monk with the ascetic look of a malnourished angel trying to make himself understood by my companions.

Yes, he has received my booking from Canada, no, it wasn't he who talked to me. The telefonista friar is away on a spiritual retreat (to a place more spiritual than this?). He will take us to our rooms. Yes, there is hot and cold water—no, not in the room, only cold in the room sink—but in the showers down the hall. No, there isn't anybody but us so we can choose the rooms we want. I feel so relieved I want to embrace this exemplar of masculine virginity, but I know my place. I have mistaken dutiful compassion for human warmth before. The fact that he is kind to me doesn't mean I exist, I am just one of the sinning flock. I don't gush in thanks, I don't want to feel like Mary Magdalene for the rest of my stay.

We walk in silence to a second-floor corridor onto which all the cell doors except three are open. There must be about thirty rooms, all empty. He has chosen the rooms for us, but we see no reason to change and choose others because they all look exactly the same. We are not asked to present any documents or a deposit, the only request is that we write our names in a guestbook on a round table by the entrance. For all he knows we could sleep and leave in the morning without a trace. The monk bids us a good stay and disappears discreetly.

We feel like children let loose in an attic. After sticking our noses in every cell, each claims her territory by choosing a different shower and washroom; we explore the library where bound volumes of *The Christian Family* are shelved chronologically from 1963 to the present. We open immense closets full of towels, bed-sheets and pillowcases, all neatly folded and smelling of sunshine. In another closet we find boxes of soap cakes, detergent, toilet paper, toothpaste, mops and pails, all still in their plastic wrappers, along with Vaseline, chlorine, salt and pepper shakers and at least two hundred plastic cups. All this hoarding gives the eerie feeling of an evacuated planet, but we feast on a wonderful sense of largesse; Clara dries herself on three towels. I keep only one for myself, mindful that we are paying only twenty dollars a night.

We remove the guestbook and some dried flowers from the entrance table and prepare ourselves for the night meal. We devour our bread and prosciutto and Clara and Violet drink one of the bottles of wine Signora Norma gave us, back in Florence.

When we finish eating, we all go for long showers in a different part of the building, wearing just a towel around our middle, behaving as if we owned the place. When we finally retire, it is late and the purity of the air and the depth of the silence are sure to enhance our sleep.

But I can't sleep, not yet. There is too much silence, punctured at regular intervals by the bells of the Abbey, every quarter of an hour. I quietly leave the room and wander down the corridor, out into a night as clear as glass. As is always the case in the country, the stars are polished and dancing all over an unhindered horizon of black hills and clumps of cypresses. The menacing cistern is over there, alive with frogs and other creatures; the swallows are in, the crickets out, the night has begun its own concert. I sit by a little wall feeling wonderfully spent; the day has been long and emotionally uneven, but my companions are asleep in clean, inexpensive, separate rooms and I am here looking at the night and breathing a slight smell of juniper and bay leaves. I look at the black silhouette of the abbey, so ancient and strong and think of the men it houses in its uncompromising cloisters. What makes those young men give up so much of their life to retire here in this suffocating little paradise with no risks, no surprises, the great happenings of the world outside nothing more than a blasphemous echo to their virginal ears? It is this negation of worldly seductions, of which I am part that makes me feel such an intruder in this precious enclave of piety.

My sister Lieta once had an affair with a man of the cloth. She always described him as a tender and compassionate lover. I certainly believe that; these communities are, at least in theory, founded on reciprocal sustenance and love.

"But," Lieta used to say, "I felt love was bestowed on me rather than exchanged, there was no equivalence of vulnerability. He loved and I got to be loved."

And maybe this is what I feel here, not so much unwanted or despised—the friar was kind and helpful——just not necessary, irrelevant. There is nothing I can give that is of any use here. What can you give to somebody who has God on his side? I once thought I knew, but it turned out not to be true. It was nuns then, but the feeling was the same.

ॐ

It all happened on a Sunday, even though nothing ever seemed to happen on a Sunday. The usual flies buzzing around the coffee cups, the window framing a sky as hot as an open oven, the hours stretching like molasses towards the promise of the cool of the evening. The ritual of preparing an espresso coffee might have killed a minute or two, cutting some bread, covering it in expensive butter and dipping it in the hot black muddy coffee. Heavenly. But hardly a worthwhile pursuit for an eighteen-year-old searching, intently if erratically, for the Meaning of Life.

Mercifully, the bell rang.

I have always been one who loves interruptions. Even in the midst of a thoroughly absorbing activity, I have to stop and unfocus every so often. Interruptions refresh me. I see interruptions as promise. They might take me somewhere I haven't been before.

So I put on my sister Lieta's dressing gown, shooed the cat out of the way and went to open the door, wondering who could possibly have come to call on a Sunday afternoon.

Two nuns stood in front of me, in black and white, like swallows on a wire. They talked to the cat even before they acknowledged my presence, bending down simultaneously, full of solicitude, making cooing noises, stroking her as if I didn't exist. Cleopatra flattened herself into a pelt at so much attention.

As young as I was, I knew it all smacked of conversion, the cat being nothing but a bridge to my wretched soul.

I dislike missionaries, particularly the religious kind. Besides, at the time I thought of myself as Marxist, and wanted nothing to do with the semantic tricks that religious militants employ in the hope of bringing errant souls back to the Right Way. Still, a summer Sunday is a summer Sunday, and even a couple of nuns is better than nothing. So I steeled myself for a lengthy discussion on the benefits of grace, picked up the cat and invited them in.

They sat on the couch at a polite distance from each other, leaving enough space for the wings of their hats to avoid bumping into each other. While waiting for them to start on my soul, I kept thinking that if they didn't dress like that for religious reasons, they would have to be considered totally insane. It must have been about 40 degrees in the Florentine summer, and they were covered in heavy black wool and white cotton that left almost none of their skin free to breathe. A large wooden crucifix hung from the cord belts around their waists.

They looked around the room my sister and I shared

with an alert curiosity, as if they had never been in a home before. Every time they turned their heads, their profiles disappeared behind the wings of their headdresses. I followed their gaze to the posters of Marx and Lenin on the wall, hoping that the sight of such heathens would stop them from any attempt at my redemption. So, I thought it rather obtuse when one of them asked me if I was a communist. I was also surprised by the bluntness of the question; direct questioning is not usual among people of the cloth. Of course, I was quite proud of my Party card, even though I was not very knowledgeable about the communist philosophy. Like most communists of my generation, I had never read Marx, but I had been studying Russian with an ex-Bolshevik émigrée who lived behind the Church of Orsanmichele, an area of dilapidated Renaissance buildings that even the communist party could afford to rent. I didn't learn much Russian; drunk most of the time, she preferred entertaining me with soulful songs of her motherland and stories of her many ex-husbands. Sometimes she received me with a despondent silence. But the visits satisfied my thirst for weird experiences.

"Yes," I said to the nuns, happy to be able to say I was something, even if I was no more than a superficial Communist. I believed I had thrown a stone in their pond of rectitude. I felt sinfully sophisticated.

But the next question jolted me out of my smugness into a state of bewilderment. I was asked for a glass of alcohol. Just like that. They didn't even pretend to faint, which was the only reason why anybody in my family would drink a little alcohol. Actually, the way the one making the request put it was: "May I trouble you for a glass of spirits?" And then she added, lowering her voice, "Any kind will do."

I didn't know what to say. What kind of spirits? How

big a glass? I went to the kitchen and from the top of the cupboard took a bottle of Marsala, a strong Sicilian wine we kept for my fainting spells. It was so old it had become as dense as gelatine.

I took the bottle and two glasses and brought them back to the living room. I was putting the glasses down on the table when one of the nuns stopped me, delicately patting my hand with her own.

"Do you have something stronger?" she asked.

My head was reeling with conjectures. Were these two really nuns? I thought of the bottle of brandy one of my sister's students had given her for Christmas. It had remained, behind the sewing machine unopened, for four years. Without a word I picked it up and brought it over together with a few small almond cookies. I fumbled with the corkscrew, wondering all the while what kind of nuns would ask for strong drinks in somebody else's house on a Sunday afternoon.

I poured some of the yellow liquid into the glasses and offered them to the nuns. They took them daintily with butterfly fingers, bent their head as if taking flight with their white wings spread around their head, and gulped the brandy down in unison. I must have looked puzzled, because for the first time they looked at me firmly and smiled tactfully. They seemed to do everything together. They must have acquired a kind of Siamese-twin synchronism after years of obeying the same rules.

Suddenly, one of them said that she was here on a visit from a southern convent, accompanying the other in her quest for alms. That sounded very strange to me because the only nuns that went around for alms were the Franciscans, the ones dressed in brown cloth looking like friars in drag. These two wore the habit of the Dominicans, a teaching order whose adherents certainly didn't go around asking for charity. In fact, the Dominicans were supposed to be the aristocracy of the religious orders. As far as I knew, they even had to bring a substantial dowry to enter the order, as if marrying into a family of better class.

Something was wrong with the nun's story. Neither of them had even mentioned God yet. My anti-missionary zeal was beginning to feel a little unused. They drank another glass of brandy each and nibbled at the cookies without conviction.

And then they stood up, thanked me and left.

I was left looking at the place where they had sat as if it could deliver an explanation. Even Cleopatra refused to curl up there and sleep, and instead kept making a nuisance of herself. It felt as if the Sunday had been cracked open and something foreign and strange let in.

Time passed and I continued with my uninspired life. I had almost forgotten about the nuns, when one evening a few weeks later, one of the nuns appeared at my door. I couldn't remember if she was the one who had asked for the drink or the one who was the guest from the southern convent; uniforms have a way of making people's faces disappear.

When she came in, I was sorry I was alone. I wanted my sister to meet her, because neither she nor anybody else ever believed what I said. Lieta thought that I had invented if not all, at least part, of the story. She believed that the nuns had come to our place, but not that they had asked for strong drink. So I wished she were here to see for herself.

I invited the nun in and asked, without a trace of irony, if she wanted something to drink. She disappointed me by refusing and proceeded to talk breathlessly, almost hysterically. She said that she wanted to leave the convent, but she had no contacts outside. She asked me if I could I help her.

My first thought was one of righteous contempt. A nun is supposed to have entered the convent because of her vocation, her love for Christ, and a peculiar propensity for poverty and chastity. My religious upbringing surfaced before I had time to remember the intervening years of rebellion and communist affiliation. In the silence that followed, the romantic and slightly dangerous aspect of the request started to make its way into my mind, and I became increasingly interested in the proposition.

Nobody had ever asked me for help. Being eighteen years old, the only exchanges of help that had ever taken place between me and the rest of the world had operated in my favour. In fact, as the youngest, my existence had always been a burden to the rest of my family.

Now, here was my chance. I was visibly growing in stature. This nun had no one to turn to but me. And here I was, willing to take risks, trustworthy and a communist. She couldn't have fallen into better hands. I only hoped that the help she was asking for did not require any money, for I had none. I depended for my living on my sister's reluctant sense of family duty, and she wasn't that well off either. We had just enough to keep body and soul together.

It took me only a few seconds to make up my mind.

"What can I do for you?" I asked.

"I need civilian clothes, some outside contacts and a train ticket to Milan."

And then, as if she sensed my financial situation, "I have the money for the ticket," she added.

I almost hugged her. But I contained myself and asked when would she need these things.

She must have contained herself, too, because after an almost imperceptible gasp of relief, she assumed the monotone voice and the economy of word and gesture that must have been the rule behind the convent walls.

She said that she would return in a week. She stood, handed me the money to buy the ticket and, after an awkward attempt at a handshake, left.

I made my plans immediately. First, her clothes. What could she wear? What looks good on a nun? Maybe something with long sleeves, rather modest, a bit like a nurse's uniform? Or, once out of the convent, would she want something that reflected her newfound freedom? Something a bit audacious and low cut? I didn't have anything sexy, on account of being a communist. In fact, I had only three items, none of which I could spare. But I had my winter clothes, tucked away somewhere in the bottom of a trunk. It was summer and sweltering, but I thought that since nuns covered themselves from head to toe in woollen clothes no matter what the season, a woollen sweater wouldn't be too much out of line. I didn't have a skirt to go with it, for the only one I had I was wearing.

So I decided to make one. For fabric, I went to the Venetian—a part time dress-maker, part time hooker, and friend of mine—who lived near the railway tracks. She had, as we used to say, a heart of gold, very generous with material particularly in light of the fact that most of the fabric on her shelves had been stolen from her clients. I told her about the nun's predicament and managed to infect her with my excitement over the clandestine project. She gave me a piece of greenish fabric and a length of elastic ribbon.

I went home and set about making a skirt. I had never sewn anything before, so it wasn't easy. I made something resembling a fabric tube with an elastic ribbon sewn on one end and a hem on the other. It wasn't high fashion, but good enough for a nun; even a little punishing.

Then, I turned my attention to the underwear. I had never known a nun intimately, so I didn't know if they wore any. Since my sister was working, and therefore could afford more things than I could, I stole a couple of knickers and a brassiere from her drawer, hoping that the nun's breasts were the same size as Lieta's.

How about sanitary napkins? Did nuns menstruate? Nuns never looked quite real to me. They appeared to be some kind of alternative beings, with different natures, like angels and unicorns. Maybe they did not menstruate. But, what if they did and the convent only gave them one at a time, and I, in my insensitivity did not provide her for this necessity? I took three of the twelve napkins that were part of my dowry and put them with the small pile of personal effects.

As for the shoes, I decided she could wear the ones she had. Shoes are shoes and don't have religious characteristics. Besides, I didn't have her size, and I was wearing the only pair of sandals I had.

I washed everything thoroughly and put all the garments out to dry in the sun. I then ironed them to perfection. I folded them lovingly, making sure that I ironed the folds flat in order to look crisp and new when unfolded, and placed them in a flour sack, after having washed that too. I took great pains in being punctiliously correct, not wanting her to think that, because she was on the receiving end of my generosity, I didn't think she was worthy of my respect. After all, my brand of communism was the Fight of the Needy against the Tyrants. At the last minute I put in a clean, folded handkerchief and a few sprigs of lavender I had picked from somebody's garden. I hid the package under my bed and went to the station to buy the ticket for Milan.

All this took no more than one afternoon. I still had one long week to wait before her return. It felt like a year.

The night before the day she was to come, I hardly

slept. I wondered if she needed me to take any further risks on her behalf. I was ready to do anything. Except for the dressmaker I hadn't said anything to anybody, not even to my sister. I wanted to go into battle alone. I planned the day so that I could stay at home to wait for her. Every time the bell rang I jumped to my feet, ran to the door and opened it. At about four in the afternoon, I took all the clothes out, ironed them a little more and put them back in their place.

I was becoming impatient and a bit worried. Lieta came home around seven and started to cook something.

The nun did not come. Nor did she come the day after or the following day, or the day after that. A week passed and the nun still didn't come.

I didn't know what to think. I took the bicycle and pedalled nonchalantly around the Dominican convent to see if I could find anything out, but it was shuttered like a fortress. I hung around for a while in the hope of seeing the nun, but only small children and their mothers went in and out the door.

I waited another couple of weeks, hoping against hope that the nun would show up. Finally, I had to conclude that either something had happened to her or she had changed her mind. I couldn't bear to think that she would be capricious enough to involve me in something as important and secretive as her escape and then change her mind and disappear into thin air, out of my uninteresting life.

I decided that something had happened to her.

I imagined dark scenarios. The mother superior had found out about her attempt to escape and had her poisoned. Stories of workmen who found skeletons buried inside the walls of convents while doing restorations were popular. These were good stories for evening gatherings; we never allowed the truth to hamper our

imaginations.   If the skeletons had never existed, we
would have hated to find out.   But this wasn't a matter of
truth or fiction.   A human being had disappeared while
plotting an escape, and I was involved in it.

I didn't know what to do.   The ticket for Milan had an
expiry date, so something had to be done soon.   I didn't
want to talk to my sister Lieta.   The nun was my adventure;
had I told Lieta she would have made it her own and I
would be left with nothing.   Also, I wasn't sure that she
would believe me.

I talked to some of the comrades in the Party cell.
Unaccountably, they didn't seem too interested in my
story.   I think they became afraid of having to abandon the
revolutionary rhetoric for a real rescue.   I took the ex-
Bolshevik émigrée into my confidence.

"Don't you ask me for money," she said.   I didn't see
any connection between my story and a request for
money, so I abandoned the subject.

The more I thought about it, the more I convinced
myself that the nun was in danger.   I knew I had to do
something.   I came up with several outlandish plans
before settling on one that seemed almost perfect.   I was
going to try to enter the convent claiming a sudden but
deep conversion to the ways of the Church—the fact that
I belonged to the Communist Party would make me
appear like a prodigal daughter returning to the folds of
the Church, an irresistible scenario to the upholders of
the Faith.   The nuns might think of it as a miracle.   This
way, I would gain access to the convent, find the nun,
give her her ticket and the bag of clothes, maybe even
help her to leave the convent and then vanish into the
world outside.   I felt intelligent and treacherous, a person
of astuteness and guile.

It took me several days to compose my letter of
application.   Actually, I didn't really apply.   I was too

clever for that. I stated only that I wanted to talk to the mother superior about religious matters, explaining that while perceiving the call of a budding vocation, I felt confused and uncertain. Talking with a person of experience in such matters would dispel some of the doubts I had about the religious life. For good measure, I mentioned that my mother and father were both dead and that I was studying to become an artist. A talented orphan. How could they refuse me an interview? If they did I could end up a prostitute.

I wrote the letter with great care and precision, signed the name of the dressmaker and took it personally to the convent. I reckoned that by the time they found out that the name I signed was not mine, I would have found the nun, liberated her and vanished into the outside world.

I cycled to the convent, locked my bike to a tree outside and entered the convent with my heart beating out a tattoo of trepidation. I put the letter on the revolving wheel, as one had to do with everything delivered to the convent, and waited outside for a sign of acknowledgement. After a time, the wheel turned towards me and I saw a little scrap of paper on it, which I guessed was the answer. The smallness of the piece of paper gave me a taste of the cruel parsimony, the suffocating denial practised by the convent. No wonder the nun wanted out. Years of living in this reduced universe would have driven anybody to thoughts of escape.

The piece of paper invited me to see the mother superior the following day, at three in the afternoon. The message hadn't been put exactly that way. It said, at three, after noon prayers. Their clocks were evidently set to a liturgical time, one not used by the rest of us sinners.

When I showed up on the appointed day, the door was opened for me as if by magic, without having to identify myself or even ring the bell. I was escorted, silently, by the nun-concierge to the parlatorio, an area where the secular world is admitted occasionally, after careful scrutiny.

The only convent I had ever known was the orphanage where I had spent some time as a child. It was a hateful little place, full of smelly children and harassed nuns, with a courtyard containing a few swings dangling disconsolately in the wind. It was also a place that was contaminated by the atmosphere of false gaiety that adults wear when dealing with children, particularly orphans.

But the one in which I now sat was in a different class. I was in a large room, with an extraordinarily high, vaulted ceiling of reddish bricks arranged in a basket--weave pattern. I wondered how the bricks defied gravity and managed to remain glued up there, my only experience of bricks being of the kind sensibly stacked to make walls. The whitewashed walls were covered in old tapestry depicting something holy and miraculous. Bricks covered the floors too, but these were polished and smelled of wax. In the middle of the room stood an immense table that appeared to be a bit arthritic with age, its horizontal surface polished until it mirrored the bricks of the ceiling, its legs carved in the shape of lion's paws. On the table lay a great terracotta sculpture in the shape of a basket of fruit, straight out of Pompeii. There were chairs against one wall, high-backed, with straw seats, covered by flat linen cushions tied to the legs with ribbons and intricate heavy tassels.

I sat on the edge of one of the chairs, looking through the open arches in front of me at the garden beyond. The doors were wide open. The white linen curtains were shaped into gigantic knots, to keep them raised from the floor. The knots swayed imperceptibly in the still air as if breathing softly. In the garden, a geometry of rosemary, mint, thyme and camomile criss-crossed and curved in a topiary of great precision. The garden was surrounded by a loggia on three sides; the fourth side opened onto a vineyard sloping in contorted rows, down towards a blue spray of olive trees. In the middle of the garden a couple of nuns, their hats like seagulls among the lavender and basil, were busy doing something with spades and scissors, singing softly with the voices of angels. It was a vision of a small, enclosed paradise, all the more beautiful because so unexpected.

I pondered briefly why anyone would hide so much beauty. Nothing I could see was not in harmony, not one jarring note in that humble music of objects and light. Even the crucifix, a symbol I always found rather gruesome, had its own beauty—sculpted in blond wood, with no graphic dribbling of blood or nails sticking out of its extremities. There were aspidistras in carved clay pots against each of the massive columns on which the arches rested and a whole carnival of whites at the foot of the Crucifix: lilies, chrysanthemums and the ivory decadence of roses.

The place had such a presence that I felt enveloped in it—palpably, like in a shroud. I was slowly succumbing to the subtle seduction of the Catholic Church by means of the sensuous. I was then, and am still, struck by the contrast between the convent's reduced existence and such understated and essential beauty.

I was left there for a long time, maybe intentionally. I was beginning to feel at ease and a bit more relaxed when a nun came in and, without a word, motioned me to follow her. We walked through several corridors, blank walls on one side, the loggia and then the garden on the other. We seemed to be circling the garden. Abruptly the nun stopped and looked at me, frozen for a moment as if something momentous was about to happen. Then she entered a room without knocking and ushered me in.

The room was white and simple as I expected it to be. More like a large cell, really. Only a desk, two chairs and a small crucifix. But on one of the walls hung a painting exploding with gold, turquoise, peacock blue, a whole sonata of shimmering colours. It depicted angels rolling on puffy clouds, pierced by arrows of sun rays; golden halos behind naked baby cherubs' heads; saints looking up and saints looking down and rainbow wings everywhere. You could almost hear its orchestral music. I became lost for a moment in the stars that glimmered in its painted sky. It was such a large painting that the little nun under it, whom I took to be the mother superior, almost disappeared.

My presence was not acknowledged. The nun who had accompanied me had silently left; I stood inside the entrance door, waiting for a sign. The mother superior was intent on mending the wing of a small bird. She was talking to it in cooing noises of encouragement, as if it were a child, handling the little beast with infinite tenderness. She had a small piece of gauze in her hand, which she was trying to apply to the bird's wing,

I remained there transfixed, looking at that scene from a Christian parable, unable to find a way to make myself noticed. After a while, almost against my will, it seemed proper for me to make a gesture of help towards the little bird as a way of introducing myself into the realm of her attention. I came forward and handed her the pieces of shredded cloth that lay on the table. Instead of taking them, she held the bird towards me, as though to have me do something with it. She did this without uttering a word or doing anything to acknowledge my presence. I didn't quite know what I was doing, but I tried not to disappoint her. To do otherwise would have seemed callous.

When the little bird at last gave signs of reviving, the

mother superior finally laid it down in a small basket, covered it with a cloth, as if it were a croissant, and directed her piercing blue eyes towards me.

"What can I do for you, child?" she asked.

The tone of her voice had hardly changed from the one she used in encouraging the bird to live. It had been a year since I had last been called "child"—that was how long ago my mother had died. This peacefulness and tenderness came dangerously close to melting something inside me. I almost didn't recognize my voice when I heard myself say, a little breathless and rather strangled, "A nun, probably from this convent, has asked for my help to escape."

I had hardly finished saying it when a sense of having betrayed the human race washed over me. How could I be such a coward? They hadn't even had to torture me. I had spilled the beans free of charge. Just like that. All one had to do was call me "Child" and I would dissolve like treacle. I felt myself blushing from my ears down to the base of my neck, as if I had lied, when for once I had said the truth.

The mother superior kept her steady gaze on me. She was looking at me not severely or, condescendingly nor even with much curiosity. Her old face was full of mild concern, waiting for me to continue.

But no more came from me. I was afraid to talk in case I should come out with more self-inflicted humiliations. She stood up and walked towards the door. She stopped for a minute to let me reach her and walked with me towards the end of the corridor.

I followed her into the semidarkness of the corridor, with a sense of relief. At least I didn't have to cope with my blushing. She opened a door into another immense room, with a high brick ceiling and heavy round columns. But there were no loggias outside, so the sun slanted right in, painting bright lozenges on the stone floor.

It was a refectory and a meal was about to be served by a couple of nuns in long white aprons. The other nuns were standing, each behind her chair, their heads bowed in prayer. I looked intently to see if I could find my nun, but I couldn't see any of their faces for their slightly fluttering wings were down. I knew I didn't want to sit through the meal with the rest of them; besides I had not been invited to do so. The place started to weigh heavily on me with its silent burden of daily denials. But I knew that my nun was there. If I could have gone and looked at them I knew I would have recognized her. I waited quietly for a while, as they said grace. Then they all sat down to eat.

And there she was. My nun took a little longer to sit than the others. She looked at me for a few seconds, her face of an opacity almost mineral. I returned her stare.

For no reason at all, I felt the sting of tears in my eyes. But when I turned to the mother superior my voice was firm and clear.

"No," I said "the nun was not from this convent."

I left silently, retracing my steps all the way to the outside door.

Nobody accompanied me. Nobody stopped me.

The Servant

In the morning we rise to the sight of clouds brooding over the hills, and the appearance of little yellow beaks in the nests stuck under the eaves. The roofs are low on the brows of the windows, so we can almost touch the little creatures. The mothers don't like us though, and fly around screeching threats at us. The morning is as cool and pungent as vinegar, the smells are damp and complex.

There is an office at the end of the corridor, but the telefonista friar has not returned from his spiritual exercises. In fact the place is still as deserted as the night before. We have decided to explore the area around the monastery, so we drive along the red brick path to the entrance portal. The restaurant is open today and surprisingly full. We have a choice of seats: by a tiny fountain, with a waterfall the size of a spurt, or on a loggia overlooking the countryside, equipped with hens and sleeping pussycats. And then there is this alcove, just outside the door of the kitchen, literally carved into a bush of climbing jasmine. We sit in a cloud of heavenly fragrance, drinking it in as if it were a bottle of young wine. The aroma tickles our nostrils until the strong smell of espresso coffee overwhelms it. And then the smell of freshly baked bread and croissants obliterates all other aromas. There are roses in the garden but, with the bombardment of the other heavy scents they don't stand a chance.

The food is expensive but worth every lira. Clara drinks her triple order of espresso out of one long glass. I don't know how she avoids a bad case of Saint Vitus dance. I, on the other hand, gorge myself on freshly baked, featherweight croissants. By the time we are ready to leave we can hardly stand any more pleasure.

Our aim is to leave Tuscany for an overnight excursion to Orvieto in Umbria. I am armed with a road map on which the route has been plotted by my husband back in Canada. I am determined to orient myself, and so avoid the torture of getting lost as we did in Provence. In France the route was Violet's responsibility, but here I must navigate.

The road we take undergoes subtle progressive changes. The poppies of the Tuscan hills give way to fields of magenta clover; the black lances of the cypresses do not guard the hilltops nor do they cluster around the terracotta villas. The landscape doesn't unfold anymore into rolling waves of fields like a quilt on display. Slowly the chestnut and almond trees appear along the road and in the countryside, in greens of different shades, and not as gnarled nor as stunted as the olive trees. The landscape is becoming narrower and rockier. It is also broken by gorges and deep ravines. The fields are smaller, of a more uncertain geometry, interrupted by pastures where white sheep graze. A different landscape, a different people, another dialect, another cuisine.

A consequence of the fragmented history of this land is this kind of drastic change between areas just a few miles apart. In not so ancient times, a man going from Florence to Bologna—just two hundred miles away— would make a will and acquire a passport. The road was treacherous and the destination alien.

On the top of almost every hill is an ancient village that's almost undetectable among the rocky outcrops. We are crossing the spine of Italy: the Appenines. The road rises, circling around steep mountainsides, and dips in secret valleys deep and cool, where torrents, swollen by the recent rains, swirl angrily against the pylons of bridges built in Roman times. We pass the Rubicon and the Tiber; it feels as if we are driving through a history book.

We are beckoned by a bell tower, rising above a small crowd of red roofs. We leave the main road and climb up to the village of Todi for a brief rest. We drive straight into the main piazza, where we take seats at the central cafe and order. I do the usual scouting of the wash-room—checking to see if it is clean enough for my companions—while Violet and Clara wait for the order to come. When the bill arrives, it is high as usual. By now I hope it is clear that main piazza cafes are expensive.

The village is rustic, stony and stage-set picturesque. It doesn't have the bare essentialness of a Tuscan village. Houses and people are more smiling, less haughty and more provincial, and therefore more open and curious about the world outside the city walls. The factional wars that ravaged most of Italy's city states spared these remote areas, leaving the inhabitants more trusting, less belligerant. The narrow streets, which sometimes look like domestic corridors, have ancient Etruscan names. History has been a little slower here. We meander in those labyrinthine alleys where children in short shorts play games I thought I had forgotten, and look indiscreetly into people's lives, through windows barred by iron grids and shaded by pots of basil. We walk on the hard cobblestones feeling like giants in a village built for lesser people, in an age of scarcity. We stop at tiny shops selling local cheeses and faded postcards of the main piazza and views of the mountains surrounding the village—the little local treasures of a half-forgotten place.

Going down a steep hill, we stumble upon a wine maker who beckons us inside to taste some of his wine. We enter his shop and are immediately immersed in the dark smell of fermenting wine. Its dankness reminds me of the wine seller below our terrace, back in the Florence of my childhood. I catch sight of his cellars that reach deeply into the excavated mountain, from the back of his store. I ask the man if we could be allowed to visit the cellars, so that my companions could see one of those ancient laboratories of inebriation. He obliges enthusiastically. He is friendly and handsome, a robust man in his late forties, with the grey eyes and thin lips typical of the people of the area. We walk into the heart of the mountain where the immense vats rest in constant coolness and where it's dark, musty and mysterious. The cellars have been here for over a thousand years, the wine maker explains. He describes the different ways of making wine, the amount of time allowed each type to age, the way it must be tasted every so often to make sure it's doing what it should. He shows us how to taste wine by sipping a little, rolling it around the mouth, and then spitting it into a vat. He dries his mouth with the back of his hand. The coolness and the earthy smell in the cellar reminds me of the shelters we dug into the soil to escape the bombing in wartime. I am a bit claustrophobic and keep looking at the far entrance where the daylight forms a welcome rectangle. On our way out of the cellar he asks me if we would like to taste some of the wine. I decline not liking the taste of alcohol, but Clara and Violet accept enthusiastically. I walk in front of both of them with the man by my side, when he, maybe sensing my uneasiness, puts an arm around my shoulder in a friendly gesture of reassurance.

We emerge in a little whitewashed room, with a small table in the middle, covered by a red checkered table-cloth—the ironing folds still in it—three bottles of wine and three glasses. It is a rather naïve little trap. Used as I am to the aggressive hammering ads from North American media, this is discreet in it spareness, almost timid. The man has not taken his arm off me yet and I start to feel a little uncomfortable, particularly because despite the demonstration of affection I have no intention of buying any wine. Suddenly he takes his arm from me and puts it around Violet's shoulder. Violet turns bright pink and starts to melt away visibly, while he, emboldened by her reactions kisses her on the cheek. I am pleased, if for no other reason than that his interest in Violet allows me to be free of him.

While he is busy with his largesse, he gives me a significant look and tells me, in his fast Umbrian accent. "Look, she is already in love with me and I haven't even started on her."

We all laugh when I translate verbatim; it all seems quite good-natured. And then he winks at me and adds, "What I have to do to get some business."

I feel unhappy at this naked admission of his use of sexual titillation in order to sell wine. I don't tell Violet about his remark. I hope that we can buy our wine and leave. While I am engaged in this bit of national embarrassment, an English couple walks in. They are in their mid-forties, he in atrocious shorts and she in no-nonsense travelling clothes. She walks straight to the wine seller, who is still busy with Violet, takes the arm that is still wrapped around her and puts it around herself.

"Me too," she says. Then pointing to her proffered cheek, she adds, "Kiss me right here."

This is the man's moment of glory. He doesn't have enough lips to kiss around. His face is flushed, his eyes are shining and his hands are busy all over the ladies. All the while he gives me that "Don't interfere, I am doing my business" look that increasingly annoys me. The English woman's husband looks on blankly, without comment. Everybody buys a lot of wine and we finally leave.

Violet had repeatedly said how, on earlier visits to Italy, she was annoyed at the obnoxious behaviour of Italian men. I have been told about Latin lechery so many times by so many people, that I think who am I to disagree? When I want to elicit a chuckle, I always declare myself a sexual refugee from Italy.

I have sunk again into an apologetic mood. I decide I owe some kind of explanation about what was going on in the shop, so when Violet says, "Do you know when the man put an arm around you back in the cellar?"

I am ready to apologize for the man's behaviour, because I am sure she, no fool, understood his ruse.

"I was jealous." she says.

I think I am missing something. I better keep my mouth shut.

❦

We arrive in Orvieto at the scorching hour of four in the afternoon. By now the stones of the piazza have absorbed the sun's heat for several hours and have started to reverberate it back, like a pizza oven. We begin to search for a modest hotel, and, having been spoiled by the abbey's abundance of space, we decide we will get three separate rooms. Also, Clara needs a good night's rest since she has been driving most of the day and will have to drive most of tomorrow. Sleeping alone will be our only luxury.

We search around the town where we are confronted by a series of horrible, suffocating, modern hotels that look like downscale versions of a Holiday Inn, minus the glamour.

We finally find almost what we want: a little hotel in the main piazza, which, because of its central location, will certainly be noisy tonight. But it has potted palms, a fat dog stretched across the entrance, and a cuckoo clock on the wall. When we open the windows of our rooms, we are entranced by the sight of the cathedral, which is one of the finest examples of Italian gothic architecture. After dragging our suitcases up to the rooms, we are exhausted, hot and famished.

I am interested in the local cuisine, so we walk around looking for a place that serves boar and venison, which has been the specialty in these parts since Roman times. We are horrified by the prices, so we content ourselves with plain, boring chicken.

We retire early. As soon as I finish my shower and set myself to write a few notes, the choir starts. It's a group of young people rehearsing songs for the coming celebration of some saint or other. The voices are young, untrained, enthusiastic and out of tune. There are also two guitars and a mouth harmonica. All are being conducted rather erratically by a young man wearing nothing but a pair of blue jeans. The singers and players keep trying, again and again, laughing and teasing each other.

As they do, the pigeons are awakened by the cacophony and start cooing and flapping their wings, flying short, uncertain circles around the saints' statues on the facade of the cathedral, in front of which the choir is practising.

Sleep is out of the question, so I listen absentmindedly to that assemblage of soloists unable to meld into a half-homogeneous choir. I stand by the windowsill thinking myself concealed in the darkened room, when I see the hotel owner just below me tilted back on his chair, looking comfortably at me, as if he had paid the ticket. He makes no bones about his lack of discretion; in fact he winks at me and asks me how I am liking the performance.

"Fine," I say tersely, withdrawing a little further inside, to hide, belatedly, the fact that I have no clothes on. I am almost ready to go back to bed, certainly not to sleep, but to listen from a more discreet position, when the voices stop and the mouth organ starts a solo trip of its own, soaring easily above the silent piazza.

Suddenly everything is magic. The facade of the cathedral, which was always beautiful, now becomes ethereal; its mosaics glitter in the moonlight like sequins. The proportions of the architectural elements are a music of rhythmical forms, and the colours exist only in tones, for the moon dips them in blue and paler blue. There they are, the young people, hushed and close to each other on the white marble steps like pots of geraniums. The sound of the mouth organ is plaintive, breathy. There is a longing, delicate bending of the notes, like thin filaments not knowing where to land, a lagoon of unbearable tenderness that puts a chill into me in the heat of the night. Even the pigeons have stopped cooing, the sound has lulled them into blind animal reverence. I am nailed in front of the window, a bed sheet clutched around me, hardly believing this gift from the night, the thing one hopes for, when travelling, but which seldom ever happens. A fortuitous conjunction of place, time, and events that together shape an epiphany of delight.

I notice the police, evidently called by somebody wishing to sleep, waiting on their bicycles at the edge of the piazza for the solo to end before intervening, not wanting to miss out on the night's entertainment. When the solo ends, applause comes from windows that look dark and deserted, from the hotel owner, from me and from the police.

After that I cannot sleep, I don't want to sleep. In fact I don't want to sleep for the rest of my life, who knows what I might miss when wastefully unconscious. I hear the choir members and the police chatting away in the night, their voices slowly becoming fainter in the distance.

In the morning we walk around Orvieto, a small historic town of rough grace and provincial countenance. Mass tourism has mercifully missed it. During the day the cathedral is even more majestic than at night. Looking at it, I wonder at the financial effort that the building of such a complex structure must have taken on a population that had, at the time of its construction, an economy no more substantial than that of a developing country of today. The cathedral testifies to a society with a common purpose, having an amazingly long-lasting absence of personal corruption that would be very difficult to find now. The funds for such structures were made available in a continuous flow for several centuries, from people who were living at a subsistence level, and sometimes, during famines and plagues, well below it. In fact those great cathedrals were not built by philanthropists, or the papacy, but by the townsfolk who believed in the desirability and necessity of art and religion, concepts that transcended their rather miserable everyday lives.

Although I am not religious, I am moved by this kind

of dedication, particularly in small towns like this one that show no sign of historic wealth, and where the personal sacrifice that must be made to keep up such structures is quite heroic.

By contrast I feel quite self-indulgent, walking around in what I think is a search for myself, which would be almost a holiday if I hadn't decided to write about it. When I look at that cathedral I almost want to commit a heroic deed of my own.

We finally give up on saving and venture into a restaurant that serves only wild game. I feel daring and, since I have never eaten any, order some hare. It tastes like a more masculine rabbit, a bit chewier, with a tinge of goat in it. But then anything wild always tastes like goat to me. I am definitely not a gourmet.

Walking around the town, we notice a great number of wooden sculptures placed everywhere: as ornaments in the main piazza, as benches squeezed along the walls of the narrow streets, as supporting elements of small balconies. The city is bedecked in those lovely works that appear to be contemporary and of local manufacture, for we haven't seen anything like them anywhere else. The sculptures are of high artistic quality, a felicitous mixture of sophistication and folksiness. Refreshingly, they do not attempt to make any intellectual statement. Some dolls and furniture evidently made by the same hands are for sale in a large shop, in the centre of the town. Outside the door of the shop is a small Trojan horse, on which children climb happily. I am so intrigued by this lovely wooden exuberance that I walk into the store and ask the salesgirl for information about the sculptor. The "sculptor" turns out to be three sisters, who have learned their art from their grandfather, who was a coffin maker. I am also told that the three are well known in Italy and abroad and have a thriving workshop in the town.

I am inordinately pleased by this discovery and set out to find their workshop on my own, since Violet and Clara do not feel like walking with me. The workshop turns out to be a small factory, larger than I had imagined, and well equipped, with a dozen men working in it. I am disappointed that none of the sisters is there, I would have loved to talk to them.

Going back to the hotel I see that the three sisters have inspired at least one other wood carver in the town. On a little descending street I find an old man who calls himself a "pinocchier" because he does nothing but carve Pinocchios. His work is crude and naïve, done solely with the help of an axe. He works sitting on a chair in front of his house, a couple of cronies giving him advice from the wings, the smell of rosemary and garlic wafting from inside his kitchen, where his old wife is cooking. Since I could not afford any of the three sisters' dolls, I buy one of his Pinocchios and feel like a victor of sorts.

We are ready to leave, but I don't quite want to. I love this little town, and would be very happy to spend more time here, alone, talking to the people, stepping out of my daily life, entering theirs.

While I wait for my companions to pack their suitcases, I go for a short walk on my own. I'm in the mood for solitary musing, so I walk on a sloping road behind the cathedral, away from the city centre.

Suddenly I am in the country, which is dotted with tiny ponds of water twinkling in the sun like blue sequins. There are sheep in the valley, too. I hear the whistle of the shepherds and the barking of the dogs. The scene is bucolic to an operatic extent; I feel I have stumbled onto a tableau from which I will have to awake sooner or later. But I have stumbled on a memory instead: the day of my conversion.

It was on a day like this, in a countryside of safe and familiar shades of tame greens and yellow, a sky untouched by clouds. I don't recall now if it came upon me suddenly or gradually. It was a feeling of utter completion, the world being as it should be, good and bad, the future and the past in a continuous ribbon of purposeful days. I hadn't felt like that ever. I was only eighteen and my life had been an existential struggle since I could remember. The fights with my mother had ceased with her death, but the bitterness of her disappointment in me still stung my emerging conscience.

And then, for no reason at all, came that moment of simple glory, a day like no other, of clear, unhindered vision. It wasn't as if somebody had given me a passport to a better part of myself, or that I saw clearly a path to follow. That would have been easy and prosaic. That moment was a gift the nature of which was almost impossible to define. Nothing seemed to have changed and everything did. And then I knew what it was. For the first time in my life I didn't feel guilty. I hadn't stolen anything, I hadn't lied, I hadn't masturbated or desired anybody I shouldn't have. I hadn't gossiped, I hadn't shirked any of my duties. I felt clean and laundered, the day was innocent of sin.

It was as if a new me had been born. I had other similar epiphanies, other moments of communion later in life, but none ever came near to that first humble moment of utter acceptance.

When the moment dissolved, I didn't feel deprived; something had been given to me, and then passed away. What had been given was the knowledge of what all those years of confessions for my sins had done to my soul. How the simple joy of being had been gradually replaced by the complicated burden of not being enough. It wasn't a decision that I made right there and then, but I never again set foot in a church for religious purposes.

❦

We are on the road heading for Spoleto. We pass the Tiber again, which, this early in its course, I had assumed to be a small river. Instead it is already of considerable size, teeming with barges. It occurs to me that if we left this wretched little car here and boarded one of those languid barges we would land in Rome right under the Milvio Bridge. But I have been in Rome many times and never learned to feel at ease in it, maybe because it is infested with priests, bureaucrats and the jet set of Europe. But then, if I went now, I would perhaps find it quite different, for I am continuously surprised by this new Italy I am experiencing.

We drive up to the little city of Spoleto and arrive right after lunch time. I always wanted to see Spoleto, a leftover from the Middle Ages, out of the way, in the middle of the Umbrian mountains. But my companions will not budge from the cafe in the main piazza. In fact, Clara looks around displeased and declares the place grotesque.

I have only a short time to make an exploration of the area behind the modest cathedral. So I quickly walk along a few streets so narrow that the walls have to be kept apart by aerial bridges. The sun hardly knows the bottom of these mazes, only the top floors are fortunate enough to open into the light. Suspended washrooms balance precariously on rickety wooden posts, like aerial second thoughts. I am looking up at displays of washing and geraniums hanging out of windows, when I feel a tugging on my hand. I look down and see a miniature girl with round brown eyes and a moustache of milk under her pink nose. She is holding on to my finger, with complete trust.

"Let's go to the fountain in the piazza," she says.

"Why do you want to go to the fountain?" I ask.

"We go and have a little bath," she says. I am trying to understand the difference between a little bath and a large one. Meanwhile I try to direct her gently towards an open door from which, I think, she has come. But she is not so easily diverted. The piazza is where she wants to go, not her house.

A barely older girl, whom I take to be her sister, appears and takes charge of the situation by taking hold of the little one's hand and dragging her away.

"What's your name?" I ask as they go towards their house.

"Clarissa," says the older one, "but this one," she adds, indicating her sister, "has no name."

"Yes, I do, I do," cries the unnamed one, and keeps crying all the way to the house. I still feel the velveteen touch of the child's hand in mine and feel a little blessed, but I remember the cruelty of older sisters.

When I go back to the piazza, I exhort my companions to come with me to see this mediaeval village that looks frozen in a Christmas scene—not the northern kind, with the Druidic tree and all the glitter—but one replete with mystical, poor shepherds and peasants still seen in the crèches of old. Clara doesn't quite want to but then surrenders, and they both come with me. My companions are not impressed. This poor town is nothing compared to Florence or even Siena. I walk around, with them trundling behind me, trying to explain what cannot be explained. I feel more stupid by the minute. Finally, I give up and try to re-enter the piazza by another route. I can't find my way and circle around the town trying to get to the base of the hill where we have left the car. Twenty minutes later we arrive at the bottom. I am acutely aware of how bad I am at directions and how I don't know where I am most of the time.

We are late now. I sit next to Clara, with a map spread out on my knees, preparing to navigate us back to the Abbey of Monte Oliveto. It is a long drive and we must arrive before dusk because of Clara's problem with the dark. I do not know the road but concentrate very hard to avoid making any more mistakes. The road goes through Perugia, where we manage to have a quick coffee in the main piazza, and then on through lovely countryside. I am too nervous to enjoy it because I want to navigate us back in safety. When we finally discern the bell tower of the abbey in the distance, I am relieved and feel a great sense of accomplishment. We are tired and hot and look forward to lying in the cool of our empty cells.

When we come to park the car in the inner courtyard, we find the whole space, except ours, is taken by four large buses. Our abbey is crawling with German students armed with easels and drawing pads, who are spread among the cypresses sketching every root, leaf and branch with the diligence of the neophyte. I try to strike up a conversation but they speak none of the languages I speak, so I smile wanly keeping the art teacher in me from giving them advice. They are polite, reserved and respectful of the surroundings, but our wonderful isolation is shattered. Gone is our wandering around wearing only a towel and singing indiscreetly in the shower. As it turns out, we don't have to worry, because when we enter our corridor, we are regaled with female nudes walking around in statuary nonchalance. Germans have never been ones to consider nudity a sign of orgiastic tendencies. Only we Italians do. The men have been segregated on the floor below, but even there, where one would expect more noise there is only a discreet silence.

I cannot help comparing my art college students' boister-ousness to the discipline and silence of these budding artists.

We eat our supper in the entrance tower restaurant, just outside the kitchen door, where a pack of local women is busy cooking traditional masterpieces. The food is superb, though the service is slow, casual and rather surly. A couple of pussycats keep polishing our shins. Oddly enough, the restaurant is always full, every day of the week, even when the abbey's dormitory is empty. People from the surrounding villas come here for a rural and mystical outing.

I converse with the restaurant owners and ask about the monks. I make the mistake of referring to the poverty of the monks, something I have come to believe, since the Church has been informing the world for years about the economic decay of its holdings.

"Poor?" the lady says, as if she were being made the object of a not so funny joke.

"Poor my foot. They own twenty-seven farms, most of them highly prosperous vineyards," and plops a bottle of their wine on our table as though to prove it. Her face is a smaller version of a Mount Rushmore face, a sculpted hardness permanently etched there. The Tuscans have been at war with the papal states for centuries, and no love is lost between the two.

When she is in a softer mood, the restaurant owner tells me that her establishment was a family business until her younger brother died, just the previous week. I feel the presence of personal pain like a scar on this little Paradise of jasmine and roses.

We are about to leave for Venice. At the last moment we visit the basilica. The cloister surprises us with its fugue of elegant arches. On the internal wall a series of frescoes by Signorelli and Sodoma look as if they were painted yesterday, because of the lack of pollution in the area. In the middle of the cloister, a well is surrounded by rose bushes, the primitive ones found in the mystical paintings of old times. We enter the large basilica, but do not find it particularly exciting except for the high-backed stalls, decorated by masterworks of marquetry.

And, oh yes, we find a little shop, equipped with a chatty friar and all the products that have been the specialty of the Benedictine order through the centuries. The liqueurs distilled from walnuts, chestnuts and local herbs, the herbal remedies; and, to be in touch with the times, some ancient beauty products. It is unfortunate that they have also added some bad reproductions of the Signorelli frescoes and some awful little rosaries probably made in India. It isn't Disneyland but I wish it had been somewhat more chaste.

We are packing, the dormitory is empty again, and I am looking for somebody to pay. I am in the process of leaving our money in an envelope, on the desk of an empty office, when a happy rotund friar appears with our bill. He is the telefonista friar, who has finally returned from his spiritual exercises. He talks a stream, in a warm, rascally way, as extroverted as a young boy, even though his hair is completely white. He is busy telling me about his experience in the Swiss retreat where he has been, the food he didn't like and the wine he didn't drink. I love him instantly; if he goes on for another half hour, I think I will end up confessing to him. My soul recoils at the thought of confessing forty years of sins.

He has got the bill all wrong. We have been charged for less than our stay. Maybe they are so wealthy they can afford to be disorganized. I point it out to him, and he genuinely looks as if he wanted to be wrong. Maybe he was testing my conscience.

I am reluctant to leave, I have been pleased by this

sacred place, and nobody has pushed religion on me. In fact the experience has been so discreet and restorative I promise myself I will come back again. On our way out I shudder for the last time at the cistern, breathe in the jasmine fragrance and wave at the cat lying with its four legs open in an obscene homage to the morning sun. Goodbye Monte Oliveto.

🐛

On the way to Venice I retreat to a private corner of my mind, to rekindle some childhood memories. There are so many now, mostly pleasant ones. This surprises me because I have a tendency to remember only the painful ones, and those can wait until I reach Milan.

We surrender the car in Siena, with a sigh of relief. I do not feel responsible for the road anymore, I can relax and enjoy the countryside from the luxury train speeding towards Venice. Everything is first-class: the cool compartment, the window shades installed between the glass panes so that the glare can be dimmed while the landscape is not, the food in the restaurant car. The clothes the other passengers wear make me feel shabby and underprivileged.

Right before Bologna a train conductor appears to check our tickets. I present my rail pass and he finds that I have not put the date in the right slot, which a passenger is supposed to do every day that the pass is used. But since it is his business to put a hole in the slot to invalidate it, I don't worry too much.

Not him. He embarks on a vociferous lecture about how passengers try to get away with freebies on his train by not putting the date in the right slot. I am trying feebly to make him understand that once he has put his damn hole in the damn slot I can't use it anyway, date or no date. I don't see how he can possibly believe that I am trying to get away with anything, when all he has to do is make it right. He doesn't have to yell at me. But he is turned on by his own aggression and keeps on and on in a louder voice, giving me a sermon I don't need. I finally fall silent, since I don't know what else to say to placate him. The rest of the passengers are looking at me as if I were a thief, while he continues in a fit of bureaucratic frenzy. My two companions also look at the two of us as if it were a disagreeable performance. The conductor finally leaves but comes back several times, looking at me intently. I feel generous and am tempted to put my feet on the seat in front of me, so that he can start on me again and have some relief from the boredom of a life of punching little holes in rail passes, but I am sleepy and want to rest. It might just be that I have met a particularly awful bureaucrat, but unfortunately this behaviour is familiar, reminding me of the reasons I left Italy and didn't come back for so long. I know the little holes have nothing to do with his anger. He felt macho beyond his wildest expectations. The behaviour of some men towards me does not always call for charitable consideration. I am hurt and humiliated.

I do not really want to go to Venice. If it weren't for Violet and Clara I would avoid it and stop in Bologna, one of my favourite cities. But the train flies along out of Tuscany, through the fertile plains of Emilia, and finally into the Veneto region, of which Venice is the main city. We are already seeing the glittering of the sea in the distance and people are starting to take their luggage from the racks. Venice is a great magnet for international tourism, the capital of ersatz romanticism.

There is always a great deal of expectation around Venice. People really think that the sea comes right up to the curbs, which of course it doesn't. In fact the water

—dank, dark and tamed—is a few feet below the curb. It doesn't glimmer as in the grand canals, but because of the narrowness of the waterways, remains a silent black presence, mysterious and uninviting. The gondolas are as black as the water, gliding noiselessly under the bridges, furtive and funereal except when full of tourists. Venice has always been a bit of a whore, wholly for sale, knick-knacks at every turn, vulgar little glass trinkets, and singers belting out the Neapolitan "O sole mio" in the night, as if the city didn't have its own wonderful music. But then there is also the Venice of the alleys, away from the lagoon, a Levantine labyrinth, intricate and endless, designed to puzzle, a place of surprises and enchantment, rather seedy, but intensely sensual and intimate.

Venice has been dying for so many years that it has become its way of living. Its grandeur has faded into a penumbra of crumbling stucco and corroded marble, but it still manages to support a cultural life equal, if not superior to, less decaying cities like Florence and Milan.

We walk around becoming more and more tired, Venice is such a large city. We always end up sitting in a cafe to rest—one time it is in the sixteenth-century Cafe Florian, and the bill for a couple of cappuccinos and a glass of water is equal to our budget for a week of food. It is because of the music, the bill states. If it was music that we needed, I could have sung "O Sole Mio" for nothing.

I try to explain to my companions the intricacies of the architecture of Venice, from the baroque, to the moorish, to the plain expedient, but I can see that they are put off by the oldness, the sheer crumbliness of the city. Half the monuments are covered in scaffolding for repairs, and the great horses in the San Marco Cathedral are shrouded in plywood. I feel bad because I cannot summon the energy to arouse their enthusiasm. Venice is an architectural showpiece, but Violet and Clara feel the urge to hunt for trinkets to take home, since these are their last few days in Italy.

The room in our hotel is small and hot. Again we seem to be in a space too small for the three of us. Its ugliness is almost obscene; there is a perversely excessive use of ceramic tiles, and on the wall's expansive whiteness there is nothing more than one forlorn little print—ugly enough that nobody feels like stealing it. Next to the rickety beds are those awful upright coffins that are a poor excuse for closets. The lacquered elegance of Provence and the quaint coziness of the English seem totally unknown here. And that is a pity because the old Italian houses were truly magnificent in a spacious, unadorned way. The floor tiles in our room are a speckled burgundy and white, a kind of slippery stale salami. Anything that drops on them disappears into mottled infinity.

We go out and stop by a street vendor to let Violet buy some ice cream. When she puts her hand in her purse to take out her money, she finds another hand searching for the same thing. The hand is attached to a well-dressed fellow in a cream suit, a camera slung across his chest. He seems to be with two equally well-dressed men. They all look like tourists. By a stroke of unbelievable luck, another man suddenly comes towards us from across the street and grasps the thief firmly by the arm with one hand, while showing his police badge with the other. The whole affair takes place in such a short time that Clara, who is looking at some glass beads a little further on, has missed the whole thing.

One of the thieves, for some reason, believes that I can intervene on his behalf with the policeman, so he begs me, in broken Italian, to let him go. I ask him where he is from, "Algeria," he says. Suddenly his well-dressed demeanour collapses into a beggar's stance and he tells me a story of poverty and misery while the policeman is telling me not to listen or talk to him.

Finally Clara notices that something is amiss and comes over looking worried.

We are all frozen for a while, nobody knowing quite what to do. The only one who seems to be in his element is the plainclothes policeman, who keeps his hand firmly around the thief's arm.

We wait for the police launch, which is to take us all to the police station. But the lagoon is jammed with traffic, and the launch requires a long time to make its way through the tangle of crowded canals.

I muse about what has happened to Italy that we must now import thieves from Algeria, as if we didn't have enough of our own. In fact I heard that, not so long ago, the thieves in Naples formed a union. When the Neapolitan police became uppity and started to make arrests as if they had the right, the thieves went on strike, demonstrating in front of the city hall and stopping their bribe payments to the authorities. The police, thank God, came to their senses and resumed taking the bribes, as they always had done, and the thieves went on with their craft. Bloodshed was avoided. If the story is apocryphal I would hate to know about it.

Finally the police launch arrives and we all pile in for a wonderful ride on the Canal Grande—a ride that we wouldn't have been able to afford on our own. The arresting plain clothes policeman is a good-looking rogue, and the three of us find it difficult to hide our admiration. Unless he is from another planet he must be aware of his effect on the ladies. I try to strike up a conversation with a mousy-looking second fiddle who keeps telling me he wants to immigrate to Canada. I tell him that Canada is closed, they closed it some years ago.

At the station the three Algerians are taken into

custody. Until they tell the police who they are—since on being frisked no documents of any kind were found—due legal process cannot be started. We are taken to another part of the city for our deposition. We enter a cool, monumental building, curiously unlike a police department, and are received by the police commissioner. Perversely, he is even better looking than the one we have left at the other police station. It is almost more than we can bear. At least this time we can look at him while he labours at the computer, asking us pertinent questions. To a man with looks like this, we are ready to confess anything, anytime. When he finishes, he reads the report back to me, his long dark lashes lowered on his tanned cheekbones. I find, with relief, that his Italian has some grammatical errors. It would have been unbearable if he had also been capable of impeccable prose.

The whole affair is over almost too soon. We enjoyed the ride and the sense of mild danger. But, really there was no danger. The police were extremely gentle and the thieves looked more like impersonators of *Casablanca* characters than menacing criminals. The mousy second fiddle takes us back to the centre of the city, after which we sit in a cafe and wait to see a regatta.

It is the last day in Italy for Violet and Clara. Tomorrow they will leave for Strasbourg. I will remain in Venice for a couple of days before heading south to visit my relatives. Their train leaves at six in the morning, so I ask the hotel owner to wake us up at five. He looks at me as if I had suggested that he jump in the lagoon. He goes to sleep like the rest of the civilized world. So he gives me an alarm clock set for four o'clock. In the morning I wake up at about five-thirty and the alarm clock sounds just fifteen minutes later. We all get up rather groggily and start preparing ourselves for departure. Clara has asked me to help her carry her suitcase to the station, because she has a bad back. Her suitcase is not very heavy so I don't mind.

I finally put Violet and Clara on the train and say goodbye.

I walk back from the quays towards the main station. On passing the Information Office it occurs to me that I should find out about trains for my journey south, the day after the morrow. At this early hour there is already a line in front of the door, so I take a number and I put myself in line. Behind me on the wall is a large black scheduling board with departures and arrivals clicking in every few seconds, but half of the board is not working. I keep turning around to see if the half-board has come alive, so that I can get my information from there instead of waiting in line, but no luck.

In turning around to look at the board, I meet the eyes of a man who smiles at me, in an expression of solidarity against the usual Italian inefficiency. I smile back and turn around to mind my line. It is almost my turn, so I lean on the door waiting for it to open and let me in, when a gentle tap on my shoulder makes me turn around. It's the man behind me.

"Do you want to go to bed with me?" he asks.

His accent is pure Oxford, his tone neutral and his demeanour courteous, civilized and contained. He has grey hair and grey eyes, and is dressed decently. I open my mouth not quite knowing what will come out, when the door opens and I tumble into the Information Office. I gather my wits somehow and ask when the train for Bologna is leaving. I am given the schedule, and I leave from another door without once looking back. I walk out of the station, up a bridge, down another and sit next to a tarpaulin-covered gondola, swishing idly in the water. I want to take time to think about the man.

I am mad at him because his crude proposal forced me

to flee when, really, I would have loved some male companionship. I had been in the company of women all the time I had been abroad and would have welcomed a bit of flirtatious repartee, particularly because the gentleman was good-looking and his English seemed that of an educated person. I was not interested in anything as intellectual as sex, just a bit of interesting conversation. I ask myself why didn't he ask to join me for breakfast, for instance, or for a cappuccino in one of Venice's thousand cafes. A request like his was almost made for a refusal, unless he thought I was so sophisticated as to do away with the preliminaries and come down to the real issue. He thought wrong: not only am I not that sophisticated but I am pathologically shy. The fact that I am married does not really justify to me my evasion of a sexual proposition. My reaction is not a moral one, it is an emotional one. I also feel mad at myself for not being able to answer with some slick and funny line. Where is my wit when I need it?

I cheer myself up by thinking that, had I answered, "Yes, of course," he could have replied, "Thank you, I just wanted to know. Have a good day."

And then, to save my honour, I would have had to strangle him.

A gondolier comes to take the tarpaulin from his gondola and smiles at me, thinking that I might want to hire him.

"No," I say, "I am too poor."

"Then you row," he says, "and I sit down and sing for you." We both laugh and I get up to go, feeling a great affection for this corpse of a city.

Back in the hotel I find that the owner has taken my suitcase and transferred it to another room. In anticipation of my companions' departure, I had arranged for a single room without a private bath, so that I can save some money. I am surprised when I see that he has given me a large double room with a shower for half the listed price. I feel unaccountably good about it. I thank him and order breakfast. He serves me, with avuncular care, chatting away with ease about the world's problems. He plonks his cat Tintoretto on the chair in front of me.

"For company," he says.

The cat is obese because it has been taught to eat the rims of pizzas, since the owner likes only the middle where most of the toppings are. He is taking good care of me because, he says, I am in my late fifties.

"How do you know it?" I ask him, horrified at the thought of my age being that obvious.

"I have seen your age in the passport," and he adds, "I am curious, I always read the passports," as he pours more hot milk in my cup. I feel so good I become expansive, I speak about my life in Canada, my son and my husband, and he talks about his children, two grown girls, one a psychologist, the other an engineer. Since he is a little older than I am (the bastard doesn't reveal how much older) we exchange our wartime experiences, he with his elegant Venetian accent, me in an Italian that has lost almost all of its colourful Tuscan irreverence.

I almost don't want to go anywhere. I have a large room to myself, and Tintoretto purring in front of me. For the first time in a long while, I can go where I want at the pace I feel comfortable with, if I feel compelled to explore.

From my new room I see nothing but a patchwork of roofs, clay tiles that started out as a terracotta red, but are now a bleached pink, a putrid green and a sooty black sprinkled with the emerald green of weeds all the healthier for being where they shouldn't be. On the roofs, as far as I can see, is a rickety ensemble of loggias of various sizes built for no other purpose than to catch the evening breeze. When the weather is very hot people hoist their mattresses up to the roof and sleep in those aerial nests. But during the day there is no sign of life except the gentle movement of the washing drying on the line. The walls I see disappearing into a dark courtyard have been patched so many times that graffiti would be an improvement.

I find out that night that there is a restaurant right below me where cooking starts around three in the morning. I hear the clanging of dishes from the courtyard and the strong smell of herbs in oil proves to be too much for me to sleep. I don't mind though; these domestic comforting smells keep me company, and the human noises have an everyday modest familiarity that makes me feel safe, like a tuck-in at night.

During the day I walk at random through the old Jewish ghetto called Giudecca, a place of tiny shops and tinier houses. Even the canals are no more than black ribbons undulating lazily at the silent passage of a boat. There is washing hanging up near the sky, and cats look at me from above, like tame gargoyles. I hope Italians will never stop hanging their washing out of their windows. I would miss the sight of their intimate garments. I suppose I am still curious about people's lives. I remember the underwear of Silvio's mother back in Florence when I was about eight years old.

We all laughed at the size of the knickers of Silvio's mother. We laughed, not only at their size, but also at the flowery fabric she used for a garment that was supposed to be most discreet. Silvio's mother was very sick. She had something wrong with her blood circulation, but I am not sure now what it was. She was enormous and could hardly move from her house, where she lived with her husband and the two children, Silvio the older, a terror at twelve, and Alberto, a timid little fellow about my age.

We all feared Silvio. He was aggressive, boisterous, pitiless and domineering. He treated his younger brother as if he were vermin, and the rest of us pretty much the same.

When we played it was he who decided who was going to die, or who was going to pay the price of failure. He had an easy time; our group was made up mostly of girls, so there was hardly any challenge to his bullying. We humoured him, thinking our vassalage a kind of payment for the generosity with which he showed us his body. He wasn't shy about letting us see his pink penis every time he had an erection, nor did he mind if we watched him peeing, and when he started to sprout a few pubic hairs, he showed us them too. It was worth it, particularly to me, who had no brothers.

One day we were playing at something very serious, when his brother Alberto came looking for him, bawling so desperately he could hardly speak. We were used to him crying because Silvio never let him play any significant role. But we had never before seen him cry like this.

Silvio, mean and busy as usual, didn't want to be bothered with him, so he told him to go and cry someplace else. But Alberto got our attention, even if he didn't get his brother's. Finally even Silvio lost his cool and asked him what was the matter. Alberto managed to stop crying long enough to blurt out, "Mom is dead."

We recoiled almost physically, leaving a little space around the boys out of respect.

Silvio went on doing what he was doing, as if he hadn't heard his brother. Alberto stopped his desperate crying, but went on whimpering, looking pathetically at Silvio, waiting for a sign. Finally Silvio stopped playing, looked at his brother as if he were seeing him for the first time, and without a word, took his hand, in an unusual gesture that was half resignation, half unintended affection.

We looked at them going home, suddenly small, suddenly like the children that they were, diminished, alone.

The adults went to the funeral. We children were supposed to go, but if I remember it right, my sister and I couldn't go because one of us was sick.

Not long after that Silvio came to sleep at our house. His father had been called out of town, so the children had to be left with neighbours. Alberto stayed with other people, while Silvio stayed with us. He could board only with us. The reason was that both he and I wet the bed. Besides being shameful, and therefore a secret, my mother was the only one who would have provided a bed equipped with a rubber sheet. She was used to it. Not that she was cavalier about my bed-wetting. She thought that I was as evil at night as I was during the day. It was not out of sense of delicacy that she kept my secret. It was a disgrace for the family to have a child of nine still wetting the bed.

I never became cavalier about wetting the bed either. In fact it was one of the great shames of my childhood. I prayed to God to make me stop peeing in bed. My embarrassment over it continued into adulthood. It finally ended when I mentioned it in self-deprecation to a friend, a Swedish surgeon, and was told that bed-wetting is caused by an immature nervous system rather than by emotional problems. Eventually, all children reach a stage at which their nervous system and the rest of their body are balanced and the bed-wetting stops. Until then, absolutely nothing can be done about it, except putting a rubber sheet on the mattress.

But back then, Silvio and I shared a shameful secret that, like all secrets, was very hard to bear. Neither of us ever talked about it, we knew we belonged to some outcast species that had not managed to be like others.

Out of delicacy for the boy, my mother sent me to wake him up in the morning, so that he didn't have to face my mother with a wet bed. Whenever the unmentionable did happen she would change the bed and wash the soiled sheets later, when Silvio was out playing.

So it was that one morning, not long after the death of his mother, I went into the living room where Silvio was sleeping on the sofa, to wake him up. I called him several times before I was able to make myself heard. When he finally woke up, he didn't quite remember where he was. He looked around a bit dazed, a bit cross-eyed, looking at me as if I were a stranger. Then he seemed to remember and got out of the bed to go to the bathroom.

I looked at his pillow, because something caught my eyes. It was a garment of some kind. It was neatly spread around the pillow. I looked at it and tried to recall where I had seen it before. And then I remembered. It was a pair of his mother's ridiculous, oversized, flowery underpants.

☙

I sit for a while in a small park—what isn't small in Venice?—and watch children, pigeons and dogs chasing each other. In front of me is an area where posters are hung, and I read idly the ads from the political parties running candidates in the forthcoming elections. There are twelve official parties listed, ranging in stance from the far left to the far right, with every silly nuance in between. It doesn't seem to matter because according to every person I have talked to the level of political corruption in Italy is such that the best solution would be to take the business of governing out of Italian hands and farm it out to somebody more sensible like the Swiss. But I don't think the Swiss would want the job.

Through an opening between houses, I see a funeral of gondolas pass by, each carrying big floral arrangements that make them look like floating gardens. The old men in the park remove their hats as a sign of respect.

I have nothing to do, nowhere particular to go, no deadlines. I can sit here and melt into the background, as if I were one of the pigeons. This is so strange and new to me. I am usually a workhorse of titanic energy. I think I might like to get used to this idling away the hours, hearing the city's breath without really listening.

Just before it's time for me to leave Venice, I sit down at the rickety table in my room, trying to write down a few impressions. When I start to write, another episode from my childhood leaps to my mind. I think it might have to do with just having observed a few nannies in the park and some old people accompanied by young servants. But I am not sure. I strain to find the real cause for the memory but don't find anything other than a probable visual association, so I accept it and write it down.

❦

My father did not consider his womanizing a trait to be ashamed of and my mother was not inclined to ignore it. She couldn't anyway since my father was not reticent about his conquests. On the contrary, he wore them with pride; as part of his personal baggage, like his Socialist party card and his undiluted German accent. He had come to Italy from his native Germany, from a village called Reynach, near the Swiss border, as a young engineer, at a time when Italy imported professional personnel from more technically advanced nations. My father had come reluctantly, expecting to complete his job and go back, but he fell in love with my mother and Italy, not necessarily in this order. Like most northerners he had failed to understand the complexity of the Italian character. He had adopted with a vengeance the ethical negligence of the Italians, but failed to acquire the humane personal warmth that must accompany it. He had applied his precise German intensity and physical lustiness to his philandering in an effort to acquire a social passport of sorts—one that would make him acceptable to the male Italian population. In the process, he became a caricature of a southern Don Juan.

To be charitable, his compulsive womanizing might have also been a consequence of death always being just a short step away from him—he had advanced tuberculosis. Or it might have been his "generosity," since his lovers ranged from the very young—he seemed to have been in trouble for a dalliance with a minor when he was younger—to the overripe: a woman who was in her late forties when he was only twenty-eight. Whatever the reasons for his sexual reconnoitring, my mother must have been of a stubbornly exclusive nature because she insisted, unaccountably, on marital fidelity. I say unaccountably because marital fidelity in my part of the woods and during my childhood was considered something pertaining to women, like breast feeding and worrying, but not at all to men.

The scenes between my parents were colourful, dramatic, tearful and, to the neighbourhood, highly entertaining. Once or twice some dishes flew about, crashing against the kitchen wall, but I don't remember who threw them. I like to think it was my mother.

My father was probably making a decent wage, but his

illness was expensive and so were the presents he lavished on his lovers. There was never enough money, certainly not for more spacious living quarters. Our apartment consisted of a room where we ate, sat listening to the radio, fought, and received our few friends; a bedroom for my sister Lieta and me with pink curtains and a basin stand in case a visiting doctor needed to wash his hands; and my parents' bedroom.

My parents' bedroom was always dark and mysterious with its black marble-topped bedside tables, reading lights with glass fringes and the sewing machine, shrouded by a doily, under the window. On my father's side was a large shelf containing his books, which we were forbidden to touch. Actually, we were forbidden to even enter my parents' bedroom, or touch anything that belonged to my father. He was never at home, but his presence was felt through a web of prohibitions effectively fencing in our tiny space. It was in the kitchen that we felt safe and reassured. That was where we did our homework; where my mother cooked our meals and sewed, washed and ironed our clothes, and where we had our bath in the winter, since it was the only warm place in the apartment. In the summer we children had our bath on the terrace. The terrace, just outside our kitchen door, was our sum-mer resort, it was our children's room, our only large space. To most observers the terrace would have looked like nothing more than a large backyard sitting on top of the wine merchant's roof. But to us it was where we could move and run with ease. We spent the winters looking longingly at the empty terrace, washed by rain. Our terrace meant winter nostalgia and summer celebration. My father never set foot on the terrace; we had our barriers, too.

Lieta and I were playing on the terrace when Ines knocked at our door. We were expecting a friend to come and play, so when the bell rang we ran to the door. But instead of Carla there was a small young woman, a suitcase by her side, smiling uncertainly at us, as if she was supposed to be known. We called my mother and retreated to the side, ogling her with our usual shameless curiosity. My mother came from the kitchen with a ladle in her hand, unsuspecting, apologizing as she always did.

The girl said, "I am Ines," and walked in. She looked at us expectantly, the head slightly tilted, chicken-like, to one side. My mother invited her to sit down, waiting, no doubt, for the visitor to say something. She was busy in the kitchen and didn't have all the time in the world, yet she didn't want to appear harried, the girl must have some good reason to be here.

"I am your servant," she said, as if it were perfectly natural for us to have a servant, "Your husband has hired me."

During the silence that followed, I got busy imagining what a servant would do for me. Maybe I could order her to make my bed, or even wash the dishes. I imagined delegating all my chores to her, including setting the table and cleaning my shoes. I wondered also if she could be on my side in an argument and be so kind as to beat my sister should the need arise. My mind was travelling fast through all kinds of possibilities.

"I don't need a servant," said my mother, forgetting to smile.

"Well," Ines said, "here I am."

My mother took a deep breath and put on the smile again. Would she like a coffee with a few drops of Marsala wine in it? I always knew when my mother disliked somebody because she smiled for no reason while extending this extra kindness, in a futile attempt at masking her real feelings. She would also deprecate her lack of facilities, and send me out on unnecessary errands, while apologizing for my appearance. I hated it when she did that; somehow I would always find myself on the receiving end of her sense of inadequacy.

The moment the guest left she would start on them with the sledgehammer of her condemnations. I never understood why she didn't tell them to have the courtesy of leaving because their very presence was unbearable to her.

Meanwhile Ines was sitting on our sofa completely unaware of the subtleties of my mother's kindness. In fact she was smiling back as if she already belonged, her suitcase firmly planted by her feet, and a multicoloured something that could have been a cardigan rolled up in her lap. The suitcase was held together by a cord looped through the handle and tied in a knot, which left some of the cord hanging down like a leash. Part of the cord seemed to be a stocking. I looked at her legs to see if one of her stockings was missing, but her feet were naked, with the toenails painted in scarlet. I thought it was very refined, to paint one's toenails. She wore platform shoes with ladders of black thongs laced all the way up to her ankles, like a Roman legionnaire, making her feet look too heavy for her skinny legs.

Even before my mother opened the sugar bowl, I jumped to my feet expecting her to send me to fetch more sugar in the kitchen. I didn't want to be described as forgetful by my mother, as I usually was. I wanted the servant to think the best of me. I was already hers.

"One spoonful or two?" I was starting to squirm. The sweet hostility of my mother was beginning to show through even to the most obtuse of observers. But not Ines, she had a creature's stance, expectant and stolidly optimistic, which would have been moving were it not for the fact that it was also unsettling. It was obvious that my father had employed her for purposes of his own, which at the time were not very clear to me. Certainly not because my mother needed a servant. First of all, we didn't seem to be in the economic bracket that could afford a servant, and even if we were my mother's obsession with cleanliness and order would not have accommodated another person's idea of how to keep house. Secondly, we lived in such a small place, a servant would have had to practically live on top of us. In fact, the only place a servant could sleep was on the living room couch. Think of the manoeuvres that would be required in the morning, to avoid bumping into one another as she dressed and we prepared for work or school. The more I thought about it, the more I liked it.

I could see that while I was increasingly rejoicing at the idea of Ines joining us, my mother was trying hard to avoid hiring her. I could see her eyes going from the sofa to the girl, then back to me, trying to find something wrong with me in order to become legitimately mad, then back to the girl, all the while holding her coffee cup with her little finger in a rigor mortis position that spoke volumes about her tense state.

"So, what kind of help do you intend to give us?" asked my mother idly, not really expecting a reasonable answer, for she didn't want anything reasonable from Ines.

"Whatever you want," said Ines, sinking her teeth in a biscuit. "I am a servant."

I am not sure, but I think I detected some pride in this statement, and I think this pride sent my mother into an atypical bout of silence. What weapon does one have against such reasonableness? Even my mother, who was a person of great resourcefulness, was running out of hints. It was time to stop being subtle and tell the girl something she obviously didn't know.

"I'm sorry, but I have no need for a servant. Besides I can't see where you would sleep. We only have two bedrooms and they are both occupied."

Ines must have been an imaginative little beast because she looked at the sofa on which she was sitting and patted it with one hand. Then she looked at my mother with a look that plainly said that my mother was bluffing. My mother chose another tactic.

"What did my husband say about your job?"

Ines came immediately alive at the mention of my father and said, "He said that you were in need of some help, what with two children and a man with tuberculosis. He thought that you would have liked a little respite from family chores while you were studying for your exams."

Evidently my father had not been shy about the details of my family's problems and had taken this stranger into his confidence to the point of mentioning that my mother was preparing for a competition to gain entrance to the public school system as a teacher. There had been heated arguments about it between my parents, because my father didn't want her to work. He liked his life cushioned by the exclusive attention of a wife and the rest of us, but my mother was looking at life as a future widow, for my father's illness had been declared incurable.

My father also saw this type of planning on the part of my mother as an ominous calculation of family economic matters in which his own demise figured prominently. He didn't seem to care about what happened to us once he had gone. But my mother did, and even though it might have seemed indelicate to prepare oneself for an awful eventuality, she wasn't going to be caught penniless with two children to sustain. But she was very insecure about the outcome of her exams. She didn't want anybody to know about them, so that if she didn't succeed she would avoid the humiliation of having to admit to her failure.

But when Ines mentioned her upcoming exams, she knew that her husband was engaging in a sort of subtle revenge, spreading the information around, to a stranger even, while also engaging in a bit of libertine titillation with this young girl sitting on our sofa as unaware and stolid as a cauliflower.

I didn't know any of this while I was looking at Ines. Only after the death of my father, did my mother finally speak against him, and all of this became apparent. I was shocked by the callousness of a husband who would bring a flirt right into his family's house.

For the time being I kept looking at the extraordinary aspect of Ines.

There was almost nothing about her that wasn't red. Her hair was a cloud of red mist tamed at the top by a red ribbon, and then let go in a minor explosion that caught the light like flaming dust. Her skin was hidden by freckles so profuse that it was hard to know if her skin colour was blue-white or red-brown. A shaft of light had also awakened a gauze of red dawn all over her face, softening the stark sharpness of her features. Her eyes were large and pale, the colour of acorns. Every time she blinked they disappeared under those eyelashes which were of the same hue as her freckles, leaving nothing but her mouth to speak for itself. Her lips were painted bright red with two little gothic cusps on the upper lip, in a sort of permanent kiss, while the colour of the lower had been eaten up until only the rim was left. Her nose was small, curved at the base and a little flared. She was an angular, nervous little creature as different from us as if she were coming from Mars. She clutched her knitted purse with both hands and kept crossing her legs from one side to the other as if she had to pee.

When my mother finally said, "Let's wait for my husband and see," I knew that Ines had won and that she would be staying. I almost leaped to my feet and embraced her.

I knew that she was going to be on my side, even though the reason why she should be was rather vague. Maybe the fact that she looked so odd would make her a natural ally of somebody that was as unacceptable as me, or maybe with an outsider's instinct she would ally herself with the most vulnerable member of the family. In retrospect I think that Ines must have looked at me as her safety net, for she probably understood that my father, far from being her ally, would be a danger to her. I was to be a cushion between her and my father's lust.

When my father came home, he greeted her with a studied indifference. There was no discussion between my parents, or if there was it must have occurred behind closed doors. Ines was here to stay.

My mother knew that to confront my father directly would get her nowhere; her weapons had to be directed at Ines herself. What those weapons would be were soon revealed.

During supper that evening nobody spoke except Ines and my father. His bonhomie was designed to mask that ozone of sexuality between the two that was as palpable as if it had been declared. My mother answered his questtions in monosyllables with a tight voice that betrayed her tension and readiness for battle. But both my sister and I knew that this was not going to be an open battle. My father would always be the winner if she tried to tell him her feelings, or worse yet, make him feel guilty. The more wrong my father was the more irascible he became, and now that he had really trespassed he would have to find some reasons to behave the way he did. Since he was intelligent and creative, he would be able to find a whole bag of fancy punishments to inflict upon my mother and the rest of us.

So my mother, who was also creative and intelligent, found a marvellous way to trivialize Ines. Ines was allowed to do absolutely nothing; she was being served at the table as if she had been a guest of honour. More spaghetti? Perhaps a little more Parmesan cheese? There was no end to the kindness of my mother. Anybody witnessing this charade so atypical of my family, where tact and subtlety were considered forms of hypocrisy, would feel as if they had entered a different space, the space of the Hollywood movies where mothers apologized to their children for having neglected to bake something as odd as an apple pie.

Meanwhile, the object of all that commedia dell'arte was eating her spaghetti as if it was her due and looking at me conspiratorially. I felt myself growing new wings of authority, mentally listing all the things Ines could do: peel potatoes, clean the canary cage, cut the newspaper in squares to hang on the nail in the washroom, look out of the window for my father to appear at the end of the street so that the spaghetti could be lowered into the boiling water, and once he was in, take his shoes and bring him his slippers.

But we had no experience with servants; we didn't even know anybody who had one. The English, up the hill, had servants all dressed up in black frocks and white sillinesses on their heads. Maybe that's what we should do, buy Ines a uniform, so that she could be told apart from the rest of us. We could have bought a black frock in the market, but where do you buy a head silliness? Also, there was the question of how to address each other. Were we supposed to call each other by our first names or was it necessary to maintain our master-servant relationship by calling her by her first name while the rest of us would be called something else? Fine, my mother would be called Signora Natalia, but what about us children? To be called by anything other than our first names would have been quite ridiculous; imagine Ines calling me

Signorina Giovanna and then discovering that I still peed in bed.

What about the day off? Would she hang around doing nothing, watching us do what she usually did? What if she got sick and died? What would we do with the body? It was enough to take your sleep away, even if the situation didn't have all those darker overtones.

When night came and we prepared to go to bed, the situation became excruciating. Nobody knew when to start to disappear discreetly to give her the time and the privacy she needed. For my father that was easy; doing what he always did, he went out to the cafe to be with his friends. The rest of us engaged in a ballet of sensibility in which nobody understood the other's role or appropriate behaviour. The toilet was off the living room where Ines was supposed to transform the sofa into her bed; so going to and from the washroom became a logistical problem. Ines sat on the couch demurely with her hands folded in her lap, looking with interest at a place on the floor, becoming invisible for a while, until all of us disappeared behind closed doors. I didn't sleep right away, the excitement of the day had taken its toll, but I listened to her unfold the sofa, open her suitcase, go to the washroom (I wondered if I had left it clean) and lay herself down on the bed, with the movements of a mouse, so delicate and silent as to be almost incorporeal. I never heard my father come home, but I wondered how he would negotiate his way through the room where Ines was sleeping.

When we got up in the morning, Ines was already up, dressed, painted and ready for anything. Her suitcase stood beside the sofa and her cardigan lay neatly folded across the sofa's arm, next to her. We understood that she was waiting for orders, but none came; on the contrary, there was my mother with a steaming cappuccino and a brioche on a freshly laundered serviette, fussing over her as she had certainly never done for us. And there was Ines smiling and accepting graciously all that kindness while my father looked inscrutably at the newspaper.

While Ines was eating breakfast, I sat in front of her, looking at her to ingratiate myself. At the same time, my mother was braiding my hair tighter than usual. After my father left for work and my sister left for school, my mother prepared herself to go out for her daily food shopping. I hoped with all my heart that she would go alone and leave me with Ines. When, after a great deal of tinkering, she finally left, the look Ines gave me was one of conniving relief. It was the first unspoken task Ines had been given, looking after me.

Ines asked me to put my coat on and we went out together like two little girls. I walked with my hand in her bony one with a sense of wonder and adventure that I had never experienced when I went out with my mother. We didn't go anywhere dangerous or forbidden, nor did we care about a light rain coming down. We just walked around, looking at shop windows, trying on shoes as if we were going to buy them, inhaling the smell of pastry outside the baker's shop, counting the number of wagons on the train clanking above us in the under-passage. Good, interesting, meaningful things like these. By the time my mother came back we had bonded for life, my cheeks pink out of love, her hair a bit less crazy for having been drizzled on.

But my mother wasn't about to relent. The same pantomime she had engaged in in the morning and the previous evening went on for the rest of the day. She cooked, served the meal, took the dishes into the kitchen and washed them noisily and pointedly, while Ines sat on her corner of the couch. The rest of us were starting to wonder how long my mother was going to keep making her point, at the same time feeling quite elated at the fact that my mother in her diabolical masochistic fervour was forgetting to ask us to do our part of the chores.

This went on for a number of days. I was getting increasingly attached to Ines, and Ines was getting more adventurous in her walks in town with me. We even went as far as the slaughterhouse to look at the pigs being delivered there. My life couldn't get any better. My mother didn't use the wooden spoon on my head as she usually did, because of the stranger among us, and my father was distracted by Ines and forgot to order us around; the lack of privacy among us had created a temporary civility to which we were not used.

Though my mother's effort to render Ines superfluous seemed as if it could go on forever, we all knew that the situation would have to change sooner rather than later. All of us, that is, except Ines who didn't seem to find anything abnormal in the situation.

Towards the end of the first week of Ines's stay with us my father was arrested. We were used to it. Every time a fascist big shot came to town, my father was put into what was called "preventive incarceration." It was because my father was a card-carrying socialist, and the fascist government felt threatened by the Party's reluctance to lie down and die. The arrest might also have had to do with the fact that my father was Jewish, but we had no proof of this. My father would keep a small suitcase ready for such occasions, and follow the *carabinieri* uncomplainingly for a couple of days of enforced holiday.

When the policemen came to the door, my mother opened it and immediately knew who they were, even though they always wore civilian clothes. We knew them well, since they had been to our house many times. They wore plain clothes out of consideration for my father, but everybody in the neighbourhood knew about them. My father was not the only person being arrested. In the area where we lived there were several so-called agitators who would be locked away for the duration of the top dog's visit.

They came in, their hats in their hands, as usual making kind noises of regret and behaving, in front of us children with great, ridiculous tact. My father saw them from the table where he was finishing his coffee and invited them in to have a cup with him. The men refused politely and waited by the door as if they were being punished. Ines, who knew nothing about it, was looking at them without understanding what was going on. The men looked at her curiously and greeted her as if she was a relative of ours.

When my father was ready, he kissed Lieta and me, reminded my mother to go to his firm the next day to tell them that he would be away for a couple of days, shook Ines's hand—who shot up from her seat and almost curtsied for lack of knowing what else to do—and left us to our own devices. At the door he turned and looked at Ines, without a word. In that look I saw, young as I was, that my father had more than a passing interest in the girl. The look had a halo of intimacy that Ines felt emanating from my father, and I believe my mother felt it too.

When my father was in prison, my mother cooked his meals and brought them to him. She cooked them at home, the special things he liked—cheese ravioli and veal—since being in jail deserved some solace. She brought them with her to the visitor's lounge where they ate together. She was allowed to stay there as long as she wanted, since political prisoners were treated better than the criminals. Sometime she spent most of the afternoon with my father, for she knew how much he hated to be in the company of other prisoners, particularly the communists. My father hated them. He used to say that communism gave socialism a bad name.

I always felt very insecure when my father left for the night, be it for the sanatorium when his illness got worse, or the prison. It took me a long time to fall asleep. When I couldn't sleep I took leave of my body and floated above the room, close to the ceiling, where anybody with bad intentions couldn't see me. I stayed there for what seemed to be half the night, looking down at myself and my sister in our bed, sleeping. Now that Ines had entered our lives and had become my friend, I took her with me on my floating adventures; I even dared to go in the living room and flit above the chandelier where it was fun to look at the lightbulbs inside the glass bowls and the dust that collected at the bottom. But even with Ines I would never have dared go into my parents' bedroom.

I don't know now if these were dreams or if I was experiencing some kind of hypnotic state, where I felt a certain dissociation between me and my body. If it was hypnosis, I am sorry to have lost that ability. I would like to feel again as I did then, a unanchored Peter Pan on her way to see a different universe. I never tried to explain this space wandering to anybody, since I knew I wouldn't be believed. Nobody believed me when I was telling ordinary, everyday lies; in fact, I wasn't even believed when I was telling the truth. I was so used to not being believed that sometimes I lost sight of what was true and what wasn't. I became confused by my own imagination, not knowing anymore which lie was a sin and needed to be punished and what was a leap of my mind into a different reality. Both lies were punished the same way, so that I was left with no tree-house of the mind into which I could climb safely. The adults in my life wanted my feet planted firmly on the ground. My problem was that I insisted on being a traveller and an explorer.

But with Ines I could go where I wanted. She was a

receptacle of true stories and lies. She would pop her caramel eyes out in disbelief and ask a barrage of appropriate questions. I would dig up answers out of the recesses of my fears, hopes, likes and dislikes. I told her all kinds of forbidden things, about my parents' fights, my mother's muffled crying, which I could hear from their bedroom, my sister's pubic hairs that had begun at the bottom of her belly like a little goatee, my father vomiting blood in a basin. I told her everything. Then I would start on my inventions: the night I escaped a fire in my bedroom, the time I ran in front of a train until I was overcome and flattened myself between the rails, while all one hundred of the carriages rode over me—I was able to count them—and when I was in Fontesanta with my mother and saved all those children from drowning in a pond and almost drowned myself. My mother cried for days at the sight of her youngest daughter dying. Dying was always my favourite way of getting attention. She asked me to forgive her for all the terrible things she had done to me, but I remained with my eyes closed for a long time. It was when my sister promised to stop torturing me that I finally came to and forgave everybody.

Ines listened to me like nobody had ever done before, egging me on with comments of her own, always helpful when my imagination failed me.

With my father away, the situation at home became more anarchic, possibly more cruel. There was no fear in any of us, except of each other, and my mother was starting to notice me again, with the result that my friendship with Ines lost its openness and became more secretive, more defiant. If my mother gave her a particularly good morsel of food, Ines would share it with me. Chewing on it, I would give my mother a round-eyed look of utter provocative stupidity. I think it was then that my mother finally realized that what she was doing was not good for her children. Although my mother and I were at war, I never knew her to be manipulative; she was not one to throw subtle, deadly hints. With regard to me, she had never tried convincing or cajoling; the wooden spoon over my head was her argument of choice. This continuous making a point that everybody understood, except the person for whom the point was intended, was starting to take its toll on her patience. On top of it, this alliance of mine with Ines was irritating her, while not giving her enough ammunition to explode into her usual screaming battle.

Few days after my father was arrested, my mother went to visit him in jail and, although she hadn't stated how long she was going to be away, the fact that she had cooked our lunch and left it on the kitchen counter and covered it with a serviette told us that she would be away for a long time.

Since my sister was in school until early afternoon, Ines and I were left to our own devices for most of the day. I don't remember now whose idea it had been to go into the sanctuary of my parents' bedroom. We entered it gingerly and, like two conspirators, started our investigation by opening my mother's side of the closet. I know I didn't suggest it, because I never had any desire to do it. But Ines started to take out my mother's dresses, hats, shoes—anything that could be found.

I was happy to see Ines so excited, her eyes darting from one garment to the next one with the greed of the deprived. To her, it must all have looked like wealth. I almost felt a bit rich myself, seeing Ines explore my mother's wardrobe with such high regard for what she found.

Before long, Ines had taken her clothes off and was trying on some of the garments. Except for me and my sister, my family was not inclined to parade itself naked.

And even Lieta was starting to insist on a privacy, that, given the close quarters in which we lived, was rather unrealistic. Still, I had managed to see my mother's body every once in a while when she had a bath.

I was used to the bodies of my mother and my sister: one heavy, her breasts round and nurturing and smelling faintly of yogurt, her armpits like black secrets, her skin opaque and solid with no transparency, the other a young adolescent beginning an early travel into womanhood, her breasts for some reason, already at her young age, looking dismally south.

But the body of Ines was another matter. In the first place she had no sense of being naked. She didn't have to take all her undergarments off but she did, and with a startling unawareness, as if it was the thing to do. She sat at the mirror, looking at herself with an uncritical eye, absorbed in choosing the dresses in front of her. Her body was as extraordinary as her face. Her nipples, redder than was seemly, were perched on top of breasts so pointed they looked like two Pinocchios. The little red patch at the beginning of her thighs was tiny, almost discreet compared to the grand pubis of my mother, which started with a whisper somewhere in the region of her navel and ended in a rolling crescendo until it almost took the place of underpants.

I can see why my father had fallen for that pointed nervous little body. It had a strangeness, a mixture of boyish immaturity and a crude sexuality that promised not exactly fulfilment as much as challenge. Ines's body was an aggressive little frame, with no cushion of tenderness or compassion, not an ounce of fat to cover her fragile bones, nowhere for a man to hide. Her colour had the descriptive variety of a chameleon: reddish around the elbows and knees, blue paths around what passed for her belly, gossamer white on her breasts and overall, that scattering of freckles that looked as if she had rolled herself in wet bran.

But what I remember most is her smell. In our family, we had a bath every Sunday. So, from Sunday morning, when we smelled like roses, moving on towards the end of the week our body odour was incrementally stronger until on Saturday night it was solid armpit. We didn't seem to mind, probably because we were accustomed to our own smells. Although we punctiliously washed our genitals every morning in the rickety bidets we had, and washed our teeth and our faces, we never noticed if our armpits were marinating in their own sweat. Before the Age of Deodorant everybody smelled pretty bad—it was just a matter of degree.

But when Ines came among us, our family's smell became noticeable as being other than hers. Her smell was redder, delicately mustier, foreign, like an aura of difference that announced her comings and goings as if moving within the dust of her own freckles. Now that she was naked that smell was stronger, almost visible; I remember breathing her in like a dog. By sniffing her I felt I knew what it was to be her. I am still convinced that one's own essence is not known until one enters this magic circle; the physical secret emanation of the body.

When Ines got up to put on one of my mother's dresses I noticed that the coat of arms of the House of Savoy was imprinted on her skinny arse in a hue redder than that of her skin. It came from the cushion on which she had been sitting, one of my mother's embroidered homages to the Italian reigning house. My mother was a monarchist, to my father's great annoyance.

When Ines wore my mother dresses, it was as if I was seeing them for the first time. They changed their nature, suddenly assuming a more elegant aspect; whereas before there had been a body slightly straining against their seams, now they looked opulent, more dress than was needed; the fabric flowed and draped. Ines was almost as tall as my mother but had a body of such reduced dimension that she looked taller; her fragility was emphasized by her slightly stooped shoulders and the wide space between her thighs. She looked like an exotic red bird.

I loved to see her in my mother clothes. I felt emboldened and began looking for more clothes in the trunk at the foot of the bed. I dug up hats that had been abandoned long ago, some with little fogs of tulle to pull over one's eyes, some with feathers stuck jauntily on one side like those the alpine soldiers wear, some with shades so large they looked like mini parasols. My mother never wore hats now, but she must have had quite a past to have been able to wear all that elegance. It surprised me to discover an aspect of my mother that must have existed once, one of almost daring chic. A life apart from us, a time unto herself, where we didn't exist. A mysterious space away from her kitchen and the market.

Then there were the shoes. Unfortunately, my mother followed the family tradition of having large, wide feet and Ines's feet were way too skinny for my mother's shoes. She tried on a few before giving up. Another item in the trunk was an ostrich boa that could be wrapped around one's neck, an item of great beauty and ticklishness, which had been sent to my mother from some distant relatives who lived in America. I had seen it before in a collapsed, compressed state, but when Ines wrapped it around her neck she looked like a Hollywood Star.

I became totally absorbed in dressing Ines up. I felt part of a great aesthetic adventure. I kept handing her new things, out of forgotten drawers, from above the closet, from under the bed. It was like creating a new whole creature. When I ran out of my mother's clothes,

I went to my room and retrieved my most precious posses-
sion: a little rabbit skin that could be worn around the
neck and fastened at the side by having its mouth bite the
base of its tail. A small clip hidden under its nose made
this amazing feat possible. And it also had glass eyes that
looked just as if they were real. Because the tip of the tail
and paws were black and the rest of the fur was completely white, my rabbit looked like an ermine. A work of
art.

Ines, after discarding a good many dresses and hats,
settled for a brown dress covered with little white flowers,
a small hat in the shape of a worker's beret with a feather
coming down on the side of her cheek in a mauve caress
against her freckles, and my ermine hugging her delicately
around the neck. She left her own shoes on, since she
had no choice, but wrapped an embroidered shawl
around her shoulders that gave her the appearance of
being longer and narrower than she already was. I had
never seen anybody so beautiful. I felt I had had some
part in creating this elegance since I had chosen some of
the clothes and lent her my ermine. Ines kept walking
backward and forward as if she had stepped right out of
an American movie.

With a sense of preservation quite rare in me, I remembered that in a short while either my mother or my
sister would be home. Ines and I were able to put back all
the clothes in the manner we had found them, just in the
nick of time.

When my mother came home, she found us chasing
the pigeons out of the terrace. Ines and I kept exchang-
ing significant glances; we were both thinking about
possible forbidden pleasures for the day after. In fact we
felt we hadn't even scratched the surface of what we could
try on once my mother had gone. There were more
clothes and hats, and at the last minute, in the bottom of

the trunk, I had even found some swimming costumes that I had never seen anyone in my family wear.

I found myself so excited that I didn't even much mind the usual tension around the table that seemed to grip us more when my father was absent. I had my own private kingdom and Ines was my accomplice.

But life is never that tidy. Throughout my childhood I seemed to have had to cope with inexplicable turns of events. I don't know if my mother asked Ines to leave that very night or in the early morning of the next day. I only know that the day after our clothes rehearsal Ines was gone. I don't mean left for a few minutes or for a while. She was gone for ever out of my house, out of my life. When I asked my mother where Ines was, my mother said cryptically that she had left taking a brown dress of hers, the one with a spread of little white flowers, a shawl and a hat with a feather. My mother kept on talking as if the disappearance of Ines was a matter of no consequence.

"I think the girl understood that she was not really needed here," my mother said. "Maybe she was not as stupid as she looked."

Ines, stupid? Did my mother really think Ines was stupid? Ines was wonderfully intelligent: she could listen to me for hours, she knew where to go for a walk, she knew all the right things for us to do together. I loved Ines, and although she shouldn't have taken them, I was happy that she had helped herself to a few of my mother's things. It served my mother right for not liking her.

For a while I refused to resign myself to the fact that Ines had gone. I thought that she had only gone for a little while. I was sure that she had loved me as much as I had loved her. I kept waiting for her return even though with the passing of days, it was becoming more and more difficult to keep up hope.

When my father returned from the jail, he didn't seem

surprised; in fact he seemed slightly relieved. He made no comments but gave a quick look to my mother and went on with his meal.

It was about a couple of weeks later, when I was looking over my winter things—the summer being almost spent—that I found that Ines had left with my ermine.

Evangelista

I am packing, but with reluctance, I have been happy these last few days in Venice.

I have promised my relatives that I'll be coming to see them near the beginning of June. Now it is the seventh and I know that they have been waiting for me, lasagne at the ready, since the end of May. I don't really want to go.

There are cousins I have never seen, uncles I would rather not see, nieces and nephews I have to kiss, snotty children I have to hug, and the inevitable realization, in looking at them all, of how fast time goes. But in the midst of all these undesirables there is my eighty-five-year old aunt, Zia Giusta. More than anybody else, she is the one I want to see and talk to. If I can stand the effort, that is. She is almost totally deaf and shouting doesn't come easily to me. I have a naturally low voice.

I board a train and then another one. There are no direct routes to that part of the country. Fontesanta, my destination, seems to have been forgotten. It sits in a corner on the other side of the Appenines, as if under a glass jar. When I arrive at the train station in the city of Fano, I am left on a sun-flattened piazza, in a tiny and comatose place. No taxis or buses are about, since it is the witching hour of two in the afternoon. I am well south of Venice, and the temperature has risen proportionally. There is no train to Fontesanta and the bus depot is nowhere near the train station. In fact it is a few miles away, under the Augustean Arch. I drag my suitcase along the damn cobblestones for what seems to be hours and arrive exhausted at the bus depot, only to find out that there are no buses until seven in the evening.

It shouldn't but it does amaze me how this part of Italy hasn't changed. It is still backward, somnolent, disorganized and terribly uncomfortable. I have avoided coming here for many years, and for good reason. It takes almost a day from anywhere in Italy to reach this mountainlocked area. I spend my waiting time reading a couple of local newspapers and drinking an espresso in the local cafe. When the bus finally comes, it fills up quickly with country folk and their lumpy luggage. For the journey I am seated uncomfortably next to a man who sits with his legs so far apart it feels like sitting next to an open umbrella.

The bus zigzags along gorges cut by the Roman army centuries ago and stops at hamlets so old they look like archaeological sites, appearing almost invisible against the rocky background.

I doze for a while until I am awakened by the bus's final stop. When I get off, I am surprised to see that nobody is waiting for me at the station. Since it is late, almost night in fact, I reason that they must have tired of seeing buses arriving without me. Again, I drag the little wheels of my suitcase over the cobblestones, all the way up to the house of Zia Giusta. I ring the bell and knock on the door for what seems forever, while I look at the lights in the second-floor windows, and hear the full blast of my aunt's television. But, because of her deafness, she doesn't hear me, and I am becoming embarrassed in front of a group of men looking at me from the cafe next door. Finally, the door opens and the whole of Zia Giusta appears in front of me with a garbage bag in her hand because she is on her way to the metal dump. She looks up, startled, against the fading light, sensing more than seeing who I am, and bursts into tears. She also tries to hide the garbage bag and take care of a few strands of white hair. I can see she has been caught off-guard.

We walk in, slowly, because she has already started on her litany of illnesses. There is something wrong with her heart, her bones, her eyes; she is a walking pathology textbook. It is a family tradition never to believe old people's complaints about their illnesses. The old folks have been around so long, the rest of the family starts to perceive them as imperishable. Because of this lack of attention, when I arrive the floodgates open to release an avalanche of pent-up hypochondria, peppered with a few real illnesses. I wish I could take her seriously, but I have heard it all so many times before. Zia Giusta has been complaining about old age as long as I can remember, which goes back to a time when she must have been in her late forties. Her old age and the illnesses attached to it are not a condition of time, but a lifelong vocation. Out of kindness I sit in her kitchen, bone tired, with a face so intent on commiserating, my kindness muscles start to ache. I am not ungenerous.

However, I am the guest of honour and Zia Giusta is mindful of my well-being too. In fact through her complaining she is busy putting food on the table, rag at the ready to wipe away invisible horrors, wine bottle un-corked. No use telling her that I don't drink alcohol, I am too tired to eat, and all I want is a hot bath and a bed.

But since I have just crossed the Sahara Desert, in her anxious mind, I must be fed, if I like or not. There is a dish of lasagne in front of me, enough for an army of teenagers, a hunk of bread, a monumental glass full of mineral water and a smaller one full of red wine. She gives me a fork, forgets the knife, and sits in front of me, to make sure I get revived.

She is already starting on the family feuds. In my tiredness I am trying to memorize whom I should hate, to whom I must show indifference and to whom I must show respect. I also am clued in on what I am supposed to know and when to show surprise, even though I already know about it, because Zia Giusta is making sure I do. I am not supposed to know about any of the affairs or divorces. Basically I am supposed to know nothing of other people's problems; Zia Giusta's are overwhelming enough.

To be mildly and nonchalantly condescending, to keep a kind of ironic distance, would be so offensive I don't dare do it. I am rapidly and, I confess, not too unwillingly, plunging into a web of old vendettas, gossip, lies that nobody believes and secrets well known by every-body. Welcome to Fontesanta.

By the time I am ready for bed my head is reeling with genealogical battlegrounds I can hardly keep straight. I vow not to get involved in their mean disputes, but I know it will be impossible. By dint of distance, both physical and cultural, I have become a referee, a kind of Solomon with no power but a lot of unwanted authority. Suddenly I realize I have become an adult. The pathologi-cally insecure, selfishly shy creature whom nobody would understand, let alone like, has blossomed into a pathologically insecure, selfishly shy something else, which I cannot define, except that she seems to command a respect that thirty years ago seemed unthinkable. I wonder if I had stayed and if everybody else in my family were not dead, would it have been so? I left because I was such an outsider, a person so odd they would invent stories about me, to create a context within which they could communicate with me. Now I am not even sure who "They" were. I feel my trip is just beginning.

Zia Giusta takes me to the bedroom and shows me the monumental bed in which I am to sleep. The sheets were handwoven a couple of dowries ago and have been washed and dried in the sun so many times they have acquired the consistency of suede. I undress half drunk with tiredness, emotion and the wine that I didn't have the heart to refuse, and sink into the heady fragrance of linen dried in the sunshine. In my late fifties I am not used to being taken care of by people older than me. I feel like a child, tucked in and blessed, wallowing in an atmosphere of benevolent tyranny. Suddenly I am less responsible, less in control, less the rock I have always been. If I weren't so tired, I would cry a little. It doesn't happen often that one is so irresponsibly happy.

In the morning, I wake up not remembering where I am, I have been in so many different bedrooms. I am slow to figure out who these people staring at me from the walls are. The bedroom walls are covered with photographs of my ancestors, all looking frightened and frozen in their Sunday best. In a corner all by themselves are the portraits of my mother, my sister and my father. Below them is a lit votive lamp. I am not sure if the lamp is always there, or if it has been lit because I was expected. Either way, it is a mute reproach to my lack of interest in my family's afterlife. I don't go to the cemetery, and I don't have memorial services for them. Nobody dares complain to me openly, because now I have become some kind of an oracle. But I understand that silent condemnation and pretend not to notice.

I dress and ready myself to see the rest of my relatives. A cousin, Marco is already waiting for me, sitting in the kitchen with a cup of caffe-latte in his hands. When I see him, I am reassured. He is one of the black sheep of the family. At the age of fifty, he has left his wife of twenty-five years for one of his students, a mixed-up girl of twenty-two who seems to have appealed to the protective side of him. Since he has no children, maybe this is not a bad thing. We all need a pet.

I know the whole drama from his desperate letters to me. I was the only one who told him to leave his wife and stop torturing everybody. He finally moved out, without having really prepared himself, either psychologically or physically. He ended up in a friend's empty apartment, totally destitute, since out of guilt he agreed to leave everything he had to his wife, whose only training had been taking care of a man. I feel a certain embarrassed affinity for this reprobate cousin, having myself left Italy to marry a man whom I left after eighteen months. The fact that I married again, and have been married for the past twenty-five years, has made some difference. I am now a notch higher up than my cousin on the ladder of acceptability.

I embrace him warmly and sit at the kitchen table expecting to hear about his new life with his new love.

He has gone back to his wife.

I am stopped in mid croissant and have to change my expressions of encouragement into those of, what? Condolences? I am a bit confused.

Underneath my words of understanding is a practical assessment of what made him go back. I had obviously underestimated the power of good meals, unquestioning adoration, a clean house and tears of love every time he returned to pick up something conveniently forgotten. What happened to the young girl he has just left remains unsaid. In fact there is so much that remains unsaid, the whole scene could have been mimed. I munch on another croissant, becoming more and more engrossed in a game of avoidance that makes a soap opera script seem perfectly viable. Zia Giusta has gone on the balcony to avoid making any comments.

I change the subject, asking about my cousin Gentile. She lives in Milan now, is also a professor and has recently thrown a philandering husband out of the house.

And cousin Petra? Oh yes, her husband has gone crazy and has to be watched twenty-four hours a day, because he has on occasion wandered the streets at night totally naked. What about Uncle Giorgio, the communist big shot? What happened to him after the fall of the Soviet bloc? He has returned to the fold of Mother Church. Uncle Giorgio? In church?

Italy has indeed changed. I have lost touch. Suddenly I am confronted with people I don't know anymore; their paths have taken directions I never anticipated. A tapestry of unbearable transformations is unfolding in front of my eyes, and I don't want to look at it. I feel without an anchor, marooned in an ocean of doubts and readjustments. I almost want their disapproval back, the old way of looking at me with the suspicion accorded to the artist, the outsider.

I wonder why I am being so silly. I left because of an overwhelming feeling of being rejected by everybody. I come back and find that I have jumped into another space. An honoured and acceptable space. Isn't that what I wanted? Why am I unsettled by my new position?

Maybe I know. I am not the *enfant terrible* anymore. Certainly I am no longer an *enfant*. Age rewards the ones who have rebelled long and hard with a forgiving acceptance. Time erases the thorns of youth. I have become yesterday's radical. Only I hadn't noticed.

I know I have to meet the rest of the family, but I am not ready yet. I leave my cousin Marco talking to Zia Giusta and wander around the town to search for the events of my past among half-forgotten sites. I walk past the piazza, on to the little park where at one time there was a mangy eagle in a cage. There used to be eagles here, when there were enough lambs to steal. Also, wolves roamed freely at the time of Saint Francis, who, if I liked saints, would be one of my favourites, talking as he did to the animals like a hallucinating ecologist. There were also foxes and hares, and down a little south of here even bears. The people were also wild in these parts. The men had lovers who bore children and wives who took their revenge in refusing to die, surviving the men by whole lifetimes.

My grandmother Antonietta was a teacher in these mountains at a time when, for a woman with children, to have a career was thought disrespectful to her husband. My grandfather was so in love with her that, when he declared his intention to marry, he passed out cold and had to be taken to hospital with a concussion. He was afraid that she wouldn't marry him because he was shorter than she was. Besides being tall, she was a woman of beauty and fierceness. But with all her fierceness her genes must have been weaker than his, because most of the family is short. Either I was adopted or I took after my father's family of tall gangly Germans. The fierceness, on the other hand, was passed on to all the females and skipped all the males. We women have fought all the wars, the men merely went to the front lines.

Uncle Giorgio was the beauty of the family. I have photos of him, looking slightly gangsterish, his lips properly licked. He came up with the only singing voice in a tone-deaf family. In fact, he was going to be a radio singer in Naples—the contract had been written and signed—when Mount Vesuvius erupted and put five inches of ashes on my uncle's career. I definitely come from a family of losers.

Back in the town I finally go and see everybody. I do what is required of me, listen to their stories, say almost nothing about my life—they are not interested anyway—and eat obscene quantities of food.

But my favourite place is with my Zia Giusta. She is the only person of the generation of my parents, the only cushion between me and my own mortality. In a few years I will belong to the generation with the longest memory. But for now she is the high priestess of the family mythology, and I listen to seven hours of stories a day.

Both my sister and I had a sketchy knowledge of my parents and their time, and when we talked about them and their times, we would merely confirm one another's few memories of them. But when my sister was killed in a car accident twenty-five years ago, a curtain of silence fell on my youth. So I sit in Zia Giusta's kitchen, and open gate after gate on a nebulous and mysterious past.

She speaks in a dialect that can hardly be called Italian, which for some obscure genealogical reason I manage to understand. Her language is theatrical and naïve, the world being neatly divided in "them" and "us," the bad and the good, the rich and the poor. There is comfort in this orderly division, this certainty, and in the knowledge that heaven is waiting to open its pearly gates for the just and the thrifty.

Zia Giusta comes from a degree of penury that is difficult for me to imagine. She remembers little things like having been given a chicken at some ancient Christmas, and having given a bedsheet to somebody who never offered any thanks.

God knows, I have been poor too. During the war we had to kill a cat and eat it to survive. But we knew that it was temporary, and that eventually times would improve. In other words there was hope. But the day-to-day grinding poverty of the times of Zia Giusta seemed hopeless and never-ending.

What I find fascinating is the effect extreme poverty has on the personality. Because her life has been nothing more than a blind coping that reduced any kind of human interaction to a matter of material gain or loss, her memory is a pixillation of resentments for what she was owed and didn't receive, injustices that couldn't be erased even with the passage of time. I am struck by her violence, her lack of both forgiveness and compassion, by the queer intelligence of the underdog, who sees with pitiless clarity only the worst in others, neglecting the best. I see, with pain, that a good solid intelligence that could have been used in the service of real understanding has been, for defensive purposes, put to the service of cunning. And cunning Zia Giusta is. You can see this when she squints her eye in a gesture of conspiratorial understanding. She couldn't have survived otherwise.

I sit in her kitchen and I ask myself if I am not being manipulated by this old woman who knows paths to survival that I cannot even begin to discern. This morning she talked me into buying a whole lamb from the butcher, saying that it would cost less whole. I can see through her little scheme, but I let her have her way. Part of me likes to be used that way. She is eighty-five years old, why not allow her her little triumphs? I hear her say in astonished tones, to other relatives who come by to see me, "She is so good, so generous."

Every so often I take a break and descend from Zia Giusta's house into the village to look around and be looked at. The buildings are made of a local grey stone so roughly cut it seems a miracle the houses are still standing. Much as I look, I find no sign of mortar between the stones, not even in the church's large vaults. In my wanderings I pass a fire department. I wonder why they bother keeping a fire department here. What could possibly burn? Even the sinks are made of large slabs of stone, hollowed in the centre to catch the water. On the floor the stones have been given such high polish I tell myself I must remember to wear black underwear, lest my under carriage show in the reflection. The well-to-do have wood on the floor, which in this ancient deforested land has been a luxury for centuries. The very rich, on the other hand, use the polished local stone that the poor use. Slumming in stone, you might say.

The day is swaddled in sheets of heat, courtesy of the Scirocco wind. This is a wind that forces its way through a corridor of connecting valleys, all the way from the Sahara Desert. The Mediterranean Sea in between doesn't seem to lessen its suffocating breath. It shakes the olive trees, exposing now the silver, now the black sides of the leaves, until the contorted trees start to look like mediaeval flags. It brings no coolness or scents, only blasts of heat drying everything in its path. It is sometimes called the Suicide Wind, because it is said to drive people who are teetering on the edge to take the final step. This is actually supported by statistics.

Strange how my memory has left out the wind. My past is a series of tableaux, deprived of movement, like dioramas in the museum of the mind. There is the cold of the winters and the heat of the summers, also the rain and the snow because it was so rare. But I forgot the wind.

I go down to the river. In place of the old shaky suspension bridge that used to be there, I see an immense concrete arch joining, not the river banks, but the edges of the valley. This over-structure dwarfs the ribbon of water below. Quays have been built around the river's edge, with children's playgrounds and a small zoo of baby goats and a llama. They have domesticated my river. It has become promiscuous, its swampy secrets obliterated. The children playing here are now of every colour, like a Benetton ad. This is the river to which my mother and I used to come to do the heavy washing, when we spent some time in Fontesanta. The river has a memory tied to it.

Back in Canada the cold is sometimes more than one can bear. There are no mountains between the Arctic and where I live. Because of that the day can change from leaden stillness to blinding snow, and then, after a silence, the wind. But that wind is a killer of a different kind. It finds cheekbones where you didn't think you had any, and polishes them to a Tartar prominence. It yodels through cracks in the windows, it reduces the trees to black blasphemies against the sky.

This Canadian wind dries people's minds, it kills memories because it obliterates smells, it shrinks the language. Names become contracted to mere utterances. Richard and Alexander become Dick and Al. It takes obduracy to hang on to a passionate name. I wonder what would happen in Canada to a name like Evangelista.
Evangelista, the old man by the river.

He belongs to a landscape so unlike the wintry plains where I live now that I might as well be living on the moon. The moon, here in Italy, is always reddish, because of the volcanoes. A minor sun really. But the sun was like an enemy in the summer sky. A hot persistence in the dead of the afternoon, nothing alive except the cicadas, their songs as dry as acronyms among the burnt-out fields. Even the snakes and the chickens were asleep in those suspended hours. In the villages people went into a dreamless coma behind closed shutters.

All except me. I was seventeen and had come to this southern village to get a taste of freedom. It was a place of old widows and a few old men still clinging to that squander of stones, but fading fast into a sepia reality, overlooked by the rest of the world.

All the young had left for other lands, many of them for Canada, preferring icy winds to that burnt-out indolence of a village without a future.

I had been there for four days and had talked to nobody, except for a few words exchanged with the antique couple who had reluctantly accepted me as a boarder in their house. My small payment had bought a rickety bed in a room full of photographs and their southern food, but no conversation. They were a Gothic couple of profound mistrust, afflicted by a total lack of curiosity. So I walked the quilted hills in solitude, feeling like an ambassador without a message.

It was on one of those walks in the furnace-like afternoon that I considered the river.

I had left the village behind, to follow a road by a shallow valley dense with fig trees, towards a half-ruined steeple quivering in the distance. I didn't know what the steeple was, but it was a destination.

I had started to menstruate. Of course there wasn't, there among the cicadas and the snakes, anywhere I could buy a bit of comfort to put between my legs.

The river had been by my side for a while. It had flashed the sun double in open spangles between the trees, sent its swampy smell up the road and whimpered when vexed by a couple of large rocks in midstream. It could hardly be called a river. More like a mountain stream, boiling in winter, almost dry in the summer, except for a few pools of green broth, just enough for the women to do their washing and a few boys to drown in. But the bed was deep and the fig trees hugged its banks like a pack of zebras, away from the Africa above.

I left the road to follow the river's promise of cleanliness down a steep track, hanging on to the caper bushes, dislodging small catastrophes of gravel and earth with my clogs. The immature fig trees cried their white sperm on my hands, and the mint bushes sent off their heady smell on being crushed. Deeper into the trees the heat dispersed itself among the leaves and the smell of dank water became stronger.

When I reached the river's edge, it felt as if I had opened a door and stepped into someplace else. It was cool here, and deep and dappled, like the inside of a silent green well, with two skies: the one above, distant and white, the one below in the water, green, breathing a baby's breath.

Nobody around, nothing moving, a room of my own. The garden of Eden before they kicked us out.

I took my clothes off slowly, folded them one by one and placed them carefully on the dry pebbles of the bank, in sacramental reverence for that silent place.

When I stood tall and naked, I felt slightly disintegrated, as if some of my substance had dissipated with the shedding of the clothes.

I am not naturally naked.

I took my underpants with me, to wash them, and entered the river. The water and I oozed into each other acceptingly, reassuringly, my blood and sweat carried away downstream.

I am no swimmer. I like my water tame. No depth beyond my waist, no waves, no surprises. But when the water is courteous I let it embrace me with a moderate amount of trust.

Once in, I rolled on my sides, I spraddled my arms, I scissored my legs, I turned over on my back and let my nipples float like pink periscopes. I allowed the water to finger my hair and fan it out in black rivulets of its own, laughed aloud and liquefied my laughter under water. I sang out of tune, to violate the silence and watch the water ripple.

I knew I was receiving one of life's momentary gifts.

I found a flat stone to use as a washing board, to clean my underpants, the way I had learned to do when I helped my mother with her washing, a long time ago, in the river that ran through Fontesanta.

All of a sudden I started to cry.

Strange how clouds can come on in the middle of a luminous afternoon.

My mother had died three months earlier.

I didn't know why I felt like crying then, three months after her death, when I had not cried at all at the time. But then, I never seemed to do anything right. I had even learned about her impending death the wrong way.

I had gone to my friend Carla's house, a few doors down the road, for a bit of gossip and a handful of roasted chestnuts. Then Carla and I had ambled back towards my place, our cheeks stretched over mouthfuls of chestnuts. I was trying to eat them before I would have to share them with Lieta.

When we started to climb the stairs, I could see my sister's feet sticking out from the upper landing, thrumming. It didn't promise much good. I new the sign of my sister's displeasure. I surveyed my recent conduct quickly, looking for sins, but uncharacteristically I found none. But when I reached my door Lieta was fuming.

"Where were you?" she yelled "I have been waiting for you for hours. I have no keys."

Had it really been hours? And even if it had, how was I supposed to know that she had forgotten her keys? And where was Mamma, anyway. She was always home.

I kept chewing on my chestnuts, ready to give her a piece of my mind, when she added in the same angry tone, "Mamma is in the hospital. She is going to die. Maximum three months."

I can still see Carla bringing her hands to her mouth as if to muffle a blunder, and then running down the stairs, without a word.

I gave my keys and the rest of the chestnuts to Lieta.

Once in the apartment, I went into the washroom, took the chewed chestnuts out of my mouth and flushed them down the toilet. I closed the lid and sat on it for a while.

I didn't know what to feel at first, and when I did, I wished I hadn't known.

It was an unmistakable sense of deliverance.

No more fights, guilt, duties, preachings, predictions of my future as a whore, the dusting and the sweeping, apologizing, the evening rosaries, the mascara and the lipstick thrown in the garbage. I still feel the weight off my shoulders that the impending death of my mother represented.

When my mother came back from the hospital, a bit mad at so much attention, Lieta and I began a cheery prattle that didn't end until the day of her death. We talked incessantly about everything: my school, Lieta's math tutoring, the dress I chose for my mother, for when she was going to be up and about. Anything to avoid the silence waiting for her on the other side of the door. We were all too shy to talk about her death.

She withdrew fast into a room full of memories, her feistiness and courage all but spent. She died quickly and silently.

Neither Lieta nor I cried. When they started to shovel earth on her coffin, my sister looked mad as she did on the day she thrummed her feet on the landing, and I passed out on the wreaths of somebody else's grave. They thought they had another dead person on their hands.

We really didn't know how to behave. But I was seventeen and my sister was twenty-one, and we didn't have a script telling us how to cope with the betrayal of my mother's death.

We were free now.

We went to the movies, sometimes twice a day, we ate when we wanted, we never cooked. We bought food from the cooking stalls like the single men did. While my sister gave private math lessons to the students she had inherited from my mother's part-time tutoring, I lolled about doing nothing. Now I could even travel.

So I had come to this village, for no better reason other than that Carla's godparents had accepted me in their home for a week.

And here I was, washing my underpants on a flat stone, sobbing away in a river, of which I didn't even know the name. I cried in loud, obscene, chest-rattling sobs. I cried for the freedom that had proved to be nothing more than another betrayal, in the middle of this green, silent gift.

I immersed myself in the river several times to wash away the tears. It was in re-emerging, while I was trying to shake the water out of my ears, that I saw the man. I rubbed my eyes, to clear my vision, and there he was, sitting quietly by my clothes.

I stopped in mid-sob and stared at him, in disbelief. Making such noise with my bawling, I had not heard him come.

I felt acutely embarrassed at being seen crying so unashamedly, with my hair slicked back behind my ears, looking like a wounded otter.

Then I remembered that I was naked and standing well clear of the water with no more than a few yards between him and me. For a moment I felt alarmed at the possibility of being harmed, but then I saw that the man was very old. His head was bent with years, his hands dangling between his legs were like small oaks, and even from where I was I could see through his cord sandals, his feet blue with veins.

He had folded his jacket and put it by his side. He seemed both calm and expectant as a child as he looked at me coming out of the water, like a minor Venus emerging from a pagan diorama. Not an insignificant gift on a hot afternoon.

I knew I had a beautiful body, my breasts full and high, my hips round, my waist thin and flexible. Being a virgin, only my mother and my sister had seen me. Not a particularly appreciative audience. Since my face was not much to look at, what beauty I possessed had been a secret yearning to be revealed. It felt good to show myself off. I came slowly out of the water, all five feet and ten inches of me. I might have been flaunting myself a bit.

I twisted my hair on one side to squeeze the water out, released it and shook it like an impatient mare. I spread my underpants in a sunny spot, making sure that I bent facing the old man and sat myself on a patch of absorbing grass. Out of belated modesty I covered myself lightly to let the air dry me.

He kept his gaze on me, a knowing, indulgent smile crinkling his eyes.

"My name is Evangelista," he offered, as if the circumstances called for a gracious introduction. His accent gave him away as a stranger to these parts, probably a Venetian.

"My name is Beatrice," I lied. Lying seemed in keeping with nakedness, out of an unnamed river, in a strange place. Besides, I liked the name Beatrice.

Here in Italy lying comes easy, not so much to conceal, as to savour the taste of it. Reality doesn't always comply with the more acceptable fantasy. In lands of truth-seekers people don't usually lie, and if they do, they lie to conceal. We almost never do that, and if we do, we have the decency to look shifty. We like to take liberties with the prose of reality.

"Where are you from?" asked Evangelista.

"Guess," I said coyly.

"Why were you crying?" he then asked.

"Oh that," I said, feeling embarrassed by the speed at which my mood had changed.

"That's because of my mother. She died three months ago."

Evangelista remained sympathetically silent for a while. Then he took a hunk of bread and a couple of dried apricots from his pockets, and offered them to me, gallantly leaving none for himself. I made some polite noises of reluctance, but then I gobbled it all up. I didn't know I was so hungry.

"My mother loved my sister," I said. And then I added in a softer voice, because I knew it to be not entirely true, "Me, she didn't love."

"Why do you think your mother didn't love you?" asked Evangelista. I shrugged my shoulders. My mother and I had fought for so long that the reason for it had been forgotten, only the memory of the battles remained. I saw an opportunity for consolation.

"Because I am ugly, an artist and I don't obey rules," I said vaguely.

Evangelista took a galling long time to come up with the expected: "But you are beautiful." And then he diluted the compliment by adding:

"At your age, everybody is beautiful."

If a boy my age had paid me a compliment, my shyness would have provoked a sassy, rude answer, but with this old man, I felt I could take the liberty of focussing his flattery a little better. "No," I said, "Carla is not. She is my age and she is certainly not beautiful."

But he didn't seem to be interested in comparative beauty.

"What did your mother died of?" he asked, after a pause.

"Tuberculosis," I said. I couldn't say the word "cancer" yet.

"And your father?"

"Oh him," I said. I had forgotten about him. He had hardly existed in my life. It surprised me that somebody would ask me about a father. "He died when I was eight years old. In the war. He was a womanizer," I said breezily, as if I had been speaking about his profession or the colour of his eyes.

I had completely accepted the family mythology, with my father as a womanizer, my sister beautiful and good, my mother a saint and I rotten to the core. It occurs to me that one must avoid dying young, lest one remain stuck in a myth not of one's own choosing.

Evangelista's eyes were wandering to the far side of the river. I enjoyed his presence. Like the water I like my men tame. I don't like waves that I cannot handle. My body is timid.

A silence enriched our company now. He kept his eyes unfocused in the distance, lost in his own thoughts. His head was a calico leather softened by tufts of white hair around his ears. His great nose gave him more profile than facade, but under the thatch of his eyebrows, his eyes were as green as the river. His shoulders were still powerful like those of a spent boxer and his open shirt revealed breasts almost as big as mine, only droopier and covered in white wool. There was something of a monument about him, a granite purposefulness to his slow movements. He had a solemnity.

I was looking at him, expectantly, like a puppy. It was not often that I had an audience, I wanted him to converse with me some more.

And then something unexpected happened. Tears welled up in his eyes and started to roll down the grooves of his cheeks. He was so still that the appearance of the tears felt like one of those miracles that happen from time to time, in the remotest parts of Italy. You know, when a saint's statue suddenly starts to spurt blood from its painted wounds, or tears out of wooden eyes, and folks start to throw away their crutches and walk. We had grown accustomed to these hysterias.

But this old man was no hysteric. His tears were real. I was beginning to believe that there was something wrong with the river, something that turned happy moods into painful ones.

But most likely it was me. I felt deeply embarrassed at having made the old man cry.

I should have had more reserve, more dignity. My sister was right when she said I was a whiner. I should have taken my sketchbook and showed him some of the villagers' portraits I had done. Anything but reduce him to tears with pitiful stories, as if it was any of his business.

Evangelista and I retreated into our personal spaces, his silently tearful, mine perplexed, straining for something to say. He took a handkerchief, the size of a small hand towel, and wiped his head, his eyes, his nose and the back and front of his neck, in one slow movement of his oaky hand. Then he looked at me, with his freshly laundered eyes, as if he had just noticed that I was still there.

"You see, young woman," he said hoarsely. "I can't

get it up anymore."

At first I didn't know what he meant. Then I followed his gaze down to his crotch, his hands open around it, in an ancient gesture of loss, as if a child had been there and was no more, and I understood.

We both looked at that emptiness of his, both feeling orphaned for different reasons. A new and different silence separated us now.

Suddenly I felt a need to cover myself. I went to where I had put my underpants to dry and donned them quickly. I put on my dress too, braided my hair loosely, and retrieved my clogs.

Then I stood in front of him, ready to leave, but trying to find something to say.

"I am from Florence," I said, "and my name is Giovanna."

I don't know why I felt the need to say that. But then, I never did know how to behave.

The Visit

I have come to the piazza to see the procession of the Corpus Domini. I ask Zia Giusta what it means.

"It's the Body of our Lord," she explains condescendingly, as if I were slightly retarded. As opposed to His Mind? I am definitely a heathen. I remember almost nothing about my religious upbringing, I might as well have been brought up a Buddhist. When I enter a church I make the sign of the cross, since it seems polite to salute on entering someone's house, but I feel like a trespasser. I admire the beauty of the old churches. While music wafts from the massive organ, the well-choreographed hieratic rituals and the incense spiralling in blue coils against the coloured light streaming from stained glass windows enrich me with an aesthetic experience.

I remain puzzled by the devotion shown by the faithful. To me, to ask for favours from a God who has shown enough indifference to human suffering to make it clear that there is no point in asking for anything, seems overly optimistic.   Given the celebratory quality of religious rituals, I would rather come to a church to thank God for what I received. It would seems more in tune with the beauty of the architectural context. I walk into a church as a voyeur. Still, I lower my thoughts and walk silently, careful to avoid stepping on the mosaic floor.

The church is full of children dressed as angels and adults trying to keep them from becoming bored and breaking into an activity of their own—activity that would be inappropriate to an angel. Some, the preferred ones, are dressed as little saints, with lipstick stigmata on their hands and cardboard halos. It all seems so pagan.

Outside, the whole village seems to be participating in the procession or preparing to witness it. The women have picked forsythia blossoms and wild rose petals during the night and now they are scattering them on the road in artistic patterns. But the Scirocco keeps dispersing the petals and the pattern is ruffled into a salad of hues. The women keep re-dividing the colours, with moving patience, but the wind's hand continues to ruffle their efforts. I walk amid the women, feeling strange and foreign. I would like to be part of the festivities, but I don't know anybody, although everybody knows who I am. The women smile at me, as if trying to engage my sympathy in their battle against the wind. I smile back, but am too shy to join them. They are too shy to ask, and we keep circling around each other, with this thin thread of impertinent wind holding us in tentative smiles.

Some children are sent to fetch watering cans and the petals are soaked in water to add ballast against the wind. The colours become impossibly vivid, and the throwing of the water becomes a side show.

From the main portal the first banners appear above the heads of the crowd and immediately unfurl with a snap like great sails, unbalancing the bearers momentarily. The little angels are also having some trouble. Their wings, which flap around their ears, threaten to take off on their own and leave the children grounded. The mothers follow the procession holding on to the loose wings like protective puppeteers.

The band has no problems. It marches on with its tubas and drums, entranced in its own cadence, mindless of what happens behind it. Finally the Eucharist appears, a burst of golden rays surrounding a white wafer representing the body of Christ. The priest who carries it above his head is so short that the Eucharist appears to levitate above the spectators, as if by a miracle. But as soon as the priest steps onto the wet flowers, he stops dead, creating a domino effect of confusion behind him. He is in his eighties and has no intention of walking on wet flowers in his light leather shoes. Had he been informed ahead of time he would have worn rubber boots. His arthritis is bad enough as it is. Somebody is sent to his house, behind the church, to fetch his rubber boots while he, in the middle of this most sacred procession, is showing his soaked black socks to his congregation, who are becoming more irreverent by the minute.

The policemen or carabinieri, who are dressed in their black and red ceremonial uniforms, are authoritatively trying to put the procession back together, while the band, having lost contact with the rest of the procession, plays on, on its own, in another street. A younger priest, an adjutant I guess, takes charge. In fact he is so much in charge he yells at everybody. My Uncle Giorgio, who has joined me, tells me that the adjutant priest doesn't want to appear disorganized, since his lover is in the crowd. I shock my uncle by asking him, what gender the lover is.

Some German tourists beside me are recording the scene on their video cameras with pitiless concentration. I am reassured by the unfolding chaos. It would have been disappointing if my Italy had become sane.

I go back to Zia Giusta for some visual rest. There is so much I want to ask her that I keep interrupting myself and jumping around with my questions like a grasshopper.

I ask her about my mother, I want to know who she really was. She died when I was at an age of frenzied self-absorption, in the midst of my teenage rebellion. But Zia Giusta is not much help when I need information about my parents. She talks about the dearly departed with a reverence that doesn't do justice to who they really were. Zia Giusta would rather talk about herself. She has the innocent selfishness of the old and the unenlightened. So, having failed to excise stories about my mother, I encourage her to talk about herself. I may as well. Maybe in telling me about herself, she might slip into other people's stories.

Zia Giusta and my mother didn't look at all like sisters. There were nine years between them. Zia Giusta belonged to a different generation and a different class, literally. When my grandfather died at the age of thirty-four—he was believed to have been killed by an assassin because of his Anarchist affiliations—he left four children. My mother, the eldest was then twenty years old and had just finished her training as an elementary school teacher. Her brother, my Uncle Marcantonio, was thirteen. He had been taken out of school when he was twelve and put in a seminary to become a priest; no questions asked about his vocation or lack of it. His tuition was paid by a mysterious benefactor, but the rest of the extended family knew who the benefactor was. It was believed that Zio Marcantonio was the illegitimate son of the local priest.

It was to atone for his illegitimacy that my grandmother—a woman of profound religious principles, though not of equally profound sexual mores—offered the child to the church. He escaped, after four years of undiluted misery, and became an engineer. Despite the official denials about his illegitimacy, he looked and behaved differently from the rest of the family. He was certainly saner. He was the only one who didn't disapprove of me. I adored him. He died of cancer at the age of forty-nine.

Next was Zia Giusta who was eleven when her father died. The youngest of the four children, Uncle Giorgio, was barely three months old when he became an orphan. He almost escaped the total misery of the family at the death of his father, by being so young.

My grandmother continued to work as a part time teacher for a while, but with a baby on her hands, lack of hired help which she couldn't afford anymore, and suffering already from a particularly virulent form of arthritis, she had no choice but to send the two girls out to work. My mother went to Milan, where she was employed as a substitute teacher. Soon after, she met my father and they married. Though she was good enough to send some money home, the financial burden of supporting the family fell to eleven year old Zia Giusta.

Zia Giusta was sent to Naples to be a servant for a family of eight people, two of whom were newborn twins. She arrived in Naples, a rather frightening city at the best of times, carrying her few belongings wrapped in a kerchief knotted at its four corners, and a small goat cheese as a present for her future employers. The idea of her being a servant had not yet sunk into her or her mother's mind. Manners require that one doesn't show up at somebody's house empty-handed.

When she arrived at the station, she did as she had been instructed by her mother. She found a horse cab, asked the fare beforehand, and only when the price was established, allowed it to take her to the address sewn into the hem of her petticoat.

Naples is infinitely bigger than Fontesanta and, as chance would have it, the King happened to be visiting the city that day, causing a great swell of people and a traffic snarl that was difficult to negotiate. She had arrived about midday, but at sunset the horse was still ambling towards its destination, which was starting to look more and more out of reach. Zia Giusta, who was already scared by the size of the city and the new experience, became increasingly agitated until she started to cry. The cab driver, a young lad of compassion, offered her the seat next to him, behind the horse. But seeing that the young girl was helpless and in need of comfort, he decided to take a God-given chance. He put his arm around her and opened his fly to show his goodies to her.

My aunt's naïvete was such that she thought the cab driver was trying to distract her with his penis because he wanted to take her cheese, which she still carried despite the fact that she was very hungry. She kept the cheese hidden below the little faggot of personal items, as the man groped. His groping was okay with her as long as he didn't touch the cheese.

It was almost night when she was finally delivered to the house of her future masters. But, maybe because of the enormous emotional stress she had been under, or because nature has its own inscrutable ways, she had started to menstruate for the first time. She had been kept duly ignorant of sexual matters, but her mother had put six linen napkins, embroidered with my aunt's initials, in her bundle, in the event that she should become a woman while away. My Zia Giusta knew, and didn't know, about it. She had seen her older sister naked, with a string around her belly and a napkin between her legs, but didn't think that she, a child barely eleven years old, could so soon also become a woman. The day's events added up to a frightening experience.

When Signora Manti, the lady for whom she was to work, opened the door, she was confronted by a hysterical girl, who was sobbing desperately, wearing a dress stained with blood, holding a small goat cheese in front of her, like a trophy. Signora Manti understood who the child was; they had been waiting for her since early afternoon. But she couldn't make out what the girl was saying, ranting incoherently as she was about a man trying to show her his private parts, endeavouring to rob her and taking her around the city and bleeding from below and thinking she was going to die.

The lady called her husband, and then all the other members of the family, to decide what to do about this poor wretched girl. They lost no time in concluding that the girl had been raped by a horse cab driver and needed to be taken to a doctor. On the face of it, it seemed a humanitarian gesture, but according to my aunt, it was more likely that they didn't want to feel responsible in any way, should she have became pregnant and need to be sent back.

The doctor, an old man of experience, asked to talk to the girl alone and sat her down for a friendly chat. He asked gentle, pointed questions, like, did the man lie on top of her, had he put anything between her legs? Zia Giusta was naïve and frightened, but she was no fool and had a creative mind. She took a quick survey of her situation and surmised correctly that, if she said what those people seemed to want her to say, she would be free to go back to her mother.

"Yes," she said, "he put his thing between my legs."

The carabinieri were called in and briefed. By now these details had become realistic and lewd. The lady of the house, although a pious woman and the mother of girls herself, was inclined to believe that my aunt was not entirely innocent and repeatedly questioned her about what she had done to provoke such reprehensible behaviour in the young man. The carabinieri were ready to go and arrest the man. The problem was, Zia Giusta refused to describe him because she was afraid she would be found out. The more insecure she felt, the more vehement her accusations. Finally, it was decided that an internal examination by the doctor was called for. It would have been sensible to have had one done before calling the carabinieri, but it seems that everybody had caught some my aunt's hysteria and forgot to suggest the most elementary exam.

The doctor examined Zia Giusta and, of course, found her still a virgin. That didn't stop my aunt from declaring again, even more vehemently, that she had indeed been raped, although, she adds today, she didn't quite know the difference between being raped and being scared to death. The carabinieri, feeling cheated of their arrest, doubted the doctor's competence in knowing the difference between a virgin and not a virgin, and said so without any regard for his status. In the end they left.

Zia Giusta was taught how to wear a napkin and put to bed with a hot cup of milk and a few cookies. She was not sent home. The next day, at five o'clock in the morning, her job started. Her work proved to be so hard that she didn't menstruate again until she was eighteen, when she was called home to take care of her mother— who was bedridden by then and totally paralyzed—and her seven-year-old brother.

She married a few months after she had returned to Fontesanta, to the only man who would take on the burden of a ready-made family. He was a man sick with the lung disease silicosis from having worked as a marble engraver, who continued to work for only a couple of years after their marriage, gave her a child and retired to a room upstairs in the family house from which he didn't leave until the day he died. He had been sick for so long that when it was announced that he had died, some of us asked, "Why, was he still alive?"

Zia Giusta worked at anything and for anybody. She was a cook for itinerant labourers at grape harvest time, preparing meals for up to two hundred people; she would search for firewood in the surrounding forest, carrying it on her head all the way back down from the mountain; she took care of sick people, as if what she did at home was not enough; and she embroidered, mended and washed clothes for rich people.

A few months ago she went for a physical examination. The doctor looked her over, and then, suspicious about the state of her heart, ordered an electrocardiogram.

"Your heart is not as good as it should be," he said.

Then, looking at her records and seeing that her profession was recorded as housewife, he added. "Now it's too late of course, but if you had worked out all your life, you would have a better heart now."

Then he remembered his bedside manners and said, smiling at the old woman,

"We have been lazy, haven't we?"

I don't want her to see the tears in my eyes. I retreat into my room for a while.

I am curious about the sex life of my aunt's generation. It seems not to exist in her tales. She never speaks of falling in love, or of dreaming about a man. A widow for close to fifty years—surely in her trips to the countryside, when cooking for all those farmhands, she must have been propositioned by some of the bolder young bloods.

These parts are not known for sexual reticence. I don't have to be subtle; Zia Giusta doesn't know what reticence is. So I dive right in.

"What did you do for sex?" I ask.

"Sex?" she says, looking at the ceiling, as if trying to remember something.

"Well, Luigi, God bless the name of my poor husband, couldn't get it up for too long. When he did what he had to do, he always ran a fever the day after. He was a good man though, always thinking about me and his daughter, he needed his glass of wine at night and three meals a day, apart from that he never asked for anything else."

She makes the sign of the cross in the direction of her husband's photograph, which has the place of honour above the stove. Is this it? That's all she has to say about sex? I push a little.

"Yes, I understand he was a good man, but what about you, what about sex after Luigi died?"

"Well, yes, of course, it was quite a liberation. I was happy I didn't have to make love anymore." This is not what I had in mind. I wanted to know about her sex life, not the lack of it. I use another tactic.

"Did you ever fall in love?"

"It wasn't a matter of falling in love, I couldn't choose. I had a bedridden mother and my kid brother. I had to marry a man who saw in me somebody who was used to taking care of people. He knew he was sick, so he needed a wife who would take care of him. Falling in love is for people who can afford it, and I couldn't."

"But did you fall in love with other men?" I push on, quite exasperated.

"Well," she says, "Once I was going for firewood, and a man was waiting for me at a crossing. After that he would always be there, always at the same time. He would say good morning and fall in step with me. After a while he would say goodbye, jump on his bicycle and leave. After a while he started to talk about things."

"What things?" I ask.

"Oh, you know, the crops, the hares that were jumping around like grasshoppers, the grape harvest." I would get off the bicycle and walk along with him for a while. "Then, what happened?" I ask, hoping for some kind of revelation.

"Then, one day he appears with a dead hare and a basket of eggs. He was all dressed up as if ready for a funeral. 'What's with you?' I asked him, 'are you getting married?' He didn't answer and didn't seem at ease.

"Finally, he said, 'The hare and the eggs are for you. If you want I can skin the hare and tan the pelt for you.'

"I knew then that he had something in mind.

"'Who have you taken me for?' I asked. 'I don't accept presents from men.'

"'No, no' he said. 'This is not because I want to do those things with you, I really want you to have these as a present.'

"He put the basket and the hare in front of me, jumped on the bicycle and left. I never saw him again." And then she adds with a sigh, "I think he would have been a good man for me. Sometimes I think of him. I think I hurt him."

I find an excuse to go to my room because I can hardly bear to be with her. I recognize myself in her. The many times I have sounded distant and missed an opportunity for closeness—because of nothing more than garden-variety shyness. I muse that not knowing how to behave must run in families. That man with the basket of eggs and a freshly killed hare was also too shy to see past other's shyness. We who are shy seem to be walking around looking in mirrors. Looking at others looking at us. For the timid ones an offer of eggs not promptly accepted must suffice for a lifetime of romantic possibilities.

When I return to the kitchen there is a silence between us. Something is cooking on the stove and it smells wonderful, as usual. Her kitchen is a concert hall of aromas. After a while she says, "If you want to come to live here with me, I will give you my house. When I die it should be worth something."

I don't know what to say to such an offer, she must know that I can't possibly accept it.

"But Zia," I say, "what about your daughter, and what about my husband?"

She smiles silently, her hands always busy with something; today it's lace.

"You are so good," she says, "you are so good. A person like you would know how to take care of me. When you are old, nobody wants you, nobody listens to you."

"We old folks," she says cryptically, "we don't even sweat anymore."

I contemplate old age from a place far from where I am now, and yet not far enough. I hardly know how to tell her that it's time for me to leave. It seems so cruel after the gift of her stories.

I am all packed, everybody has been seen, embraced and given a present. Everybody's story has been listened to.

I am waiting at the bus stop in front of Zia Giusta's house. When the bus shows up at the top of the street, Zia Giusta puts a little basket of baked rabbit in my hands.

"You eat it in the bus," she says and starts to weep. I kiss her cheeks, bitter with tears, and run on the other side of the street to board the bus. Once inside I stand up to wave goodbye as we start to move. Suddenly the bus bumps into something and I am thrown on the floor and slide all the way to the side of the driver, with a number of suitcases, from the overhead nets, falling after me. The driver is cursing a little Fiat that has crossed his path. He is revving up the motor to swerve away from the stalled car.

A lady gets up from her seat and helps me back on my feet, but I can hardly move. I feel that one side of my body has been knocked out of consciousness. I slowly make it to a seat near the lady, who addresses me by my first name. I am surprised and ask her how she knows me. She tells me she is my cousin's wife. The one he left and now has gone back to. I can hardly believe my eyes. I remember her as a scorned wife, a mouse of a woman, wallowing in abnegation, always busy cooking something. But before me is this lovely woman, with a mane of black hair sweeping across one side of her face. She is thin and tall, a real siren. I now understand why he has come back to her. The transformation is breathtaking, she even speaks differently. She is going to Pesaro to meet some girlfriends, and from there they are all going to Spain. To Spain?

"Yes," she says, "We are going with our priest to the Sanctuary of Campostela."

So, I say to myself, that's what the crusades were for, giving people a holy alibi, an excuse to get away. A bit like taking a kid along to Disneyland. She is so busy telling me about her new life and I am so busy listening to her, that we forget for the moment that I have just been knocked to the floor. I avoid the subject of my cousin. He will have to work out who, when and how he is going to love.

When I try to get up from my seat at Pesaro, I find that I can hardly move. My cousin's wife asks me if I would like to be accompanied to a hospital. I refuse, saying I will be all right. The reason is that, from my experience,

Italian hospitals used to be more like lazarets than places for curing sick people. They probably have changed in the intervening years, but I am not willing to take a chance. Italian friends have advised me that, should I need a hospital, the best course would be to go to a private clinic. But I don't think I am willing to pay what a private clinic would cost—not unless I feel in real danger.

On the train to Florence, which I have managed to board at Pesaro, I feel faint with pain and grow a little scared. When I go into the washroom to look at myself in the mirror, I see that one side of my body is a dark shade of Prussian blue.

I am going back to Florence, but I have changed my mind about returning to the pensione Norma. I will search for a luxury hotel with a doctor on call, just in case. I am also ready for some comfort, since I have saved money by staying with my aunt. But when I ask the receptionist at the Grand Hotel about the price, I decide I don't need that much comfort. One night there costs as much as two weeks in a hotel for mere mortals. So I hop on a bus that is just leaving from the station square and a twenty-minute ride takes me to Prato, an ugly little town of smoke stacks and crumbling walls. But it is a textile centre with many good hotels for business people from all over the world.

It is raining and I feel rather miserable. The hotel doesn't help. Being luxurious means that a lot of marble has been thrown around at random, on stairs, tabletops, the floor and the reception desk. It looks like a marble sample room. The architecture is atrocious, a mishmash of contemporary ideas in a zabaglione of visual languages with no connecting concept or even concern for creature comfort. In fact, the only comfort comes from the espresso coffee machine, hissing the smell of delicious strong coffee, through the well tended potted palms by the entrance.

The bedrooms are a showcase for the most outlandishly slick furniture to come out of the mind of unemployed architects, playing at designing furniture. Everything smells of plastic upholstery and newly laid carpet. I feel that, if I do need a doctor, they'll send in robots.

The weather is so bad that I have no choice but to watch television. I see Robert Redford open his mouth in English and it comes out Italian. I change channels and get a revue of gyrating naked breasts and Neapolitan songs.

I feel splurgy and order supper in my room. I sit in the grand, vulgar bedroom, eating a dish of fried octopus and calamari, while somebody on television is belting out a song of love and betrayal. Outside it is raining hard, and the city lights come on like a necklace of bright oranges. What more can I ask for?

I have come back to Florence in order to visit three places: the Library, the Orphanage and the Place-Where-I-Was-Born: 31 Fanelli Street. The next day, the sky doesn't look too promising, but it has stopped raining for the time being and I am feeling a little better. I have decided to go first to the place of my birth. It will not be too difficult to find. Old derelict buildings have a way of surviving if the surroundings have the good sense to remain derelict.

It starts raining again when I get to my old neighbourhood. The building is at the edge of an old railroad track. No improvement has been made to the track that I can detect. The weeds still break through the disconnected stones and the stucco still reveals patches of bricks. It is almost two o'clock in the afternoon and the street is deserted; everybody is having a siesta. By the time I am ready to ring the bell, I am drenched and look like a bag lady.

I almost don't want to do it. It is an indiscreet hour and I look like hell, but I have come two thousand miles to this landmark of mine, so I must at least try. I ring the bell and although nothing happens right away, I feel a flutter above me, behind the shut blinds. I know I am being evaluated, I hope curiosity will prevail and they will open the door. If nobody comes though, I will retreat with relief and assume that fate has kept a door closed. The intercom makes a raspy noise and the door opens automatically. I am a bit uncertain as I enter, because there is nobody at the door, and start climbing the stone stairs.

A little woman peeks from behind the landing wall and asks, "Who is it?" I draw my breath and say, with a gentleness I know the woman is not accustomed to and, thus, could not fail to impress her, "I am awfully sorry to disturb you at this awkward time. I am sure you were resting. I was born in this house almost sixty years ago and would appreciate it immensely if you could be so nice as to let me look around for a few minutes." And, since I don't see any softening of her face I add humbly, "For sentimental reasons."

I see the idea penetrating her consciousness. I can almost follow the neural path my request takes, a sequence of emotions as subtle as water ripples showing on her tight little face.

I feel I have to encourage this beginning into a more promising result, so I increase my charm volume and add: "I would, always with your permission of course, be happy with just seeing the terrace, the one with the skylights over the wine cellar and the pigeons on the upper eaves."

I smile at the memory of the pigeons. I want to make sure she understands that I really am who I say I am, so I add details to enhance my credibility.

"The wine cellar is not there anymore," she says, as if this fact had some relevance to my request. I am running out of charm and don't know what more to say. Suddenly she says: "It's very unusual, what you ask, but come in anyway. You must understand that I didn't expect anybody, so the house is in disarray, I haven't cleaned it yet."

"Oh, please," I say with a sigh of anticipation, "I don't mind the way it looks, I just want a few minutes."

I enter the cleanest, neatest place I ever saw, it even smells of detergent. I ask if I should take my shoes off.

"Oh no," she says, "it's so dirty anyway."

I indulge her in her dirt fantasy by not commenting. I immediately recognize the living-dining-entrance room, which I had expected to be small, but not that small. The perception of size changes with time. It is hard for me to believe that four people lived in a space no larger than my entrance hall, back at home in Canada. And at the time of the servant, Ines, we were five.

Nothing of what I remember as our decor is left. The arrangement of the furniture is the same—one could hardly invent another layout in such minimal space—but the furniture is afflicted by the current fashionable plague of chrome and glass that I so dislike. The green wooden blinds that filtered the midday sun, have been replaced by metal blinds that are drawn shut, slitting the light into thin lines, giving the place a faint tropical flavour. Over the table a crystal chandelier dangles drops of refracted light in an attempt to convey a pretence of luxury, defeated by the smallness of the area. Everything is sleek and hard-edged; the new language of poverty is glassy and polished, a private war against the dandruff of dust.

She shows me to the bedroom, the one where Lieta and I slept. There is only one bed here now and one large chest of drawers, so shiny it looks as if it is made of white nail polish. Again I ask myself how we accommodated two beds, one chest of drawers, one wardrobe, a table for my sister to do her homework, and a marble basin stand. The room must have been filled with miniature items. But here I see that the floor has been left the way it was, red bricks polished with cinnabar and wax. Of the whole apartment, only those few bricks on which a stripe of sun lies, like a pointed finger, give me an emotional jolt, which I try to hide by talking nonstop to the small woman. I wish I could be left alone for a few minutes, but I can hardly ask her to remove herself from her own house, so that I can emote in peace.

The kitchen has suffered more aesthetic effrontery than the rest of the apartment. It has been totally remodelled. I don't know where the pots and pans are kept, but they certainly don't festoon every available area as they did when it was our kitchen. As for the great marble sink and the equally vast hearth, both have disappeared. And, where there was once only one faucet, now there are two, one for cold water, one for hot. The woman even shows me the washroom, bless her soul. I tell her: "We kept a chicken in here, during the war, and believe it or not, it laid eggs."

"Why not on the terrace?" she asks.

"Because on the terrace, it would have been stolen."

She looks at me as if I am talking about another country. Of course, I am.

We go onto the terrace. No surprises about size here; the terrace is twice the size of the apartment, exactly as I remember. There are still the pyramidal skylights opening onto what used to be the wine cellar but is now a garage. The smell of gasoline has replaced the smell of wine. I tell her about the horses that hauled the huge barrels from under us, foaming at the mouth, their hooves sparkling on the cobblestones, their round eyes almost popping out of the sides of their head because of the strain. Some-times the men would let us ride on the cart around the block and we would shriek in ecstasy.

I wish I wouldn't keep talking and talking as if I owed this woman a stream of memories that belong only to me. I wish I could be silent and open a few doors onto my past and then quietly savour them. But I can't, I am embarrassed by my emotions, and try to cover them up with conviviality.

I say goodbye to the woman a bit too abruptly. She was starting to enjoy my company and is taken aback. She offers me some refreshments, a few candies in a dish, an espresso, but I want to run away. I am almost resentful of her. I shake her hand and give her my card.

She glances at it and asks me what all those letters after my name mean. I explain that they are my profes-sional degrees. She becomes flustered with respect and is determined to hold me longer in her house, while I become more determined to leave. I say goodbye again and go.

In the street I walk along the curb until I trespass onto the railroad tracks and sit among the brambles, on a dead rail, to clear my head and engage in a bit of well-deserved wallowing in my past. The railroad is where I used to play with Riccardo, who, though younger than me, I had elected to be my best friend. I was supposed to look after him, which shows how naïve parents can be. His mother and mine used to put us out in his great garden in the morning, together with the house cat and the aspidistras, and retrieve us at meal times and for the night. The garden was part of an industrial school where Riccardo's father worked as the janitor and night guard. The garden—it seemed immense then—bordered the Institute of Applied Chemistry on one side and the railroad tracks on the other. At the far end, completely out of sight, was a more secret garden, with a fountain at its centre. But no water spouted from the fountain's stone shell; the water in the basin must have been there from antiquity, mephitic, still, green and dangerous; it was a soup of algae, with some water lilies displaying their whiteness to nobody. Riccardo and I almost never went there, we found it too enclosed.

Our parents thought we were safe in the garden, surrounded as it was by walls three metres high. But I was not the kind of child who would be stymied by enclosures. I found a hole at the base of the wall that allowed us to wiggle directly onto the railroad tracks. There the horizon enlarged to vistas of coming and going trains, with whistles and steam, and the opportunity of counting wagons, an activity I found hypnotic. I always held onto Riccardo's hand, because although I was only five years old, I knew that he would be in danger if I let go.

I found all manner of entertainment on the tracks. There was the placing of little stones on the rails, then waiting for a train to pulverize them. Different materials met different annihilations. Flowers became instantly pressed and, when dried, long lasting. Dead lizards didn't become something very nice to look at, just a splat. Glass became totally shattered and sticks multiplied by their individual strands.

Once, looking around for new stuff to offer to the pounding wheels, I thought that metal would be an interesting material to use. But hard as I looked, I found none around the tracks. I grew quite frustrated, until I remembered the key to our apartment that my mother always left hanging on a nail, just outside the door. I knew that my mother was out, since every morning she went to the market to buy food. So, I took Riccardo by the hand, parked him in his kitchen, and ran up to my door. I took the key and ran back to retrieve Riccardo and then went back to the tracks. I put the key on the track and waited for a train to come by. Every so often I would put my head down on the rail to hear if a train was coming. The key was a big, clumsy affair of solid iron with a large ring on one side, a jutting, dented protuberance on the other, and a hollow tube joining the two sides. A bit like what one imagines the key to Heaven might look like.

A big international train came along—forty-seven wagons and two sleepers. Some of the passengers waved at us and we waved back. When the train disappeared after the curve past the bridge, we went to retrieve the key. It still managed to look like a key, but was three times as long, twice as wide, as thin as a metal wafer, and quite hot. Both Riccardo and I were intrigued; nothing had performed its transformation as well as the key. We were in fact elated. We kept fingering it to feel its heat and it's thinness, we could even bend it a little.

After a while I realised my mother would return eventually and look for the key. And I knew that if she didn't find it, she would have known immediately that I had taken it. So, I ran fast to my house and hung the key in the place where I had found it.

I wasn't home when my mother returned so I don't know how she got into the house. She probably asked one of the men in the wine cellar to come up and break the door down. But when I came in she was still livid, not so much with anger, as with puzzlement. She kept looking at me. I could see her brain wheels working, suspecting that I had had something to do with it, but not able to unravel how I could have stretched a solid iron key into a long wafer of metal. I kept looking at her, innocently, angelically; I almost felt as my sister must have felt most of the time: not guilty. It was my first victory over my mother and I savoured it. I never told her how the key had been transformed. It was one of my rare triumphs. It was also one of my rare secrets.

❧

I am going to see the library. I think I remember where it is, but on my way I am distracted by the market. I want to taste again all the cheap forbidden things I used to buy with the money I stole from either my mother or my sister. I still wonder why my mother kept putting her money in the kitchen drawer, where I could easily find it. Poor as we were, my stealing couldn't have escaped her eagle eyes. Maybe it had to do with the fact that I was very cunning.

Sometimes I played close to the fire. Intermittently, I would steal a bit more money than usual, so that it would be noticed, but then put the money someplace where it could be easily found, like under a stack of dishes or in a coat pocket. First, I would be accused of taking the money, since it was a family tradition to think of me as the culprit. Then, of course, the money would be found and apologies had to be made. Meanwhile, I was in a corner crying that I had been accused unjustly, believing every word of it.

Not that I stole much. But since my mother thought that I was a cross sent to her by God for the purpose of making her expiate sins that she hadn't even committed, I wonder what she would have thought of me, had she known of my pilfering from her already meagre resources. This leaves me with the puzzle of my evilness. I feel I deserved my mother's animosity, but since she didn't know I was stealing I have come to the rather logical conclusion that honesty would have won me no love anyway. Morality never entered my innocent mind. Morality came into question only when I was caught.

Time has indeed changed me.

The money was usually for apple fritters, the occasional movie and, later in my teens, mascara. I look for the apple fritter shop at the end of the San Lorenzo Market and am happy to find that it is still there. It isn't really a shop, but a little window with a few fritters and rice rings on the sill. In order for the man to leave his niche, he has to lift the sill and turn the window into a door. That's how small it is. A bit further on, the cord maker and the tripe vendor also, I see, still hang onto their decrepit little enclaves. I am pleasantly surprised that these tiny enterprises still exist.

I order some apple fritters and rice rings and ask that some extra sugar be sprinkled over them. I take my little parcel of historic lemony tastes and sit on the stone steps by the fountain to pause for pure delight. I watch the crowd of people engaged in their daily habit of feeling and touching the merchandise with suspicious, intent looks, absorbed in the ancient pleasures of trade.

A man in a wheelchair appears, pushed by a young man who looks no older than seventeen or eighteen. The youth pushes the wheelchair carefully to a prominent but shady spot, out of the way of the traffic. He puts a coverlet over the legs of the man and a wooden crate he has been carrying, upside down, next to him. He climbs on the crate, clears his throat and starts to address the crowd. I expect him to ask for money. Though they are decently dressed and do not appear to be beggars, I can't think of any other reason for the young man to address the people in the street.

"This man is my father," he says, "and, as you can see, he is paralysed from the waist down." He motions to his father to remove the coverlet, so that people can see his useless legs. "He has worked all his life to support a wife and four children. My family never wanted for anything, he never missed a day of work and never spent a cent on himself. The firm he worked for threw him out like a dog, with no compensation or pity. This is a good man," he continues, with an almost imperceptible catch in his throat "and should not have been treated like that. What do you think he can do with his useless legs now? I want you all to know that my father has been done an injustice and he doesn't deserve it." He stops for a minute to wipe his brow. A little crowd has gathered around him. I am still eating my fritters waiting for him to come to the point. The youth looks at his father now and adds. "He has been the best father. I am proud of him."

He doesn't ask for any money. He has finished. He folds the coverlet and puts it on his father's lap, takes the crate and slowly pushes the wheelchair away. I get up and give some of the fritters to the pigeons. I'll have the rest later.

Sometimes, not often, I find it hard to eat.

I find the library with some difficulty and hesitate a little in front of it. Since there are road workers making repairs at the curb, I can hardly see the facade. I enter and go up the few steps to a landing I do not recognize. The mosaic floor is still there but everything has been white-washed and cleaned up, to an antiseptic degree. It looks like a dentist's waiting room. The two statues of Dante and Petrarch are whiter than I remember.

In the library proper I am confronted by a turnstile, one of those horrible contraptions that just about rapes you every time you try to enter. I walk over to a table and sit at it, in order to look around. A skylight has been opened in the roof, flooding the area with a slanted shaft of crude light, and giving the area the feel of a mini shopping centre. The books have disappeared, presumably into the bowels of the building, and a large number of students sit at the reading tables in silence, while others sit inside carrels at ticking computers. I can't see the garden with the magnolias that used to be at the right of the entrance. Maybe that's where the new bookshelves are.

A squat, efficient lady librarian approaches me and points silently to the computerized card catalogue.

"I just want to sit here for a while," I whisper, "I used to work here when I was a child."

"All right" she whispers back. "But you are not allowed to eat in here," she says archly. I realize then that I still have some of the fritters in my hand. I get up and throw them in the wastepaper basket and go back to my seat. But on second thought I decide to leave.

If I want to remember the library, I must get away from this cleaned up "resource centre" and sit by myself someplace where I will not be disturbed. I go back to the fountain, sit on the stone step, lie back against the column and close my eyes to the sun until I start to see golden spots. I go back to a day in spring more years ago than I care to number. I want to remember it all with clarity, and for that I must get the atmospherics right. It all started with the rain.

❦

When I was twelve years old, I found myself a job—not a paying one, but a job nevertheless. It happened because of the weather. It had been a heavy spring day. First the clouds descended to the level of the saints' halos above the cathedral portals, obliterating the great dome and Giotto's bell tower. Then the pigeons had started to behave as if they were gulls, flying aggressively for a last-minute peck, before disappearing inside the saints' niches. Finally, after a few premonitory sparks, the sky unzippered itself and threw a tantrum onto the city.

On my way to school, I had ran from cover to cover until, mercifully, I found an open door and tumbled in, without looking, shaking myself like a Saint Bernard, squeezing my eyes to clear them of water, and stamping my feet on the marble mosaic of Neptune and frolicking mermaids.

At first, because of the size, I thought it must be a church. But it didn't smell like one. I knew the smell of churches well, because it was a smell that made me faint. When we went to church on Sundays, my mother had to to take along the salts and a cream puff. The cream puff was to be eaten after Communion, for Communion had to be taken on a respectfully empty stomach. But the combination of the smell of incense and an empty stomach made me collapse. Then my mother would take the salts out, and look around apologetically, lest people think I was having visions. That was all she needed—she would say with weariness—to have to cope with rumours of a miracle."

Nor did the place I was in look like a church.

All I could see were the faint dishes of light that green-shaded lamps threw onto massive tables, arranged in an orderly manner, all around the room. Only after a few seconds—my eyes having adjusted to the gloom—did I see the books.

They covered every inch of the walls, all the way up to the ceiling. On the ceiling a landscape of tumbling classical temples and other pagan images were half revealed in the semidarkness.

The smell was of a gentle putridness, a scent in keeping with the accumulated detritus of centuries of unrequited knowledge wrapped in gilded leather, parchment, silk, exotic veneers—all the artistic bindings we bestow on books we do not read.

Through the great arched windows, a courtyard of

shaking magnolias gave the dusty silence of the library the appearance of an archaeological enclave.

Florence had several such libraries—long forgotten bequests from private citizens in search of a place to dispose of a lifetime of erudition. They dotted the cultural landscape of the city, beside private chapels and galleries of anonymous portraits. Sometimes the municipality gathered enough funds and found the will to dispose of the books and transform those buildings into something useful, like an orphanage or a brothel, but mostly they languished in the keep of a caretaker whose job condemned him to terminal boredom.

At that age, although I was a voracious reader, I avoided libraries and museums because they reminded me of cemeteries and schools. But this one had the dusty splendour of a grand ballroom that had fallen into a mothy silence. The walls were so thick that individual small desks had been embedded in their thickness. Its immense windows were half covered by sun-bleached curtains, held back by silk ropes with tassels the size of upturned buckets.

No one seemed to be around. Still, I tried to make as little noise as possible, as one should in a library. But my wet sandals squished loudly with every step. I was about to decipher the Latin inscription on the fascia above the shelves when I was startled by a voice from above me.

"Can I be of help?" it said.

Voices have a way of revealing their owner's nature. This one was reedy, muffled and dusty like the rest of the place. Had I been sinning, it could have passed for the voice of my conscience. It came from a desk as tall as a pulpit, and it belonged to somebody whose head stuck out from the edge, like a gargoyle. He had the mien of a gentle vulture, his open-winged ears so transparent I could almost see the outline of the magnolias through them. I was about to answer something at random, when he preceded me with a bout of coughing as thunderous as the storm outside. He took a handkerchief out of his pocket, and dabbed delicately at his forehead and the rest of his face. He raised himself slowly and came down a few steps, to my level.

I realized then that he was a priest. His cassock was so old it had acquired the colour of a young cockroach, with small masterpieces of darning in deeper black around the neck and on the edges of his sleeves. He had an appealing ugliness about him, a smile full of teeth, mostly vertical. His eyes were heroically cheerful, given the dignified disaster that was the rest of him. He could have been thirty or forty years old. But it was difficult to say, since his emaciated face seemed to have aged at its own sickly pace. But he had heroic eyebrows. They were like great dark, thick arches across his forehead—a little leftover tuft in the centre—permanently raised in childlike curiosity.

He led me with a flourish to one of the tables, took out a monument of a chair and invited me to sit.

I sat, in order not to disappoint him, and immediately I felt glued to the old leather chair, through my wet school uniform. I felt obliged to ask for some book, but the strangeness of the place had pushed all thought out of my mind. I looked around for inspiration, and noticed the *Encyclopaedia Treccani*—the Italian equivalent of the *Encyclopaedia Britannica*—all one hundred volumes of it, housed on a free standing monumental shelf, in the middle of the library.

"I need to look up something in the *Encyclopaedia*, for my home work," I said uncertainly.

"Of course, of course," he said, eagerly, "Here it is, right here. We lost the *S* and the *G* in the war," he added, with the expression of mourning reserved for the passing of a beloved. Should you need something in the *S* or the *G*, it will have to be found in the *Illustrated Updated Dictionary* or up in the shelves. Regrettably, I cannot climb the ladder. My lungs," he added with an affectionate tap to his chest. "But I can tell you where to climb."

'Troy," I improvised. "The city of Troy."

"Right," he said with a sight of relief, and pointed to the *T* volumes. "T has three volumes," he added with some pride.

I sat there, with the appropriate *T* volume open in front of me, trying to concentrate.

The storm was abating outside. In the garden the magnolias had come to rest, but the rain was still drumming its tattoo on the window panes. A few voices came from the street, always a welcome sound after a storm. I wanted to go, but I felt compelled by compassion and by what little I knew about manners to stay for a while. The walls of Troy were looking at me blankly from an engraved page so large that I had to raise my head every time I turned it. The priest was puttering around handling a few books of a size he could manage.

An old man came in, leaning heavily on a cane. The priest hastened to welcome him deferentially and led him to a chair at a discreet distance from me. The old man looked around with a professorial countenance, his eye glasses flashing, and asked for a book.

"Yes, yes, yes," I heard the priest whisper, while hurrying to a ledger on his pulpit. I was gazing at him absentmindedly, when I saw him look at me with an inspired look. I diverted my eyes and went back to Troy, but not soon enough. In an instant his flickering voice was by my ear.

"I wonder," he whispered, "if you could be so kind. You being a healthy, young, clever girl, I wonder if you could help this gentleman?"

"Me?" I asked, my mind reeling with puzzlement.

"The book," he said, "the book is up in the stacks. You certainly would find it easy to climb up the stepladder and retrieve the book for us."

"Oh," I said, relieved. "Sure, I will."

I took the scrap of paper on which he had written his instructions for finding the requested book and climbed up the ladder. Once up, I pushed the little wheel below the ladder, a bit more than necessary. It was like travelling in space. I could see the green lights below me, as if they belonged to a dwarfed world, the priest and the professor looking up at me, like elves. I came down the ladder with the book, feeling rather triumphant, only to be handed another scrap of paper, with the instructions for finding another book.

And that's how I became Father Benno's assistant.

Every day after classes were over, at 1:30, I would walk to the library where I ate my lunch, hang around for something to do, and when a book was requested, climb all over the stacks to find it. Mostly, I would do my homework, dust a few volumes, look up the forbidden book illustrations of overfed, nudish ladies and read about Angkor Vat. I had discovered the Temple of Angkor Vat in the *Encyclopaedia Treccani*. With its decaying ruins in the Cambodian jungle, it had fired my imagination and become come my afternoon retreat.

Not long after the start of my job, a policeman started to come to the library. He usually asked for a book, but in reality, the library had become a place for him to go. He came every day, after, or instead of, doing his daily beat around his assigned block. He brought with him his dog, a little mongrel called Carlomarx.

Middle-aged and bald, he had a pencil-thin moustache that started from inside his nose and stopped well above his upper lip, as if it had been breathed in in a moment of uncontrolled inspiration. His baldness was not the scrawny nakedness of the priest's head, but a joviality of the head befitting the benevolence of his appearance, which even the black police uniform didn't manage to dilute.

He was a man of precision. He would lay out his lunch with great care, on the table next to the door overlooking the courtyard, where—the priest, the police-man, Carlomarx and I—had taken to having our lunch.

He had two baskets, one for himself and one for the dog. He usually sat at the head of the table, and the priest and I sat on either side of him. After sitting down, out came all those little containers of his, each one full of carefully prepared food, a napkin with a border of red birds, a thermos containing espresso and a half full bottle of wine, plugged by a rolled-up page of *The Communist Voice*. When he had finished preparations for himself, he would place a prosciutto bone on the floor for Carlomarx. He would cut everything—even bread and broccoli—into polite little chunks before settling down to the business of eating.

The priest, on the other hand, would take his lunch out of a brown paper bag, put it on the table, look at it as if it were another of his daily tribulations and close his eyes for the saying of grace. He would swallow a raw egg by piercing both ends with the point of his knife and sucking from one of the holes. Then he would nibble at a bit of chicken, a couple of asparagus stalks and a prune. Enough for a rabbit. It took him no less than an hour to get through it.

I took my lunch from my school satchel, waited for the priest to swallow his egg, because the sight of a raw egg being gulped whole made me want to vomit, and then eat it out of the newspaper wrapping without bothering to arrange it in any manner. My lunch was whatever was left over from supper the night before, which my mother stuffed into half a loaf of bread, with the inside scooped out. The taste differed from day to day, but it always came out in the shape of a wedge, from having congealed in the scooped out bread. No matter, I gobbled up everything edible in those days. I would finish eating before the priest had started to torture one of his peas and the policeman had time to artistically arrange his rapini and chicken fricassee.

It was right after lunch that the policeman told his stories.

At first he kept to episodes of his professional life. Stories about the tests of wits between wily thieves and their network of accomplices and him, a lone policeman with no better mean to chase them than an old bicycle.

In the beginning we listened with great interest to his stories, but then, the repetitious linearity of reality started to make them monotonous, even though, one of them concerned the capture of a murderer.

It had been our appetite for the thrilling that had slowly edged him away from the thin stock of personal experiences to the endless resources of the fantastic.

Because he was a generous man, he allowed us to push him into the unreal.

We were not good listeners. We participated in his stories, robbed them of their endings by finishing his sentences and tried to unravel their hidden geometry. He defended himself by keeping a foot in reality, so that we were never quite sure how much to believe. Take the story of the pelican.

"What pelican?" I would ask.

"The pelican, the twins, Francesca and Anna Francesca, kept as a pet."

Right there we knew that nobody in his right mind

would give a girl one name and the other the same plus another.

"Funny, isn't it?" he said, as if he could read our thoughts. "It's like Baptist and Anabaptist. Anyway, they had a pelican, which they named Pelican."

"Where would they find a pelican?" I would ask, reasonably.

"In a savage land," was the authoritative answer. Francesca and Anna Francesca had been doing well at their trade, but then the war had come and food became scarce and expensive. They were forced to sell their furniture, one precious piece at the time, until their home became no more than an empty shell. But, of course, being women of resource they took to singing to fill the empty space. And being women of taste they were mindful of the character and size of each room. They sang operas in the salon and ballads in the study, and would sing nothing but love songs in the bedroom. In the kitchen they sang nursery rhymes, as one must."

See what I mean? He took liberties with our common sense. But we didn't care. We loved strangeness.

"So, what about the pelican?" I asked.

"Have patience," he said, savouring the suspense. "In time the twins had no more furniture to sell, nothing more to eat. All they had was their singing, but, as you know, one must eat. The time had come to eat Pelican."

Here it comes, we thought. Now we would be treated to some gory details.

"But, unfortunately, the knife could not be found. It seemed to have disappeared. So a way had to be devised to kill Pelican. Clever girls that they were, they lured the bird with a few fish bones until its head was within the door frame, and then they slammed the door shut. The pelican's head cracked like a walnut, and its little black eyes popped out and pinged on the bare floor, like marbles."

Well, he had the decency not to disappoint us, after all. But it wasn't over. As usual, we tried to anticipate his ending.

"So they opened the pelican and found the knife, right?" I volunteered.

"Wrong," he said slyly. "They cooked the pelican and ate it. They found it quite tasty."

"That's it?"

"That's it. Apart from the fact that, the twins being so poor and resourceful, the pelican beak was turned into a mail box. When it was full of letters, which it never was, the lower part of the beak stretched all the way down to the floor."

He then proceeded to pour the espresso into our cups, a little less for me because of my young age.

After lunch and the stories, we retreated to our private worlds. The priest in his pulpit, coughing up small galaxies of dust in the sunlight. The policeman would go to sleep in front of an open volume of anything, as long as it was large—Carlomarx at his feet—and I disappeared in the jungle of Angkor Vat, where I felt safe, removed as I was from my mother's preaching and my sister's goading. My homework would be done later, when, mercifully, readers would arrive to distract me.

Life went on uneventfully until, a month or so after I got my job at the library, during the general catalepsy of early afternoon, we had a visit. As happens with momentous events, I remember exactly what I was doing when it occurred. I was giving a wedge of congealed spaghetti—which had proven to be too unpalatable even for me—to Carlomarx. As I did so, I tried not to disturb the policeman, who was asleep in front of the atlas, open at the map of the Philippines.

Actually Carlomarx and I smelled the visitor before we

heard the steps on the marble floor.

It was an aggressively sensual perfume, an alluring cloud so profane and intense, it made Carlomarx sneeze.

The apparition that followed was in keeping with the scent's promise. I wasn't sure what a lady looked like, for I had never seen one, but I had seen enough American movies to have a vague idea and thought this must be a lady. She was tall and curvy, and wore a suit with great padded shoulders and a hat jauntily on one side of her head. A gauze-like material covered her face with a dark mist, making it difficult to guess her age. But under that veil, she had scarlet rose-petal lips, layers of eyelashes and ogival eyebrows pencilled high on her forehead, in chronic bewilderment. A beauty spot, applied on one of her luminous cheeks, reminded admirers that, alas, nobody's perfect. A great silver fox biting its tail was draped around her, and casually slung to the side of her long neck. The fox's little paws dangled in unison, at each undulating step.

Entering, she had a moment of elegant hesitation, and then laid her Garbo eyes on me. I was quick enough to close my mouth, rearrange my face to look as if I hadn't been looking and straighten myself up, to summon some class out of my school uniform.

I was readying myself to tell her that she had stumbled into the wrong place, when the priest came down from his pulpit and started to walk towards her. But half way he seemed to lose momentum, as if his legs were giving away below him, and sat down at a little distance from her.

"Maman," he said hoarsely.

Even possessing no more than school French, I knew enough to understand. Could that lady really be his mother?

She then walked slowly the rest of the way, stopping

in front of him and extending a gloved hand to touch his arm, but staying at a little distance, not so much in affection as in incredulity.

"Antoine," she said softly.

The priest took her hand formally, stiffly, and shook it, as if reintroducing himself. But then he brought her hand to his cheek in a sudden, unguarded moment of such tenderness that I felt compelled to divert my eyes. It was then that I saw the policeman, on the other side of them, staring, transfixed by the scene.

Now the lady started to speak in quick, incomprehensible French, too fast for me to understand. As she spoke, she touched him now and then, lightly, as one touches a pet. She never removed her gloves or lifted her veil. She did not sit. She just stood there, talking softly, a civilized pain—more like an annoyance, really—in her dark painted eyes.

He kept gazing at her from below, looking lost and shrunken, a spent creature momentarily lit by an arrow of forgotten love, waiting to sink back into his comfortable anonymity.

I thought of my mother's yelling at me, of its vulgarity compared to the civility of this encounter. I would have liked this kind of mother. When the lady had finished talking, she took his hand into her own, for a few silent moments. Then she straightened herself up and walked a few steps backwards, to look at the priest at an angle, the way one looks at a bad painting.

"Adieu, Antoine," she murmured.

She turned, giving the silver fox a spin around her shoulders, and left.

The priest stared after her, his hands stretched emptily on the polished table. Then he rose slowly and disappeared into his pulpit. Had it not been for the cloud of perfume the lady left behind, I might not have believed it had happened.

Things changed.

We looked at Father Benno with different eyes now. Antoine? Why had he never told us that he was French? Being French was of a higher order than being Italian. Being anything else was of a higher order than being Italian. It meant being more exotic, more mysterious, more peculiar even. The English from up the hill, near Fiesole, must have known that being a foreigner was more interesting, because they never tried to become one of us. Since we didn't speak their language and they never bothered to learn ours, we never talked to them. I would have loved being one of their children—taken around in prams like thrones on wheels by nannies carved out of starch, wearing shoes of iron. The French were not as numerous nor as peculiar as the English, and sometimes they took the trouble to learn a few phrases of Italian, slanting their words towards the last syllable, like falling dominoes. But they had their liquid language, compared to which our own sounded like the staccato sound of a stutterer.

If I had been French, I would have flaunted it.

How could he be French and sit in his pulpit, waiting to die of tuberculosis, in this dusty catacomb, listening to the policeman's silly stories, not even playing with Carlomarx for a bit of solace?

There must have been more to his life than we could see. I became suspicious and I started to imagine.

Maybe he was a great writer in disguise or a nobleman punished for unspeakable sins. Maybe he had contracted tuberculosis roaming around Angkor Vat, in the Cambodian jungle. At night he would engage in orgies with overfed nudish ladies, although it was hard to imagine where he would find the breath to do that. No matter. The policeman and I looked now at him as a subterfuge, a hypocrisy to be cracked open with wiles more cunning, more subtle than his.

The policeman's stories changed

He became allusive, engaging in innuendoes and parables. The locale was transferred to France, the protagonists relentlessly French. He lost his humour and his bonhomie. He ceased to be the neighbourhood's policeman, waging a friendly war against a few petty thieves, and started to fancy himself a detective, no less. Like the ones in trench coats in the American movies. He would talk of French legionnaires abandoning innocent girls, after those poor girls had given birth to children out of wedlock. These babies were then given away, either to nunneries if they were girls, or to seminaries, to become priests, in atonement for their parents' sins.

On finishing a story, he would fall into a meaningful silence, to give the priest the chance to do the honourable thing: tell us about his past. He would pour the coffee in slow motion, as if it were molasses, managing to look at times patient and indulgent, at times menacing and policeman-like.

Sometimes he was so obvious and unsubtle that even I grew embarrassed, although, of course, I was on his side. Don Benno's silence was offensive. The policeman had made us laugh, had told us stories with the right touches of gruesomeness, had allowed us to jump into his weavings and rob him of his endings. He hadn't minded our correctly guessing the answers to his riddles, or our not laughing when he thought he was funny. Surely the priest could share with us his mysterious French life. But no, Don Benno kept coughing into his towel, smiling that vertical smile of his, his emaciated face an ivory of irritating inscrutability. He possessed an obtuse innocence.

Meanwhile, out in the courtyard, the magnolias had lost their flowers and covered themselves in leaves. The wisteria, planted a century ago and trained around a circular trellis in the middle of the yard, had bloomed an umbrella of purple grapes as delicate as clusters of pursed lips. The three of us had transferred our lunch ritual outdoors, under the wisteria, in a spot from where we could watch the library entrance. We ate immersed in a cloud of mauve fragrance.

The library was quite deserted now—the summer being a time of solitude in the city—all the windows and the French doors were open to the garden, the curtains swishing languidly, like great sails, in the breath of the new summer.

During one of those glorious afternoons while we were eating our lunch, one of the glass panes of the French doors caught the breeze and, in turning, mirrored the three of us sitting on the bench, in the centre of the garden. I looked at our reflection—a lost group in black uniforms under the summer triumph of the wisteria— and stopped in mid stew-wedge, as if pierced by a revelation. The chilling realization came to me that I didn't want to be part of that tableau of forgotten people. I grew suddenly alien to the feud between the priest's morbid reticence and the policeman's morbid curiosity. I felt I must walk out of that picture, before it engulfed me in its squalid dusty destiny.

I stood up without a word, padded Carlomarx on the head, and left. The next day I didn't go to the library, nor the day after that. After a week, I still meant to go to the library and present some excuse for my absence, but I didn't. I really didn't know what to say. I never went back.

It wasn't until the end of the summer that, school having started, I happened to pass by the library, on my way to class. I was looking at the grand Renaissance door, from the other side of the street, when I noticed the black-rimmed posters on each side of the entrance. That meant that someone had died. It must have been some time ago, because the posters were starting to peel. So, the little priest had died, I thought. I was surprised that he had lasted that long. I crossed the street to see what his real French name was. The notice said:

> THE POLICE FORCE
> OF THE MUNICIPALITY OF FLORENCE
> REGRETS THE PASSING OF THE POLICEMAN
> VASCO BONETTI
> WHO DEDICATED HIS LIFE
> TO THE SAFETY OF HIS FELLOW CITIZENS.
> HE IS MISSED BY HIS FRIEND
> FATHER ANTOINE BENOÎT
> AND HIS YOUNG FRIEND GIOVANNA.
> IN MEMORIAM

The policeman? Me, his young friend? I hardly knew him. I didn't even know his name, and neither he nor the priest remembered my family name. All I did was listen to his stories. It must have been the priest who thought of adding my name to the notice, in an effort to show that somebody else mourned him.

The notice didn't say what the policeman had died of, but I knew.

He had died of curiosity.

I felt relieved that I had left. It wasn't as if I was heartless. In fact I did wonder for a long time about what happened to Carlomarx.

The Funeral

I am on my way to find the orphanage. It is in the oldest, most unglamorous part of the town, where most of the changes have occurred. But since it is an historical building, it cannot be obliterated. I find it after a bit of wandering and I hardly recognize it. I was only four or five years old when I was taken to the orphanage. I saw it for a moment from the outside—only for the time it took to approach and enter it. But I remember the orphanage accurately from the inside. I don't recall how long I stayed in it, it seemed an eternity, but a child's perception of time is skewed by impatience and anxiety, and by the shortness of his or her life.

It had been decided that it would be safer for me to be away during the time my father was home from the sanatorium. His tuberculosis put us all at risk, but since I had just been sick with double pneumonia and was a very weak child, my mother put me in the orphanage to protect me from contamination. That's what I was told, but I knew my mother also didn't want me around. Impartial as I believe I have become with years, I still think this is the case. The fact that my mother didn't want me around fills me with admiration for her. It is easy to care for a child one loves, but to care for one that is not loved must be a tribute to a woman who knew her duty.

We are not born with the right to be loved, we are born with a right to be cared for; love is a gift. We have no more right to be loved than to win a lottery. But my mother cared for me even though she could never make herself love me. In retrospect I can see her point. I wasn't that lovable, what with being sickly, difficult and certainly not too nice to look at. The idea that all children are lovable has always struck me as rather unrealistic.

But that my mother cared for me I never had any doubt. When the nuns sent her a note saying that her youngest child had tried to die, my mother came running and took me home. It isn't easy for a child of four to devise her own demise. But I was creative and not without a sense of the dramatic. At the same time, though, I lacked experience in dying; therefore here I am, remembering it all quite a few years later.

I had been bathed, talc-powdered and made to wear my best clothes. My personal effects were put in a little suitcase, and my coloured pencils and pad of paper in a shopping bag. My mother and my sister accompanied me to the orphanage. It felt as if there was going to be a celebration of sorts. I was all excited because I had been told to show a particular nun how good I was at drawing. This was the nun who had done all the drawings for my mother's portfolio, to be submitted as her own work to the principal of the local elementary school to compete for a teaching post against other applicants. Since my mother couldn't draw a straight line if she tried, she had been given the name of that nun, who sold her artistic services to people without a drop of talent, like my mother. The orphanage survived mostly through charity, in the form of donations made to the orphans, who were hired to follow the hearse of a dear recently departed. Some of the nuns also arranged the flowers for the church altars in the city and made the sacred embroideries. But the orphanage also survived by engaging in gentle criminality like taking money for supplying people with talent they did not possess. One might look at it as giving a helping hand to God, to right His not always equitable disbursement of artistic gifts.

My mother seems to have liked the orphanage, because she hired not only Sister Bianca to provide her with beautiful drawings, but she had also asked her to allow both me and my sister to participate in the little theatre productions the orphanage put on at Christmas: another source of income.

In one of those pathetic little productions I was given the role of a corncob. The likeness of this was achieved by dressing me up in yellow crêpe paper and dark brown socks. I was given a little poem to recite, about the pleasures of being a humble corncob. It wasn't very successful, because once on the stage and facing about fifty pairs of eyes, I burst into tears and had to be yanked backstage. I attributed my failure to the fact that I didn't want to be a corncob but a flower like my sister, who was dressed up in pink and blue with green socks to signify a stem. I still don't know what the brown socks were supposed to signify, but I didn't like them either. Anyway, that was the beginning and the end of my theatrical career.

But it was generally agreed that I had a remarkable

artistic talent. I could draw a flower, a cat and even a bee with all its wings. I was inordinately proud of my ability, and the chance to show it off was quite appealing to me. I had seen the drawings that Sister Bianca had done for my mother, and I thought they were wonderful, particularly the one of Cinderella dressed up as a princess.

We knocked on the door and were ushered in by the mother superior herself, an old nun with glasses so thick her face seemed to occupy another space behind them. Before the nun took me inside, she took my suitcase from my mother with one hand, and my hand with the other. My mother kissed me, admonished me to be good and say hello to Sister Bianca. She would come and see me to morrow, she said. I didn't register the "tomorrow", because it didn't occur to me that my mother and my sister would walk out of the orphanage without me.

I went, quite confidently, to see Sister Bianca, and when the mother superior left taking the suitcase with her, I showed Sister Bianca my bee. The nun was nice, as always, and praised me for my talent. I felt a warm flood of pride and asked her if she wanted me to draw her something else. She said yes and I sat by her side for a while, drawing away. It was when the bell sounded and Sister Bianca took my hand to go to the refectory that I started to understand that something was not quite right. I asked where my mother was and was told that she was going to come the next day. They said it was only a trial, they wanted to see how I was responding to the orphanage. Me? Responding to the orphanage? I thought they were out of their minds.

I happened to have two living parents. There was absolutely no need for me to be in an orphanage, let alone responding to one. I kept repeating that I was not an orphan, there must be a mistake. I asked over and over again that someone please go and fetch my mother because she must know that I am in the wrong place. They put me with other girls, to see if I would take root and stop hollering, but I was adamant. I would not play with other orphans. I felt some kind of contamination creeping up on me. It was as though I was thinking that if I consented to play with the other girls, I would catch something that would make me like them: an orphan.

After a long time I finally understood that I had been abandoned. I started to cry and didn't stop until well into the night, after all the other girls had gone to sleep in their white-curtained beds.

In the morning I woke to a place I didn't remember and started to cry again. Much as the nuns tried, they couldn't put any food into me. I wanted my mother, and I wanted an explanation. By the time my mother finally arrived, I had become totally hysterical and I couldn't even talk. The nuns were thinking that maybe it would be a good idea for me to go home, but my mother had made her decision. She said that it was for my own good and that eventually I would get used to it.

But I never did get used to it. Never.

My mother had to promise me that I would only have to stay for two more days and then I would be allowed to go home. After she left, I stopped crying for long enough to take some interest in drawing with Sister Bianca, but I refused to play with the other girls, some of whom I found unspeakably ugly, since their heads had been shaved to rid them of lice. I became testy and recalcitrant and nobody could stand me. When I wasn't doing something I wasn't supposed to do, I would cry for hours at a time.

My mother reneged on her promise and although she came to visit me, she came less and less often and when she came she always left in tears. But, still, she didn't take me home.

Life at the orphanage was bleak, almost totally devoid of joy. We were awakened at sunrise, and made to go and pray in the chapel. I didn't dislike the chapel but I didn't understand prayer, which I found to be nothing more than the numbing repetition of memorized phrases. I would look at the nuns and move my lips, but I never managed to memorize any of the complicated prayers. In my child arsenal of devotions there was room only for a prayer to the Guardian Angel and the Hail Mary, the rest was a blur of words. Being still for any length of time was torturous for me, and the smell of incense made me faint.

In the morning breakfast was a sad, silent affair with only milk, no coffee, and a slab of stale bread. The rest of the meals were even worse. At noon we had a hot soup, which I never touched. Even my mother accepted the fact that I hated soup of any kind. I still dislike soup, I like my meals solid; anything that I can't chew feels like a greasy drink to me. As a second course we had a few slices of bologna with another slab of stale bread. Some kind of green mush must have been the vegetable, but I am not sure. I never touched the vegetables either. At night just the bologna and the bread. On Sundays we had a leg of chicken. None of this ever changed. If any children became sick, they were given four cookies.

But the worst was having to go to bed at five in the afternoon, when most children in the piazza outside were still laughing and playing, and continued to do so, well into the night. Our iron beds had canopies, which held heavy white curtains. Once the curtains were drawn, we were entombed in a cube of whiteness until morning. Should it turn out that there is a hell, I think it is a white place with drawn curtains in which you must lie, while the rest of the world enjoys the summer night outside.

This monotony was broken only by the funerals. People hired us to follow the hearse from the church to the cemetery. On those occasions, we were made to wear our uniforms, which consisted of dark-blue pinafores with white collars, white socks and black shoes. We also had to wear a blue beret that covered our heads down to our ears. I think the idea was to add a pathetic touch to our appearance, so that we would benefit from more largesse, but the result was that it made us look slightly demented.

At first I experienced a rather ghoulish pride in taking part in so much sadness proceeding slowly among a crowd of people: the women making the sign of the cross and the men taking off their hats, as a sign of respect. But the road to the cemetery was long and tiring. I used to surrender myself to an irrepressible urge to laugh, which of course was strictly prohibited during a funeral. But prohibition was probably what made laughing so exhilarating. Once I started, the laughter infected the rest of the children. As soon as we were back from the funeral I would be punished with chickpeas. That is, I was made to kneel on chickpeas for a time. But, of course, I spread the chick peas so that I could kneel directly on the floor. I wasn't entirely without resources.

But I still felt betrayed and lonely and terribly sad, particularly when I thought of my mother, father and sister, all sitting down to eat a meal at our house and chatting away about things. It was also harder at night, because whereas during the day I could be distracted by the routine of the orphanage, at night the sense of loss was keener. I cried so much that it was starting to be of no interest to anyone. I was not asked why I was crying anymore. I was losing weight and becoming more withdrawn. I had lost any hope of being rescued, now that crying didn't make any difference. Only Sister Bianca sensed that I was in serious trouble and, so, took more time than she ought to have with me and my drawings and made a point of being kinder than the other nuns. But I was inconsolable and hardly responded to any prodding to play.

It was during one of the funerals that I decided to take matters into my own hands. I made up my mind to die. We had been called to participate in a particularly beautiful funeral, with lots of flowers made up in wreaths, hearts and pillows. The hearse had four horses instead of the usual two. All of them were black and shiny, with ostrich feathers on their heads. Right in front of us, a band played and moved slowly and solemnly. Other groups of children from other orphanages had also been hired; all wore different uniforms. Right behind us were the Celestini, the most pathetic of the lot, because they were children without surnames, who had been found on the doorsteps of churches and monasteries.

It was a hot day and our woollen dresses were making us even hotter. I don't know at which point I passed out, but it seems that in doing so I had managed to stop the whole procession for a few minutes. When I came to, I was placed on the hearse itself, next to the coachman.

That proved to be a momentary, small triumph. I loved it there—I felt important and singled out. It was like travelling on a tower, higher than the horses, almost at the level of the second-floor windows. When the horses defecated, their large black anuses spewed out neat balls of brown, shiny dung. I giggled to myself at the thought of the rest of the girls having to step over it. I felt quite privileged. It was all so new and unexpected I almost forgot to die.

When we arrived at the cemetery, we fanned out as usual, waiting for the function to take its course. We all sat in a row, on the mounds created by the earth of freshly dug graves, like vulturettes.

I left the group to look for one of those small chapels built by rich families to house their dead in the style they were accustomed to in life. I was looking for one where I could die, without being found out. I chose the one I thought the very best. It was one I had seen before—always full of fresh flowers and lit votive candles. I didn't want to be in a dark one, for I was afraid of the dark.

When I entered the cool, silent chapel, I was met by the smell of wax and slightly decayed roses and gladioli. There was an altar of stone and a bare cross flanked by marble angels, twice my size. One angel was kneeling, offering a stone lily up to the cross with both hands. His face looked downward, casting his marble gaze at me. The other angel was sitting on a cloud, his wings spread out on both sides of him, his hands open in a gesture of surrender. The rest was nothing but names on marble plaques and medallions of fading sepia faces embedded in the walls. Among the photographs, were several of children in sailor suits.

I went outside to pick more flowers from other graves; I didn't think the ones inside the chapel would suffice. I went back in the chapel and looked for a place suitable for my death. I laid myself down at the foot of the altar, but I wasn't comfortable. I tried several alternative places, until I found what I wanted. I climbed on the sitting angel and covered myself with flowers. I said my prayers, repented so that I would go straight to paradise, crossed my hands over me and waited to die.

I didn't happen to die because I'd made a mistake. I thought that people died because they were taken to their graves, rather than the other way around.

I was found there, asleep, after the nuns' frantic search all over the cemetery.

My mother received a note that very evening. It stated, in no uncertain terms, that the child was not fit for the orphanage. Better come and retrieve her as soon as possible.

The next day I went home.

I never learned how to die. I'm sure when the time comes, I'll have to go without knowing how to do it.

Mogadishu

I feel I need to go someplace I haven't been before. I want a holiday from my memories. I have several choices, including invitations from relatives and acquaintances. It's only a matter of choosing which would give me the greatest freedom of movement. I like to come and go in an unstructured manner, in fact that's what I think the definition of a holiday is: a blessed lack of purpose.

I climb on a train that goes to Bologna, since wherever I go north of Florence I must pass through that city. I will decide when I am on the train whether to go to Ferrara or Ancona. In Bologna I stop for a wonderful meal at the station cafeteria and decide on the spur of the moment to spend some time in this beloved city. I take my suitcase and go to the Information Office where I ask for the name of a cheap hotel. The girl, a giggly teenager with bouncy locks on each side of her head, like slinkys, looks at some book of hers and writes the name and the location of the hotel.

I read it and then read it again, because I think it's a joke. The name of the hotel is "Hotel without a Name" in the "Street without a Name." I look up at her quizzically and she says, shooting her eyebrows up in a sincerity position. "That's the real name, it's not a joke."

To prove it, she picks up a map of the city and traces the way from the station to the location of the hotel with a yellow felt pen. I think it is a good omen. I thank her and start in the direction she has sent me.

As soon as I am out of the station, I am happy. The city is as beautiful as I remember it, all painted in red, ochre and pink. It is a city of porticoes and arcades, a forest of columns of different styles and thicknesses. The colonnades go on for miles, interrupted now and then by piazzas of various sizes. Some loggias are luxurious, made of marble, with the undersides frescoed in brilliant colours. The capitals are elaborate and richly decorated, and displaying a northern penchant for mini gargoyles. Others loggias are no more than just a few vertical wood-en posts holding second floors as rickety as an assemblage of oversized outhouses. But everywhere are those high, hot colours giving the city the flashy appearance of a mediaeval banner.

In the arches between the columns are great canvas curtains in Venetian red—rolled up at half-mast when the light is gentle and let down during the hot hours of midafternoon. The curtains muffle the street traffic and create a deep shade of cool intimacy and quiet under the porticoes, broken intermittently by the glare of an unsheltered piazza. The life of Bologna occurs almost entirely in the shade of the porticoes. People sit in cafes, shop in their super-elegant stores, or talk in their rich Bolognese dialect in groups and clusters, like a tableau of convivial rites. It's a city of people, framed in mediaeval colonnades.

Trudging my suitcase on its little wheels, I walk along trying to find the Street without a Name. After a while I know I am lost, but I am a bit self-conscious about asking for a street without a name. It is, by now, well past noon and the streets are beginning to empty; the stores are being closed with the great clang of rolling metal shutters. I build up my courage and ask somebody for directions. The gentleman looks at me with compassionate contempt and shakes his head. But he wants to be of some help, so he points at a door with an official inscription at its side, and suggests that I go in and ask somebody there. I don't bother looking at the plaque and, with some difficulty, open the large portal and enter.

Immediately I know I shouldn't be there. Together with the smell of food—it is a cafeteria of sorts—a sick smell permeates the area. Because it is mixed with the smell of food this sick smell reminds me of the days I worked in a mental hospital in England. It is the odour of abnormality, an emanation of uncoordinated thoughts, as unsettling and off-putting as danger. The vast space is full of men sitting at long tables, some silent and motionless, some talking to one another, some just talking to themselves. Upon my entering, a few of them come to me quickly and purposefully, as if I was expected, and stand in front of me, saying nothing, waiting for a Godot of their own. I feel confused and a little scared, until I see one man, who is also coming towards me, but in a natural, unhurried manner. When I look at his eyes, I become aware of how strange the eyes of the other men are. He looks at me with an ironic expression, as if I had stumbled on some awfulness to which he has become accustomed.

I feel terribly mundane, concerned as I am about a

place to sleep in this place of unidentifiable misery, unsure of myself and out of place. In fact I want to be out of there as soon as possible. But the crazy men crowd around me asking me questions about myself. Not knowing what else to do, I raise my voice and ask the man who seems in charge if he knows were the Street Without a Name is. I feel like Alice in Wonderland, in a place out of context, asking for a street that doesn't exist. I think he takes pity on me, shoos away the small crowd and approaches me without abandoning his condescending smile.

"I don't know where the Street Without a Name is, but it certainly is not here. This," he adds, "is a narcotics dependents centre."

So, that's what I've stumbled into. Suddenly the crazy eyes of all those anorexic-looking men make sense, and I feel a little better. Better to know something unpleasant than to think you are hallucinating. I retreat to the safety of the outside, where even the emptied, hot city feels better than that cafeteria of the damned.

I sit in a little park to reorient myself and take a small rest. No sooner have I sat down that I am accosted by a man with arms covered in suppurating needle marks, asking for money. I get up in a hurry, I am starting to feel persecuted.

I walk away quickly, stopping long enough to figure out what direction to take. When I finally arrive at the hotel, it feels like I have overcome a dangerous obstacle course. The hotel is clean and old and the hotel owner is a mustachioed old gentleman of great kindness. I feel safe and reassured and am confident enough to ask him to tell me why the hotel has no name.

"Because you can call it what you want," he says with a smile. He reconfirms in me the love I have for the Bolognese people.

To go to my room I must go through a courtyard covered with slabs of greenish glass. The centre of the covered yard is full of potted herbs. Thyme, basil, rosemary and marjoram, I know them all well. The pots are the decorated majolica kind from Faenza, a few miles from here. The smell of the herbs is fresh and familiar, and the green light makes me feel as if I am swimming to my room. The room is small and stark: white-tiled floor, white bed and curtains, white shutters. It feels strange moving from a green courtyard to a white room. I can hardly wait to see if the dining room is all in red.

I lie in bed for a while trying to digest what I have seen of the city. My beloved Bologna seems to be afflicted by a large number of drug addicts. I hope it is only by chance that I have met so many. I am impatient to go out and be reassured that the city is still alive and well. But I will make sure that I take a few precautions. I shall go out early and retire early.

Around seven o'clock I start to walk around in search of a place to eat. I know I will have to settle for a pizza, which I dislike, but it is the only food I can afford. Also it has the advantage of being suitable to eat while walking or sitting on some public steps. I find a pizzeria and take a seat at one of the outdoor tables, in a pleasant area fenced in from the pedestrian traffic by rows of potted oleanders. I plan to order a take-out pizza and walk away but, when the waiter comes to take my order, on the spur of the moment, I order myself a whole meal of spaghetti and veal and half a bottle of mineral water. I feel I deserve it. Besides, Bologna is the gastronomic capital of Italy; to go to Bologna and order a pizza, which is a Neapolitan snack, seems quite stupid—even for someone with my limited resources.

While I wait for my meal I realize that I have forgotten how long it takes, in Italy, to be served a meal. Most of the pasta has to be boiled after it has been ordered, for pasta turns to porridge if cooked too long. While the tactical preparation of my food is going on in the kitchen, I notice an African man walking slowly by, giving me significant looks as he goes. I try to stare ahead of me in an effort to avoid eye contact, to look as if I haven't noticed him.

Evidently he is not easily discouraged, because he is circling nearer and nearer. I keep on looking straight ahead or at my hands, cursing myself for not having brought something to read. Finally my food comes to my rescue, in the form of a dish of spaghetti, brought by a waiter who fusses over me like a mother. He snatches a cheese container from some Japanese diners at the next table and holds a spoon heaped with grated cheese over my spaghetti, looking at me like a living question mark. I don't really like grated cheese, but how can I refuse his culinary devotion? I motion him to let it rain on my day. I stick a corner of an immense serviette in my collar and start putting a couple of pounds on my thighs.

I am just about to finish the last mouthful of my dish when the hedge of potted oleanders separates and the African's face appears a few inches from mine, as if sprouting from a jungle.

"Signora," he says, in passable Italian, "would you like to buy some love tonight?"

I finally look straight at him; I can hardly ignore him, the damn oleanders practically brush my face. He has tribal scars on a face that cannot be older than my son's. His eyes are spaced so far apart that they seem to be almost at the sides of his head. His nose is slightly aquiline and beautifully sculpted, his smile so shy as to almost move me to ask why he is doing this to himself. But I know the fatuousness of such a question, his life must be difficult enough without my adding smug compassion to it. Still he is so young and lovely, I would like to help him in some manner.

"No thanks," I say as kindly as I can, but without unduly encouraging him.

"Thank you," he says unaccountably, as if I had done him a favour. And maybe I have. He lets the oleanders close over him just in time to disappear before the waiter sees him.

I finish my wonderful meal, leave a small tip for the waiter, hang around until it is actually picked up, since I don't trust the place to be totally free of thieves, and go back to my room without a name.

While I walk I think about the young man selling his body to middle-aged women, for money. His face didn't look Nigerian, he had the fine delicate features of a Somalian. Suddenly I remember Mogadishu. My memories seem to follow me wherever I go. But after all, that's why I am here. I walk fast to the hotel so I can write about him.

❦

I don't remember now how and when Mogadishu entered our lives. Next to our terrace were more terraces, separated by wire mesh, so we could see all the terraces in a row, all the way to the end building, where Signor Falchi had his bathroom in a tent. The children from all the terraces would play together in one of them—which one depended on the availability of supervising parents.

But one terrace was always empty. It belonged to Signor Ristori, a mysterious man who wasn't given to sharing his terrace or his life with anybody. Signor Ristori's terrace was next to ours and its emptiness was bothersome and unsettling, for it separated me from my playmates, with a barrier of silence and mystery, broken only from time to time by the display of washing hung out on the line to dry. This was better than nothing because it allowed some knowledge of Signor Ristori via his underwear, but it was not enough to sate the neighbourhood's curiosity. In Italy, privacy or the desire for it is a capital reason for suspicion.

And then came Mogadishu. Nothing had prepared us for the sight of a black person. We had never seen anybody of a different race. We had seen the Sicilians from the south, to be sure—squat and dark, and speaking a dialect totally incomprehensible to us. Some of us had been to Fiesole, where most of the English lived. They were different enough, with their white eyes and skinny children. But we had never seen an African before.

He was there, one morning, in Signor Ristori's terrace, sitting on a little worn-out grass mat, doing something with an array of objects as unusual to us as he was. That morning we were all playing on my terrace, when one of us noticed him on the other side of the metal net. We didn't see him come. One moment the terrace was empty, the next this incredible gift from nowhere appeared, busy with an array of odds and ends.

We fell into a silence and crowded in front of him, glued to the fence as if we had paid admission. He didn't pay any attention to us, but went on with his business. It was as if we didn't exist, although we must have looked as strange to him as he did to us.

But while we weren't much to look at, snotty little brats that we were, he was as close to a miracle as we could ever hope for.

His colour was a velvety matte brown all over except on his palms and the soles of his feet where the colour looked as if it had been worn down to a pale beige. His features were delicate and well defined. His nose, slightly curved with flared nostrils, was so small it made us big-nosed Latins feel like tapirs. His eyes were placed far apart, almost at the sides of his head. But his mouth was what we liked the best. It was generous, and carefully designed with a little ridge all around the outer border of his lips, as if to contain a laughter. His lower lip was divided into two parts by a little groove of great precision. His forehead was very convex, sloping all the way to the top of his head, where an afterthought of pale brown wool stood around his head like a saint's halo. His ears were as small as those of a baby, with negligible lobes.

His fingers were thin and long like a woman's fingers, and his nails looked like opals against the dark of his skin. The rest of his body was so thin and muscular it looked woven, and his skin was as taut as a drum.

There wasn't a detail of his body that we didn't notice. We would whisper respectfully about the small-ness of his ears or, when he finally smiled at us for the first time, the whiteness of his teeth.

He sat on his haunches for hours, for he had taken to mending broken umbrellas, re-weaving the straw seat of a chair, hammering bent nails to straighten them, jobs which required great ability and patience. The nimbleness of his fingers was miraculous. He didn't seem to be able to throw away anything; he used and reused every bit of scrap of string, metal or fabric that came his way. Once I even saw him use the hollow part of a feather to blow air on his fire.

An unspoken decision had been made from the very beginning: we loved him. Our natural conservative ten-dencies towards suspicious novelties was overcome by his extraordinariness. He was a particular gift to us in the sleepy midafternoon hours, when all the adults were having their siesta and we children were left to our own devices. He could always be counted on to be there, either preparing himself a meal, working at his jobs or laughing at us with a healthy contempt for our bizarre predilection for those worms we insisted on eating. (That's how he saw our spaghetti.)

His food was just as extraordinary to us; we could smell it, different and foreign, laced with unknown spices, cooked in a discarded tin can as if anything else more domestic was not manly or ingenious enough. He had made a contraption out of a discarded large can, which he used as if it were a Hibachi. He filled the bottom with a few pieces of charcoal and topped it with a wire mesh he had made out of discarded wire. On the wire he placed another discarded can in which he cooked his beans and chicken. We never saw him eat anything but chicken, even in the morning.

We used to take our cups of cappuccino, full of morsels of bread, to eat by him. We wolfed down our breakfast in seconds, while he went through his ritual of cooking and fanning, and tasting and mixing, until he would finally declare his meal ready. Then, he slowly picked at his chicken with the delicacy and care of the craftsman that he was. He made us feel like dogs.

He wore nothing but a vest and a pair of shorts, which seemed rather skimpy for the season, early spring, but since his skin was matte and dark—it didn't blush with embarrassment and didn't turn blue because of the cold—we had no idea how he felt. He was his own weather system, different from ours.

His short pants were shorter than the end of his penis, but he was unaware of this. He was also casual about on which side he wore his penis, sometimes placing it to the west of himself and sometimes to the east. If we were lucky, he wore it to the west. That's where my terrace was. It made us giggle. It wasn't as if we were lacking in respect. We didn't have many occasions for lewdness, we did what we could with what we found. All in all, it was even better than the cobbler, who exposed himself from his upper-store window, starting in the middle of July to the middle of August, every year. At the end of this period, his wife would come back from the seaside, and he went back to just being our cobbler. We loved that. We exposed ourselves back at him, by lowering our pants and showing him our bums, and Silvio showed him his penis, as if it was something to talk about. Silvio was very proud of his penis; once he noticed that he had grown a vein on it, and he made us put a finger on the vein to feel it throb. I put my finger on it, but didn't feel any throbbing, just a very soft warm vein.

I felt I was Mogadishu's personal friend, but I am sure every one of us felt that. Since he was a man of few or no words, a smile thrilled us so much it made us do stupid things. He never chased us away or showed any annoyance at being looked at all the time; in fact, I think he rather enjoyed it.

I loved Mogadishu. I could hardly wait in the morning to go and see him. My mother could hardly keep me still while washing my face and my bum. My hair was often badly braided, because of my impatience to go to Mogadishu. My mother liked him too. In fact, I think that the adults would have liked to stare at Mogadishu as much as we did, but didn't do it out of a sense of propriety. When my mother came to retrieve my sister and me from the terrace, she would linger.

She said that she found him interesting but didn't like the way he closed one of his nostrils with his thumb, and emptied the other by blowing its contents out, a few feet from where you were standing. She said it was uncivilized, but the rest of us found it miraculous. We all gave it a try, but most of us ended up with a mess in our hands. Only Silvio could imitate Mogadishu to perfection.

This was not Mogadishu's only feat. He could whistle

through the gap in his teeth, like none of us could, and we were all whistlers of varying ability. I could even whistle backward, through inhaling.

He could also play a little mouth instrument. With it he produced a melancholy sound full of twists and turns, with no end or beginning. We were never quite able to see how the instrument was used because he had a hand in front of his mouth when he played.

And he could spit. I don't mean the horrible full blast spitting that men at the time were used to doing. No matter how many posters about the danger of tuberculosis and its connection to the habit of spitting that the Department of Hygiene hung all over the city, the men were by reason of their gender incapable of keeping their spit where it belonged, inside themselves.

Mogadishu's spitting was an art form of great precision and elegance. He would spit from between his teeth to a prodigious distance, without as much as moving his head, or even his mouth. He was a natural spitter. We were full of admiration for his ability. He, however, didn't seem to take any pride in his accomplishments, for in addition to all the other remarkable things about him, he was a truly modest man.

We never knew his real name and called him Mogadishu because we had heard the name from the news. He might have come from another part of Africa for all we knew, but one of us started to call him Mogadishu and it stuck.

We never understood why Signor Ristori had brought him back from his native Africa. We didn't really know how useful he could be to Signor Ristori. We only knew that Signor Ristori only called him in occasionally and always with another name that we didn't remember.

He certainly wasn't a servant, since he never did anything except those little tinkerings of his, and these seemed more an expression of his particular genius than a proper job. Besides, each day he did something different—he had no routine—while a servant's job implies routine labour. Mogadishu would do what he wanted when he wanted. He awoke earlier than we did, because even the earliest risers in our group always found him on his mat, doing whatever he was doing, as if he had been there, fixing the night. He would retire when he couldn't see anymore, well after sunset.

Little by little, people started taking broken things to him to repair. It is not as if we didn't have the normal itinerant repairmen, like the umbrella mender and the knife sharpener. But to have Mogadishu doing it was more of a thrill because, although we were very poor, Mogadishu must have come from an economy of an even crueler scarcity since his ingenuity was nothing short of miraculous. Besides, he never asked for any money. But people did pay him, though not in money. (Who had money in those days?) They gave him, instead, small things that would be useful to him, or food they knew he liked such as eggs and onions. Sometimes they gave him a chicken.

Once somebody gave him a pair of wonderful new shoes. The tip and the heel were made of black leather, while the rest was white. On the front, they had a flowering of curlicues, made of tiny holes. They looked like the ones Fred Astaire wore in the movies.

The shoes were a little larger than his feet, but Mogadishu, who had refused to wear any of the clothes that people had given him, wore the shoes on his bare feet with pride and great dignity. He sometimes got up from his mat and walked around in his shoes just to hear them creak. He didn't look funny though, with those incongruous shoes; rather, he looked as if he was engaging in some kind of irony, a mockery of our customs.

My mother, who had from the beginning aspired to teach Mogadishu some of our ways, was encouraged by his wearing the shoes into a bolder effort to have him use a handkerchief to clean his nose. But, since she considered herself tactful, an excuse had to be found to give him some handkerchiefs. She had taken some old sheets, cut three squares out of them, finished and embroidered them with his initial M on the corner that showed up when folded. They were really lovely. Since we didn't know when Mogadishu had been born, and a saint by that name could hardly be found—which would both have been occasions for a present—my mother had him repair some pots that were really only good for the garbage. She underestimated Mogadishu's ingenuity, though, because he presented her with the pots miraculously trans- formed— they were now shiny and looked for all intents and purposes as if they were new. My mother was delighted and found the giving of handkerchiefs fully justified. She sent me over to present them with as much grace as possible, while she looked on shyly from a little distance.

Mogadishu accepted them as he accepted everything else, nodding in his matter-of-fact way, and placing them on the edge of his mat, together with the rest of his stuff.

If my mother thought that this would stop Mogadi- shu's blowing his nose with his hands, she was disap- pointed. He never used the handkerchiefs for the purpose intended, but he made use of one, right away. He rolled it up and tied it around his head like a ban- danna. It squeezed that cloud of hair of his into what, from the back, looked like a number eight. He also used it to hold certain items, like a pencil, a piece of chalk, or a pumice stone. Sometimes he tied the bandanna around his calf, or around his biceps, all for the same purpose of storing small items he needed for his work. He taught us how to roll up our handkerchiefs and make bandannas. In his measured calm way, he was always teaching us something, and he never laughed at our attempts or mistakes, even when he taught us something quite difficult, like eating rice with our hands, or power spitting.

There was nothing we could teach him in return, but when we played, we looked at him from the corner of our eyes to see if he looked at us and admired our abilities. Our play had more meaning with him around, our aggressions were more spectacular and we cried and laughed louder so that he could hear us. He didn't return our interest, but we knew he was there. He was watching us even though he seemed always busy with his work. We were each other's theatre.

One day he disappeared. We all came to the side of his terrace as usual, and he wasn't there. It felt as if the sun had gone out. We didn't know what to think. Mogadishu was not the kind of person to go into the city for window shopping or a movie. His life was on that mat for us to admire, and the idea that he could be some place else was unbearable. We waited around until midmorning and then we delegated Silvio, who was afraid of nothing and had even been arrested once, to knock on Signor Ristori's door and ask if Mogadishu was sick. This was not an easy thing, since it was well known that Signor Ristori was no lover of children. At one time or other we had all encountered his wrath for being either too loud or too boisterous, or for just being there. It wasn't as if we hadn't been taken to task by just about everybody in the neighbourhood, but Signor Ristori treated us as if we were criminals. There was a particular meanness about him that made going and talking to him a dangerous adventure.

We all went with Silvio to the door, but the rest of us

remained well behind, just far enough to be able to hear what was said. Silvio rang the bell. We could see from his ears that he was scared. They looked taut. Signor Ristori came to the door dressed as the strange man that he was, in a crimson dressing gown and soft slippers, a cigarette in a long cigarette holder in his hand. We thought that very fancy and elegant, but according to my mother that was nothing but a pose. Anybody with any real means, she said, wouldn't live in our neighbourhood, with the smell of wine coming from the cellars and snotty children running around. Still, phony or not, it did demand respect.

Silvio asked in a voice we hardly recognized if Mogadishu was coming out.

"No, he will not. He is very sick," said Signor Ristori, who then closed the door. Silvio turned to us with a look of helplessness we had never seen on him before. We felt as if Mogadishu had already died and gone forever. We would have liked a bit more information, like what illness had he caught, how bad was he, and when was he going to die. We felt disoriented and orphaned, and hardly played for the rest of the day, except for some despondent games and a bit of dispirited rope jumping. Since Signor Ristori had said that Mogadishu was very sick, we expected him to be bedridden for a long time.

So, when the day after we saw him in his usual spot, healthy and busy as always, we were so pleasantly surprised, we could hardly contain ourselves. We crowded around him as if he had come back from a dangerous journey. We asked him what had been the matter with him the day before. He smiled his fluorescent smile, and tapped his head twice in a knowing manner that curtailed any further questions. We looked at him with extra attention to see if there was any sign of illness. The problem was that, had he been pale we didn't know what colour to look for. The signs of sickness that were familiar to us, like redness in case of fever, or paleness to indicate weakness, did not apply to a person of a different colour. We looked at his eyes, but they were the same bright bulging Mogadishu eyes we knew. He seemed as good as new. We were happy he was back with us.

One morning, so early that the day was more heard than seen—announced by the birds in the wisteria, rather than by any sign of light, I woke up with the terrifying feeling that Mogadishu had gone, and this time forever. My anxiety was so real that I even failed to rejoice at the fact that I hadn't wet the bed for a change. I got up silently and carefully, in order not to wake my sister who was sleeping in the other bed, and tiptoed through the living room past the open door to my parents' bedroom to the kitchen where the cat barely stirred. Once in front of the door to the terrace, I became a little scared of going outside, I had never been out at such an early hour. I didn't know what could happen. I sat on the chair by the door for a while, waiting for daylight to materialize. It was happening very fast, since summer dawns are quick once the sky sheds its darkness. I thought that I would go out as soon as I was able to discern the spot where Mogadishu sat. The light came in transparent sheets showing a few pigeons first, then the hammock, a little further on the planters with the basil and the parsley, and then already sitting at his mat was Mogadishu.

I wondered what time he got up. He seemed to have been there when it was still almost night. I went out to him and hung around, shivering a bit in my nightgown and naked feet. He looked at me as usual with an acknowledging nod of his bandannaed head and went on doing what he was doing, cooking his breakfast of chicken and rice.

I said nothing, not at all reassured by his presence,

and still in the grip of my anxiety. Except for the early hour and the fact that I was there without my mother's permission, nothing seemed to have changed. There was Mogadishu tinkering as usual, in his own calm deliberate way, his penis to the west of him, his shoes on the edge of the mat, clean and polished, ready to be worn. The smell of his cooking was reassuring and tantalizing, and nothing in his behaviour betrayed any change. He farted softly in the turquoise morning air. But I knew—I was too young not to know—that he was as good as gone. It was going to be a matter of days or even weeks but Mogadishu was going to leave.

The sadness, the sense of loss was already in place. He had been a gift to us—wonderful as long as it had lasted—but he would be gone, gone like the summer holidays. I wanted to say something to him that would make him reconsider and pay attention to our feelings, but there was nothing to say, because my premonition had nothing to do with anything he had done or said. Maybe he didn't yet know himself that he was going, but I did. My premonition belonged only to me. Young children sniff a betrayal far ahead of anybody else.

So, the next morning, when Mogadishu was not there, I was not surprised. We gathered around the place where he used to sit in wounded silence, waiting for an explanation. None of us thought that he was sick again, or that he would come back some time later. It was unspoken but clear that Mogadishu was gone for ever. Nothing was left of him except his shoes at the edge of his little mat—not his tinkering things, nor the tin cans he had used to cook his meals. Just the shoes that he seemed to have liked so much. Maybe there was a message there, but either it was too subtle or we were too obtuse to get it.

In the end it was I who forced the link fence up and

retrieved the shoes. I put them under my bed, so that my mother wouldn't see them. Every once in a while I would take them out and polish them with my spit as I had seen Mogadishu do. I would sniff them as if to conjure up his presence, since the memory of him was rapidly vanishing in the midst of my daily cataclysmic absorptions.

While caring for Mogadishu's shoes one day, I put a hand inside one of them and felt something stuffed far into the toe space. I pulled it out with my fingers. It was one of the handkerchiefs that my mother had given him. Now I knew what he had done with two of them.

I never told my mother about it. The shoes eventually disappeared, I don't recall how. But I kept the two handkerchiefs for a long time, I liked the embroidery my mother had done on them. I took them with me when I left for Canada, packing them with the rest of my dowry. When I gave my dowry away to friends and acquaintances, piece by piece, to make them love me, the handkerchiefs went with the rest of it.

They must have wondered what the M stood for.

Love

I leave under a torrential rain for Ancona where I will visit my cousin Petra. I have a purpose. I want to ask her about my family. She belongs to my generation and shouldn't be too reluctant to speak irreverently about people who are long dead. My aunt couldn't do that and I had to be content with a gallery of saints devoid of real-life sins and mistakes. Even my father, the irresponsible womanizer, had become a saint after his death. I want to know who my parents were, I don't want a hagiography.

My cousin Petra is not the reticent type—I don't know anyone in my family who is—and shouldn't need too much encouragement to produce a more realistic picture of my family, even though it will be tinged with the mythology typical of secondhand information. She is a few years younger than I am and she is not expected to have recollections clearer than I have of my past. But her life has been less eventful than mine, her mind has been more circumscribed by events and locale, and her interest in the family history has certainly been keener than mine.

The reason for my blindness to the events and personalities that shaped my family is that I was a nonconformist. While I was busy trying to cope with the price of being a rebel and an outsider, I didn't have the time to notice what was going on around me. Rebellion requires a lot of energy. The problem is that this energy is spent more in general activity, like dressing differently or running with the wrong crowd, than in real action; rebellion makes relationships unnecessarily difficult. The relationship with my relatives was difficult then and it's going to be difficult now.

When I arrive in Ancona it is still raining in sunny Italy, and I, the suitcase, the flowers and the box of pastry I have bought in a bakery just outside the station are soaked. I drag my suitcase on wheels along the cobblestones—I wish some of my relatives lived in one of those slick, smooth suburbia with asphalt pavement— up a little street in the historical centre and arrive looking as if I had swum across the Adriatic Sea, which lurks foamily from gaps between the houses.

It seems that every time I meet one of my relatives I feel like a giant towering over them. I have to practically kneel down to embrace Petra, she is round and short and full of concern. Her apartment is a welcome relief to the ugly interiors I have been in so far. It is comfortable, well furnished and quite pretentious. I walk around making patters of appreciation which, for a change, are sincere.

But the best part is that she owns another small apartment on the ground floor in which I can stay as long as I want. I might even be able to cook for myself, without having to rely on my cousin's services. I have visions of going to the market to choose some vegetables and bread and coming back to my miniature apartment and preparing myself a meal. It has been a long time since I last engaged in those comforting domestic chores. It will be a relief from the tired sequence of walking, seeing, eating, walking, seeing, walking, walking, walking. Travelling, I miss the variety of activities that differentiates the days, and so, I look at the little apartment as an oasis of normalcy.

No such luck. Petra has made sure that the stove, an ultramodern, efficient affair of bluish steel, has been locked shut so that I cannot use it. Petra is a pathological giver, a guest is a guest; at nine in the morning she arrives at my apartment with a cup of hot milk and a croissant from the bakery next door. I would have loved going to the bakery myself, breathing in a hundred dollars worth of bread baking smell and choosing myself some crunchy biscotti and crusty, heavy bread. But no, I must resign myself to some sweet expensive croissants and feel guilty about being served and not feeling grateful. I wish people would ask me what I want or let me get it myself.

In her apartment the tragedy of her life becomes apparent. Her husband has been in and out of mental institutions for most of his life, and now, in his late fifties he has become so paranoid that he refuses to leave the house. But he is also afraid of being left alone: Petra can only run out for a few moments to buy what she needs, while he waits at the top of the stairs for her return. If she is a little late he sits in a corner and cries.

In Italy—bless it—you can retire at the age of forty if you started working at twenty. That allows workers to take another job and retire again at the age of sixty with two pensions. Should your spouse die and you remarry and the new spouse does you the favour of also dying, you can retire with four pensions. It is all thanks to the Communists, according to my cousin. But now the

Communists have gone, and work is becoming the addiction that it is in the rest of the world. Both Petra and her husband have been retired for years, rotting away in a solitude *à deux,* that is hard to witness without musing on the benefits of work for people without imagination. The television, with its numbing stupidity, is on most of the day, while the rest of the apartment is kept in semi darkness to allow Neapolitan singers to belt out their sobbing sentimentality in total clarity.

Every morning Petra asks me what I would like to eat. I tell her and she cooks something else anyway; ritual has its place. Every day I sit in the kitchen and eat substantial meals of pasta and meat and vegetables, food that has been prepared with the punctiliousness of a person with no other anchor than the preparation of food. Her whole manner and her surroundings illustrate a compulsive attention to detail, the result of being marooned in a sea of irrelevance.

Upon entering this maniacally clean house, I must take my shoes off and hand them over to her to be put away in a cupboard built for that purpose. I am then handed a pair of slippers to try on. They don't fit me, of course, and I think I can get away with bare feet, but Petra has a larger pair in reserve for yetis like me. I am drowning in an ocean of petty rules, one more meaningless than the other.

All the rooms are kept dark to avoid the heat, and shuttered because of a bizarre fear of drafts. I decide that Italy is a country of hypochondriacs. All my relatives wear vests under their outer garments—this in weather so hot it feels like Singapore. Their medicine cabinets are textbook pharmacies, continually upgraded and updated. Their illnesses are the main topics of conversation, as weather is for the English. Their livers always seem to be roguish, God knows why.

We talk at night after her husband has been put to bed. I am ashamed of how little I remember and surprised that she remembers so much. She has kept all the photographs, and all the diplomas, my mother's and my grandmother's, written in beautiful longhand with curlicues at the ends of every word. She has kept the photograph of me dressed up as an angel with my hair forced into spirals at the sides of my head in a failed attempt to make me look like Shirley Temple and the one of me dressed as a corncob. At one time I knew Petra to even have a book of essays I had written as a child, which my mother had given her to help her with her own assignments. I ask her if I could see them, but she tells me she has thrown them away some time ago. Oh well, there goes another piece of my past.

She talks about my sister. "She was so beautiful and intelligent," she says, "I can't think why God had to take her so suddenly, so young."

I look up at the ceiling and down at the floor feeling guilty for still being around while the best of the family is gone. Petra doesn't mean to hurt me when she adds,

"You have changed, you are not so strange anymore."

Even after so many years I still feel the sting of such a remark. It doesn't seem to occur to anybody that a nonconformist doesn't necessarily want to be an outsider. Acceptance can coexist with being different. I wanted to rebel, but I also wanted to be accepted. But I was never accepted, not by my mother nor my sister. Not even by my father who as a foreigner and a Jew should have known what being an outsider meant. But he was busy with his lovers. Sometimes I wished I were a homosexual or a nymphomaniac or a prostitute, so that I would be part of a group of outsiders. But walking alone as I did seems to be an unnecessarily difficult journey.

I went away, made a comfortable life for myself and to

a certain extent I conformed, though with reluctance, to what was expected of me. But here I am, and all I get is that I am not so strange anymore. What does it take to be one of them? And do I want to? Or, better, can I? I can elicit admiration, envy—I can even be imitated—but acceptance still eludes me.

"What do you know about my mother?" I ask.

"Your mother was so beautiful," she says. Is anybody dead of average appearance? I feel uglier by the minute.

"Do you know why she tried to have an abortion when she was pregnant with me?" I ask.

'Who, your mother? She wouldn't do anything like that,' she says indignantly. "Who told you that, anyway?" I don't know if I should continue the conversation, since I am not getting anywhere.

"She did, my mother," I say.

"You know," Petra continues, "you should let go of your past, look forward to the future and be happy."

I tell her that I am very happy. Still I want to know where I come from. Being happy and wanting to dig up my past don't seem mutually exclusive to me. I am not willing to listen to advice on how to conduct my life. The time for searching is long past; I have in fact come to bury some of the dead. I wanted to make sure I understand why I have been away for thirty years.

"What about my father?" I ask, hoping for a more realistic picture.

"He was a German Jew," she says as if this was an adequate description. "He was a womanizer. We all liked him."

"Well I didn't," I say, regretting it immediately. "Your mother didn't like him much either," Petra says breezily, "because once she arrived at Grandma's door with both children asking to be taken back. But grandma said, a husband is a husband, and threw her out. Your mother had no choice but to go back"

My father now exists a little more. I don't feel either shattered or upset. Parents are people with problems, I am not willing to judge. But I do not ask for any more information.

I want to go down to the port and look at the immense oil carriers, and sit around doing nothing for a while. If I am still strange, I want to be strange all by myself.

The sea glitters like a sheet of molten metal and the great ships are so heavy they don't rock, not even slightly. The city embraces the port with a circular amphitheatre of hills; all the streets converge on the port and all the commerce both in goods and humans is geared to the needs of seamen. There are a lot of them around in the cafes and in the shops, buying expensively and unwisely as young people do, but good-naturedly and exuberantly, since being on land is their form of holiday.

I am amazed at the damage earthquakes have wrought in this part of the country. There are deep gaps in some of the buildings, others are propped up with hefty steel beams. Most seem to have been loosened of their stucco permanently, great patches of brickwork showing through the missing dressing. In areas where the buildings have been vacated because they are too unsafe, posters indicate that rat poison has been applied. It seems that empty buildings attract rats. I shudder at the thought of rats inhabiting those beautiful renaissance buildings.

Because of having been built on a fault that crosses most of Africa and doesn't rest until the formidable barrier of the Alps, Ancona has been hit by a series of earthquakes, which has left the historic centre small and derelict. But the walls, made to last millennia, are still standing, waiting for some entrepreneurial soul to rehabilitate them. Some of the buildings have been restored with astounding results, but so few of them that they don't seem to be anything more than isolated, historic gems. Ancona feels like a city full of gaps and out of sorts, half thriving port city, half archaeological site.

Still, I like to discover a city for myself. I want to go and sit on some Roman ruins and enjoy the magnificent view of the port and the ships, but that poster about rats has made me edgy. I end up in a church listening to a preacher. It has been a long time since I have listened to a preacher, so long in fact that I find it quite interesting. He speaks with the local accent, in a humble, avuncular way, giving advice that has so little to do with religion as to be almost a Dear Abby from the pulpit. I marvel at the changes here too. No more the fire and damnation, and the devils and temptations of my childhood. The Church has evidently adopted a more reasonable approach. I am not sure I like it that much; I knew what to dislike when the Church was so outrageously apocalyptic, but now, how can I dislike this pudgy fellow with a shopping bag of banal wisdom and semi-religious platitudes given out to a crowd of three people including me? I feel so sorry for him I am almost tempted to convert and make his day.

Back at my apartment I have just started to write when Petra appears with a dish of homemade something.

"What about your sex life?" I ask. If I am to be continuously invaded I may as well have some fun.

"What sex life?," she says, "I am so glad it's over."

I muse on the fact that one page would be all I would need if I was writing about the sex life of my relatives. Either they have all gone to seed or the whole of North America is on a sexual binge of priapic proportions, a fashion that hasn't reached these shores yet. And yet the ads on television here are duly sexual with naked uncensored breasts shown freely, something that is not allowed in Canada. Most men here do not consider themselves successful unless they have a lover, children with the lover—a second family really—plus the children and the regular wife, who seems to be very happy at no longer having to look after her husband's sexual needs. There is a contradiction here, the meaning of which escapes me.

In fact, the more I talk to people from all walks of life here, the more I discover that, except during youth's wild times, everybody's interests have shifted from the sexual to the existential. To them the idea of going to therapy to rekindle a vanishing sexual need seems a bit bizarre. If you don't have a need, why create it? Everybody my age here seems to be quite happy to live a rather eunuchy life.

But, of course, I am not sure of all this; people tend not to tell the truth when dealing with sexual matters. Petra asks me, "And what about you?"

"Since I am not so young anymore, I am now down to twice a day. But after this lovely holiday things should improve," I say laughing.

"You see what I mean?" she says, "you are still strange."

I look down at my plate and start eating.

I am happy when I am alone in my little apartment. I think that Petra has neglected to open the faucet to the gas cylinders on purpose so that I can't make a mess, but the view is onto a little courtyard full of potted petunias and saucy underwear hung on a line to dry. There isn't a book in the place, except a dictionary and an atlas. Idly I open the atlas to the map of Italy, I want to think about where to go next. While looking at that contorted boot that is the Italian peninsula, I notice the island of Elba, just off the coast of Tuscany. I spent a holiday there once with my mother and my sister. In fact I fell in love there. I sit against the back of the bed and let my mind slip back to my first experience of being in love.

❧

Mostly I hated my mother. She always managed to hurt and irritate me. I was made to apologize when I did something wrong, but she never apologized or asked for forgiveness, the way mothers did in the American movies. Her latest outrage had been the cutting of my hair, when I thought she was just snipping the ends. When I looked in the mirror, I beheld a boyish cut that made me look naked and silly, while my braids lay scattered on the floor.

She said it was a surprise present for my namesake day, the feast of San Giovanni. Not that I didn't want my hair cut; of course, I did. But not just then, not on that day. That day I needed my hair, because for the first time in my life I was in love.

I was eleven years old, he was thirty-eight. I knew his age because he had just celebrated his birthday right on the beach, not far from where my mother, my sister and I had established our territory within the shade of a large beach umbrella. We were staying in a secluded little place—half resort, half fishing village—with a beach no bigger than my schoolyard in Florence. After meticulous research into prices, the quality of the sand and the distance from Florence, my mother had found this tiny resort on the island of Elba. Not that we could afford it. Had it not been for my weak lungs, we would have stayed home as usual that summer. With the meagre wages my mother earned as a schoolteacher, and my father having died three years earlier, only an absolute necessity could compel us to indulge in such a luxury. But the doctor had been quite clear, "The child needs some sun and fresh air, or she will catch tuberculosis like her father."

Well, sometimes I was of some use.

So here we were, on the beach, like the rich people. I loved the water. It felt great to have every part of my body touched all at once. It was like having no secrets. And then the sun would dry me, leaving cool hidden places under my arms and between my legs. Paradise.

There were few birds on the beach, but lots of butterflies. Running among both made me feel as if I could fly too.

Then the foreign family arrived and took their place under the beach umbrella next to ours. We didn't know where they came from, or what language they spoke. They knew no Italian, but they did smile readily at us. It must have been one of those smiles, that made me fall in love with the father, or the way he called his children gently and softly, so unlike my mother, whose yell could practically be heard from the mainland. It might have been the green of his eyes, or the thickness of his lashes, which were paler than his skin. Whatever it was, each morning I found myself waiting impatiently for him to arrive. I would take my place a little distance behind him, playing in the sand, trying not to look too obvious. I sat in the burning sun and looked at his shoulders covered in foreign freckles, at the polished knots of his muscles and at the base of his neck where his hair curled.

He could sit for hours, just reading his book and smoking his pipe. He hardly spoke to his wife who was always swimming in the sea, even when the red flag was hoisted, which meant the waves were dangerous.

I never ran or showed off in front of him, since I knew I was nothing much to look at. My braids were thin and straight, my nose was too long, and my breasts no more than two mosquito bites on my ribs. But I had been told that I was talented and intelligent. "A genius," my friend Carla always said.

So, I built clever tunnels in the sand and made castles, roads, bridges, channels, rivulets of water, lakes and dams—a whole geography of my own invention, never too far from where he was sitting. One day I built a snake of sand all around him and his umbrella, but distant enough not to be noticed. I covered the snake with shells and small stones, made the scales on its body by pressing the net shopping bag that we used to carry towels to the beach, and shaped a forked tongue protruding from its mouth. A masterpiece. When he went to swim he stepped on it, twice.

I was also busy with my fantasies. I tried to imagine how it felt to kiss a man. My father, even when he was alive, had spent most of his time in a sanatorium and, when he was at home, had avoided kissing me out of fear of transmitting his illness. Boys couldn't be used to experiment on—they were a disaster to be avoided at all costs. But I had my imagination. When nobody was looking, I spread wet sand over my cheeks and slid my hands over them. That's how I thought a man's shaved cheeks would feel. I also made muscles out of my biceps, to taste a man's tautness.

In a very evasive way, so as to arouse no suspicion, I asked my sister if men were inclined to love geniuses.

"First of all," she said, "geniuses die young." I immediately made a mental note to fail religion, gymnastics and possibly even mathematics. "Second, men are not interested in things of the mind. They are essentially physical."

Being four years older than I was, I thought my sister Lieta must have known what she was talking about, but I had no idea what being "physical" meant. I felt too stupid and unsophisticated to ask. I was not experienced in things physical. I had always been appreciated for what I did, never for who I was. I had come to believe that the only way to be loved was to work my way up to it. Now, suddenly, I was thrown into this physical dimension, about which I knew nothing.

Whatever there was in me that was physical, I wanted him to have, but I didn't know what it was. Not only was I inexperienced in physical things, I had also never been very good at giving, either. As a rule, I resented giving, particularly when I was asked to do so. But now I was in the throes of an urge to give that was totally unfamiliar to me. I sat in the sun, burning and worrying.

Then something happened that presented me with an almost ready-made solution, and it came from where I least expected it.

Every Friday night, the local priest showed a movie in the garden behind the church. Usually, it was the kind of Hollywood movie that made us long for the better things in life that were unavailable to us, like linoleum, refrigerators and romance. We all loved to escape into those movies—even my mother.

The cinema in the church garden was nothing more than four or five benches on each side of a bedsheet stretched on a wire, which served as the screen.

At first, the sheet had been at the end of the garden and we all sat together in front of it. However, the boys behaved so badly—making rude comments and farting loudly, even during silent scenes—that the priest found it necessary to put the sheet in the middle, with the males on one side and the females on the other. The result was that we females saw all the writing in reverse, which was fine with us. What with the black moths and the flickering fireflies, we hardly could make out what was going on anyway. No matter, we simply loved everything that we saw.

Recently, we had seen a movie that had been particularly wonderful and tragic. So tragic in fact that we went to see it again. A younger girl loves an older man, but the man is too honest and upright. So he refuses her. Both live through a series of events designed to increase their frustration, until finally the moment comes for the lovers to part. In the final scene the girl cuts off her braids and puts them by the man's door, and then, lightly and silently, leaves him forever. I could hardly see the ending for the tears running down my cheeks. It was better than anything I had ever seen.

On the way home from the cinema I suddenly understood the connection between the young girl's situation and mine. Of course. I would wait until the last day, cut my braids off and leave them on the beach near him so that he would understand. To make sure that he knew where the braids came from, the next day I would begin wearing ribbons of a different colour on each braid so that when he saw them he would know where they came from. He couldn't possibly miss the meaning, since I had seen him and his wife watching the same movie.

But it was the next morning that my mother, in a fit of unusual capitulation to my wishes, had cut off my braids and deprived me of any means of being physical.

I cried and yelled and sobbed. My mother couldn't believe my reaction. For years, I had asked her to cut my hair so that I would look like a Hollywood actress, and now that she had finally done it, I was behaving as if she had tried to kill me. She thought I had contracted schizophrenia.

For days I felt as if something vital had been taken from me. Now, with only a few days left before our departure, I didn't know what I could do to make him understand. I sat behind him under the sun, counting the bumps on his spine, memorizing the way his hair curled behind his ears, and trying to gather enough details to remember later.

It was not until the second last day that I came up with a way that was sure to make him understand; and when I finally decided what to do, a great peace descended on me. I felt whole, clever and almost happy again.

The last day arrived. We didn't stay too long on the

beach that afternoon because we had to pack as our train was leaving the next morning. For the last time, I watched him walk towards the sea to swim. He advanced slowly into the water, until there was nothing more than a bobbing head among the waves. He never looked back. He swam on his own, daringly, as if land didn't exist. Never mind—by next morning he would understand.

That night I went to bed early to think and dream. I woke up around five o'clock, with no prodding from anyone. The house where we were staying was cool and silent, the milk bottles already on the steps. Everybody was asleep. I took a sheet of paper and the coloured pencils from my sister's kit, the safety razor my mother used to shave her legs, her little hand mirror and four small stones. I wrapped them in a towel and put it in the string shopping bag. Then I walked to the beach without making a sound. I was amazed at the newness of the world at this early hour. The beach umbrellas were closed and limp, a seagull was trying to catch butterflies, and little mysterious imprints were all over the cool sand. The sea, a breathing silk.

I walked over to the spot in front of his chair and emptied the contents of the shopping bag onto the sand. I took the paper and the coloured pencils and drew a portrait of myself. Just in case he found it too difficult to recognize me, since I had drawn the lashes a bit longer than mine, I drew myself with my braids still on. Then I took the mirror, bent over and shaved off my eyebrows, letting them fall on the page. I wet them so that they would stick to the page, and gathered them in little crescent mounds above the eyes in my portrait. I made a little depression in the sand to create a shelter, then I took the four small stones, and put one on each corner of the page, so that the morning breeze would not scatter it and its contents all over the beach. I looked around to make sure nobody had seen me.

I felt a new coolness where my eyebrows had been. I did not dare to look at myself in the mirror. I surveyed the beach, the portrait, the chair, the umbrella and the fishing boats returning from having been far at sea. Then, like a lamb to the slaughter, I turned towards my house to face my mother.

With time, I let my hair grow back, and I braided it, just in case I should need it again. But my eyebrows, when they grew back, took a different route, and came out in a different shape. They grew less arched, straighter and nearer to the bridge of my nose.

I never looked quite the same.

The Suitor

Another of my cousins, Giancarlo, has invited me to visit him in Ascoli Piceno, a little city south of Ancona where I am now. At first I refused to go because I don't know him or his family. I left Italy when he was still a baby; so he is almost a generation younger than I am. But then, in a fit of curiosity, I decide to go. I am sorry to leave Petra and the lovely little free apartment. I could have stayed longer, but I feel bad at being served three full meals a day and not being able to do anything for myself. I am being too pampered, and gratitude has begun to weigh heavily on me. I give Petra some silver jewellery I bought in India and offer to take her and her husband out to dinner somewhere. I am eager for them to get out of the house at least once. He would like to come, but Petra refuses; she is ashamed of the state of her husband's mind. That's the reason she has lost all her friends; she doesn't want anybody to know that her husband has a mental disorder.

I leave them sitting in that shuttered living room of theirs like two chained monuments of unbearable togetherness. When I am in the street, I look up and see Petra waving, while around me the city is dappled by the reflection of the sun on the water. I am immensely sad about her destiny, which I know will never loosen its mortal grip on her. There are in every family the ones who live a life of quiet desperation until finally death takes them to a better destiny. But before now I had never seen anybody of my generation locked in such a Gothic dungeon of the mind. I thought that by now each of us was, at least to a certain extent, master of one's own life. But Petra is there at the window, in a winter of her own, while the rest of the city is immersed in the summer glory of water reflections and youth in short sleeves and sandals. I wave back and escape to the station.

I am a little late, so I jump on the first train going south. There are so many passengers crowded around the entrance, I am sure they are there because they want to get out at the next stop. But the next stop comes and goes, and it's evident nobody gets out. It is, I find out a train completely packed with young soldiers. I cannot move any further in than the entrance. I barely manage to put the suitcase between my feet and hope that the train will not stop suddenly because there is nothing for me to hang onto. In front of me is a young woman with a rather provocative low-cut neckline. She is shorter than I am so I can look right into her bosom and can't help noticing an exposed landscape of flat breasts and extraordinary nipples. Her nipples are so prominent they are bent inside her brassiere, one sideways, the other upwards, and every time the train shakes her they are free to shoot in a proper horizontal direction. They look like little brown corks. She is a girl of few physical assets, her face is all teeth and her eyebrows are straight large caterpillars. But she seems pleased with the shape of her corky nipples because she keeps looking where everybody else around her seems to be looking. A tall soldier standing behind me, is also looking inside her brassiere, but his reaction is quite different from mine. His breathing is fast, and getting faster and hotter. It feels like a gentle, rhythmical hair dryer is blowing on my neck. I would like to move and let those two reach some kind of mutual fulfilment but there is nowhere for me to go.

I look down and see a little child sitting on the part of my suitcase that is protruding from between my legs. I smile at him, but he looks at me with that disconnected look that children have when they have not been indoctrinated into being nice. A soldier starts to sing and everybody tells him to shut up, it's too hot and uncomfortable for singing.

One long hour later, the train finally pulls into the station in Ascoli Piceno. When I finally disembark, it feels as if I have been reduced in size. I hope that the cousin who is supposed to pick me up at the station is actually there, and that he is at least as tall as I am. I am sick of having to bend down to kiss my relatives.

I have never seen him before but I notice him instantly. There is an imprint of the family traits that makes his face inexplicably "one of us." It is not a matter of features, more like an emanation. I bend down to embrace him.

Giancarlo is one of the younger generation who, like my sister, has made the family proud. He is a VIP in a big international firm. Because he has not followed the family tradition of being an academic, he has made a lot of money. He uses only one hand to steer his BMW, making me nervous. He works in Rome but drives three hours each way to spend his weekends in Ascoli Piceno, where he owns a house he has not had the heart to sell. I expect a beautiful house

The house is a pastiche in white stucco with an almond tree in front, the roots of which have managed to give a permanent earthquake to the entrance steps. I meet his wife Laura who is refreshingly slovenly with a cigarette in her mouth most of the time and a dressing gown that reveals most of her, since it doesn't overlap properly. I am given a meal which I can't decipher, but it seems to consist of little olives fried in olive oil.

Laura says charmingly that she cannot cook because the kitchen is too small. However, should I like to be served a proper meal I could accompany them to a banquet some friends of theirs are giving. Who am I to say no? I feel I am embarrassing them by being there so I see going someplace else as a nice way out.

The banquet, which was supposed to have been held outdoors, has, because of persistent rain, been moved to an unfinished garage, which is leaking in several places. We are late, and all the other guests are sitting at makeshift tables covered by embroidered tablecloths. There are flowers everywhere and clusters of balloons float along the ceiling like anchored clouds. At first I think it is a wedding, but it turns out to be a party for a young boy's first Communion. I think about how wealthy the parents must be to be able to seat over one hundred people at a table for something as insignificant as a first communion. But, of course I am in the south, where things are different. Everything is more emphatic, more textured, more traditional. Even the city, which I have hardly seen through the rain is different from what I have seen so far: a small baroque jewel of travertine marble, open and exuberant like a miniature Rome.

When we enter, all eyes turn on me, making me feel like the incoming floor show. I want to melt into the background and let them start talking again, but the host, a little man with a wealthy paunch feels compelled to introduce me to the crowd as a Professor from America. They applaud and I cringe. I finally sit down next to Laura, who, squeezed in a black little nothing with plenty of jewellery, looks slutty and lovable. I feel very attracted to this sample of my relatives who seems to be totally different from the rest of them.

A man sitting in front of us looks at Laura intently, almost offensively, but she waves at him, calling him by his first name. She has trouble sitting at the table, because its leg has to be accommodated between her legs.

The man in front of us asks her if she has forgotten how to open her legs. She looks someplace else, but the man repeats the lewd joke since he doesn't want his sexual wit to be lost. Laura looks as if she hasn't heard him, but I know she has. Although she looks blatantly sexual, the old training of letting the boys be boys is still alive and well. Looking stupid was one of the first lessons I had to learn when dealing with men.

I am on her side, but I am surprised when I see her throwing little pellets of food at him, as soon as he loses interest in her and starts eating his food. He is a vulgar little man with the manners of a peasant and the clothes of a gentleman. The result is one of mild impersonation. He seems to be suffocating in his shirt and tie. But he gets rekindled by the food pellets and looks around to see who is sending them. For a worrying second he lays eyes on me, but he is too clever to suspect me. I am twice his height and my face expresses no liking of him, I am sure.

Laura throws another pellet and he starts running off at the mouth with some lewdness which, this time, I don't get. I only know it's lewd because Laura becomes slightly coloured. I think she is trying to direct him to something a little more romantic than this blatant sexuality, which I find definitely overlaid with contempt. My cousin Giancarlo, her husband, is sitting next to the lewd man, beatifically unaware, stuffing himself with food.

The banquet would give indigestion to Gargantua. The antipasti alone are five courses. The pasta is cooked in three sauces and the meats are in courses separated by modes of cooking. The boiled, the fried, the roasted, and the sauteed. The vegetables are brought about in circular revolving trays with fifteen compartments. Among them are vegetables I have never seen, that are grown only in this part of the country. Some are bluish, some deep green, some almost white. I ask around for the name of this and that exotic item, but I am misunderstood and my plate is filled by well-meaning guests. Either they speak a dialect innocent of any real Italian, or my shyness renders my speech incomprehensible. By the time I have finished the antipasti, I am so full I can hardly eat another morsel.

I finally get to see the child for whom all this has been organized. He is small and gracile and at the moment being picked on by two fat girls who appear to be twins. The girls try to break his balloons but not very effectively. Their leotards keep falling down so each has to use one pudgy hand to hold onto them. Even so, the boy is no match for the aggressive girls. But he tries gamely to hold onto his balloons. He doesn't seem interested in the festivities. I can tell he is not an eater and couldn't care less about all that food.

Finally, everybody is ready to dance. The tables are pushed aside and a young boy with an accordion starts to play in front of a microphone that does nothing but whistle. No matter. The people have eaten for close to four hours and feel like moving. The boy plays with a concentrated little face and refuses to listen to suggestions for old-fashioned tunes from the audience. He has got his book of songs in front of him and goes at it methodically. He is endearingly out of tune.

Suddenly, I am seized by the thought that some of these little people are going to invite me to dance. Memories of me at sixteen dancing with short boys, their heads resting on my chest, leaving a round stain of brilliantine on my best dress, leap at me from my past like little gargoyles of embarrassment. I hope everyone can see that I am too tall to dance with anybody here. But evidently I underestimate the goodwill of these well-meaning folks. An emergency tall chap is sent for so that I will have a dancing partner. When I see the fellow come in, a bit dazed, I know immediately why he is here. I disappear outside to take a breath of fresh air in the pouring rain. There I find the child for whom the banquet has been given and we both sit silently under a jutting eave. Somehow I feel that with the two of us here the party is deprived of its main attractions. At the same time we have delivered the guests from deference and restraint. I hear them singing in the background with an abandon that I, because I am an outsider, and he, because he is a child, cannot join in with.

I detest banquets, those eating orgies full of joviality and smacking of lips. It must be because of my very first banquet. It has to do with my mother's suitor.

According to the gospel of my Aunt Giusta, my mother had been a great beauty in her youth. She was always described dreamily as a black and white numen, tall and slender, her hair a great mane of black cashmere, coiled twice around her head, and an alabaster skin of aristocratic pallor.

But after the death of my father she let herself go, her hair became streaked with grey, her cheeks sunk for lack of attention, and she wore the same dress long enough to look as if she had been upholstered in it. Her famous smile, a smile that was said to catch the light even on a rainy day, had become so rare that I had to learn to somersault and almost break my neck for the privilege of seeing it appear on her face. But, of course, being eight years old, and my sister Lieta thirteen, we never really took any notice of her appearance, since mothers are mothers—necessary but unremarkable fixtures in a child's landscape.

But she must not have gone completely unnoticed because one day she came home from the market and announced, a little breathlessly, that, having met a gentleman several times while lining up for milk, she had decided to accept his proposal that he come to our house to cook for us. It was to be a present for her birthday the following Friday, the second of July.

Lieta and I must have been slow to react, because she repeated the announcement slowly, carefully and a little louder as if we were foreigners. A gentleman? We had never seen a gentleman. If gentlemen looked like Fred Astaire, with a cane, spats and a top hat, then I had only seen one in the American movies. We knew no real live gentlemen. People we knew weren't referred to as gentlemen. They had names, and if we didn't know them by name, they were known for what they did or what they looked like. So there was the cobbler, the wine merchant and the umbrella mender. Then there was the cross-eyed widow and the red-haired orphan. People we disliked had nicknames, like Sentiments, the crooked lawyer, and Gondola, the town drunk. But a gentleman? It must be what my sister called "an irony." Besides, we asked, why would a gentleman want to come to our three-room apartment? And to cook?

"Precisely because he is a gentleman," said my mother defensively, and to prove it she produced a business card, handwritten in fine flourishes, that said:

Pasquale Torre
Business Gentleman

No mention of what the gentleman's business was. That didn't bother us since we didn't know much about business either. But we knew that someone with a name like Pasquale had to have come from the south, maybe from as far south as Naples. To us, growing up in our Florentine arrogance, someone from the south could no more claim to be a gentleman than to be an honest businessman, as vague as both concepts were to us.

His name conjured up the image of a brilliantine-glazed Mafioso, shifty of eyes, skulking around in search of innocents like us to prey on.

"He has been in America for many years," said my mother, reassuringly, "in a place called Columbusohio, where he was a chef at a famous restaurant."

That gave him the seal of respectability. People who had been to America were of a different, superior class, no matter what their names were. We didn't know anybody who had ever been there. We ourselves had only been as far away as Milan, but that had been a disappointment. With its chilly fog and the horrible incomprehensible dialect its people spoke, it was certainly not better than Florence. The gentleman was, for all intents and purposes, an American. The thought of an American coming to our place to cook was quite exciting. We became anxious and full of expectation.

My mother proceeded to make our place fit for the gentleman chef's visit with the energy of a tiger. She washed all the curtains, starching the folds so that their freshness would not go unnoticed; washed all the window panes inside and outside, leaning dangerously from the windows, cleaning them so thoroughly the flies got fooled and bashed against their transparency; and polished the brass knobs until they trapped every surrounding detail into their spherical universe. She poured wax and cinnabar onto the kitchen floor until it didn't look like bricks anymore, but more like the linoleum in American movies. Since I was artistic, she had me retouch the nicks in the plaster of the naked lady on the lion—the only "work of art" in our place—to make it look like bronze again.

Then she washed the china—not our everyday dishes, but the set with the blue peonies which was trimmed with real gold—and put it in the kitchen cupboards to give the impression that we ate from it every day and then polished all the glasses until they almost ceased to exist. By the time she finished, our place looked as if it had never been inhabited. Still she kept going around, surveying the effect of her work with a critical eye, nitpicking at imperfections only she could see. We were afraid to move.

When the appointed day came, my mother woke us up earlier than usual, put all the pots we had on the ranges, heated the water to a boil, poured it in the galvanized zinc tub in the middle of the kitchen floor, and gave everybody a bath, starting with herself because she thought she was the cleanest. By the time I got in, the water was almost cold. She told us to put on clean underwear, and she braided our hair with new ribbons, pink for Lieta and blue for me. I preferred pink but was never listened to. We washed our teeth more vigorously than usual and checked each other's breath to make sure it smelled good.

My mother's breath was hotter.

At the last minute my mother and I had one more row because I had cut the newspaper squares to be hanged on the nail in the washroom too small. I asked her defiantly how I was supposed to know the size of the gentleman's arse, and she let me have a slap in the face that left one of my cheeks looking much healthier than the other. At five in the afternoon we were all ready, sitting on the chairs, not on the couch, lest we should mark it, waiting for the gentleman to arrive.

The bells of the Church of Santa Croce had not finished their fifth toll when the doorbell rang. The three of us jumped to our feet. But then my mother sat down again to look nonchalant, while my sister took her place standing behind her, her hand poised on my mother's shoulder as if ready for a family portrait. On my way to the door to open it, I stopped for a moment to look at them. They looked so beautiful and poised I felt as if I had been adopted.

The gentleman stepped in and carefully placed two heavy suitcases on the polished floor. He went to my mother and shook her hand with a rigid little bow and then he turned to my sister and shook her hand, as if she was an adult. Since I was young, he pinched my cheek slightly. His hand smelled of soap.

He was dressed in a three-piece suit, a carnation in his lapel. His eyebrows and eyelashes were thick, long and black; in fact, he had so much fur around his eyes the blue inside looked like a vacuum. His mouth was small, almost insignificant, a thin moustache just kissing his upper lip. But a great blade of a nose managed to pull together those spare-part features of his in a concentrated vertical manner, with no promise of laughter or even a smile. What hair he had, he had combed from one side of his head to the other to cover his baldness, but a few strands hung down by the side of his chin.

I loved him at once.

He engaged in a bit of polite conversation, sprinkled with "yes" and "OK," which did not fail to impress us. After a brief but seemly amount of time, he asked to be shown to the kitchen and requested very politely if he could recruit me as a helper. My mother looked at me as if she was seeing me for the first time and agreed uncertainly. I followed him into the kitchen triumphantly, ready for anything.

Once in the kitchen he closed the door carefully and took off his jacket, his vest, his shirt and his pants, leaving on only his socks held by little garters under his knees, his undervest, his baggy underpants and a little chain around his neck holding a cross and a little devil's horn, half hidden in the fur of his chest. Then he removed his wrist-watch and placed it carefully on the kitchen counter. I thought he had forgotten that I existed and that he would proceed to take the rest of his clothes off. I didn't know where to look. But then, out of one of his suitcases, he produced an immense apron and wrapped himself in it from the little chain around his neck all the way down to his black and white shoes, and I felt reassured. He put on a high, white chef's hat and tied a little handkerchief around his neck. Then he asked me to leave for a few minutes because he was about to kill a chicken, and didn't want me to be upset by the sight of blood. He evidently had a live chicken in one of his suitcases.

I went to the washroom, avoiding purposefully the mute questioning looks of my mother and Lieta. Back in the kitchen, I was intrigued by the sight of this exotic chicken, black with tiny white polka dots, laying on the sink minus its head. My mother would never have done anything as barbaric as that; she always strangled her

Giovanna Peel - 247

chickens to avoid having to cope with the sight of blood. He was a considerate man though, because he had wrapped a towel around the chicken's neck before tossing it to me to pluck. I expertly removed all the chicken feathers, saving the tail and the wings, which I then tied up in little fans. My mother used those fans to baste the meat and dust small, otherwise unreachable corners. I was quite proud of my expertise; the little fans had never looked so beautiful with all those polka dots. But when I finished all that embroidery of feathers, I was aghast to see Signor Pasquale throw all of it, together with the head, the feet, the neck and the entrails of the chicken, into the waste bucket.

My mother would be shocked at such wastefulness, she never threw anything away. She would save the neck skin to make a casing for a sausage of liver and bread crumbs, she saved the head and the wings for herself to eat; and she would put the feet and the bones on a piece of anonymous newspaper for Garibaldi, the snarly dog next-door, in the hope that he would choke on them and die. She was an ingenious woman.

But the part I liked the best was when she removed and cleaned the guts of the chicken by pouring water into one end to push the shit out the other. Once the guts were cleaned, she cooked them a little, chopped them up and gave them to our cat Cleopatra. When we first got the cat, we fed her the guts raw and whole, but Cleopatra got rather tangled, so now my mother chopped them as well as cooked them.

Since the death of my father, my universe had been largely populated by women. I had forgotten, or maybe had never quite known, the ways of men. They seemed to be nothing more than a flimsy smell of tobacco, or a threatening display of muscular strength. Since I could remember, their ways had always looked rather strange to me.

Take that silly hat they wore when cooking. I saw no reason for it. I never saw any of the women wearing such an oddity when they cooked. I could just see my mother, trying to cook in the interstices of time between private classes and the normal school hours, sit down, don a chef's hat and start to peel the potatoes. Or toss the pizza up in the air as they did in the marketplace, or, as Signor Pasquale did, break an egg with one hand when using both made things so much easier.

But there he was, Signor Pasquale, breaking all those eggs with the flourish of one hand and his high hat becoming soaked at the rim with sweat. Some eggs were so tiny I was sure they must have been laid by a baby chicken. There were times in the midst of all that cooking when things were so strange and fascinating I would forget to do what I had been asked to, like shelling the peas or peeling the oranges. I was lost in a cloud of puzzlement.

I had never seen so many strange and exotic ingredients, redolent of mysterious, far away places. I was also surprised at the number of dishes and pots and pans that he found necessary to use. There was nothing left in the kitchen that hadn't been used, and in addition to those, he produced more gadgets and trinkets from his suitcases, like an inexhaustible conjurer. I thought of my mother who would have to clean up this devastation. She made do with as few pots as possible in the kitchen; on the table all that was needed for our daily meals were three dishes, three glasses and three spoons and forks. We hadn't used any knives since the time I had cut my lip with a knife and she had to take me to the hospital to be sewn up. My mother cut our food before she served it, to avoid any danger.

The heat in the kitchen was infernal. Signor Pasquale

kept drying his face, his neck and his armpits with a sweeping motion of the dish towel, but it didn't seem to help much. The sweat kept dripping into his eyelashes until they shone wetly as if he had used mascara. I was very jealous of his eyelashes. By the time Signor Pasquale declared the cooking finished, I was so exhausted I was practically falling asleep into the potato peelings. Finally, taking off his apron and funny hat, and putting on his suit, he went to the other room and announced the meal ready to be served.

In the dining room my mother had not been idle. The table had been covered by the damask tablecloth, with its woven garlands of roses coiling around the heads of cherubs, wings sprouting from behind their ears. The cloth smelled of juniper berries, which my mother never failed to put in the linen closet. It was one of my jobs to steal the berries from what was left of the municipal gardens. My mother had placed the naked lady on the lion in the centre of the table. She had made folded snowy peaks out of the napkins and arranged them in the centre of each dish. She had also placed knives and forks and little spoons all around the dishes, as if we knew how to use them. When Signor Pasquale came in, he took a look at the table setting and proceeded to change it. He started by removing the naked lady on the lion and putting it back on the pedestal by the door. Then he took the gladioli he had brought with him, which had been kept semi-submerged in water in the kitchen sink, and scattered them artistically in a vase, which he placed in the centre of the table. Next he rearranged all the cutlery and then deftly shook out the napkins my mother had so carefully shaped, and with a few swift expert folds, made rosettes out of them, and placed one in each glass. Having accomplished all this, he remembered that we existed and looked at us triumphantly and for the first time he smiled. I noticed then that, yes, he indeed had teeth, but they were tiny, like grains of rice.

We sat at the table, ready now for Signor Pasquale's meal. He emerged from the kitchen with his entrées, nursing each dish with both hands as if it were of a fragile nature. By the time he finished bringing in all the first dishes, he had found it necessary to remove the vase of gladioli and some of the glasses together with the napkin rosettes, which he snapped open and placed on our knees rather than inside our collar where we always put them. We were so intimidated, we let him do what he wished.

He was a man of great punctiliousness. He arranged each item on our plates with the delicacy of a calligrapher, placing a scattering of peas here, a corsage of parsley there, two carrots, swimming in what looked like brilliantine, the mashed potatoes combed in little waves as if they had been prepared by a hairdresser. Parts of the chicken were entombed in a silent transparent tremulousness, which he named gelatine, and the tossed salad had nothing tossed about it—each leaf was arranged, checkerboard-like, with a transparent slice of tomato, on which he drizzled some olive oil, in front of our eyes to allay any doubt as to its virginity.

He had made some mistakes though. Like those tiny black pellets that smelled of fish which, he instructed us, were called caviar. Too salty. And as far as the beef, he had failed to cook it properly, since some of the blood was still oozing from the centre of each piece. I tried to dry mine up with a corner of my napkin since he had also forgotten to give us any bread. He had served us some bread sticks, but they were totally useless for sopping up all those sauces he ladled on our plates. Most revolting were those baby eggs, no bigger than marbles, which Signor Pasquale had boiled and then returned to their half shells—suspiciously speckled in brown—with a caper at the centre of each so that they resembled eyes drunkenly looking in every direction. He had not let them cook long enough: they were soft inside and a little runny.

Signor Pasquale seemed not to have let anything cook long enough. He also never gave us enough of anything; all the portions were so small it felt like eating an encyclopaedia of samples. We were also given glasses of wine, which had not been mixed with water, the way we always had it. The undiluted wine stung my throat and made my eyes water; it felt like drinking gasoline. But the looks my mother darted at us made us eat or drink everything and feign great delight. We didn't question anything and, in any case, wouldn't have been able to do so because Signor Pasquale talked continuously, telling us the history, the origin, and all the regional and national variations of each dish. He was such a learned man. Lieta and I said nothing, we were lost in admiration and awe, while my mother was all agreement and smiles and little chirps of surprise; we hardly recognized her. Finally, after the last of the courses had been consumed, Signor Pasquale stood up a little labouriously, placed the flower vase back in the middle of the table, filled our glasses with a new kind of undiluted bubbly gasoline and said:

"I propose to drink to your health and your future, Signora Natalia, a lady of courage, refinement and learning, a widow with two young children still in need of your attention and care, and welcome the opportunity graciously given to me to cook for you as a well-deserved gift on the occasion of your birthday. It is on this day that, seeing that the world is a place of cruelty and hardship, insofar as every human being needs something more than just work and duty, and also a bit of support, given the fact that I am a man of honour and free from any obligation, I would like humbly, and of course should the answer be in the negative, apologetically, in front of the two innocent children who will be witnesses as to the honourability of my intentions, would like, in not so many words, to ask your permission to respectfully love you."

And then, a little winded he sat down, fixing his eyes on the remains of his chicken, looking spent and round, and as pink as an apricot.

The silence that followed was so profound that we heard the workmen returning from the factories on their bicycles outside, laughing at each other's jokes. We seemed to have frozen in the night heat until the spell was broken by a loud sob. They all looked at me as if I had farted. But the idea of Signor Pasquale taking my mother away to respectfully love her was too much for me. I had thought he was on my side. He had pinched my cheek, and even undressed in front of me, which was a bit like sharing a secret. He had allowed me to be his helper, and suddenly I was relegated to the same non-existent place I had always held in the family hierarchy. I felt betrayed.

In moments of crisis I used to faint, and the look my mother gave me made it quite clear that she was hoping I would faint and deliver her from having to give some kind of an answer. But I was no help this time, I left her to her own devices.

So she stood up and, apologizing for being such a forgetful host, announced that she was going into the kitchen to make the coffee. She left the three of us looking silently at the gourmet carnage on the dining table. My sister and I didn't dare look at each other, we kept our eyes on a spot on the table, not knowing what to do. Meanwhile, my mother had evidently decided to create a coffee of such perfection that it required an eternity. Probably, though, the reason she was taking so long was that she could hardly find her whereabouts in the catastrophe that had become our kitchen. I was becoming increasingly mad at her for having left us to broil in the embarrassing silence, waiting for something to mercifully happen.

I think it was me who heard the noise first. It was a rhythmical, soothing sound. I didn't want to embarrass anybody but soon enough curiosity got the better of me. I looked up at Signor Pasquale and as I did so, I saw that my sister was also looking. With his hands woven over his belly, his head sank into his neck and his eyes closed, he was emitting a muffled snore that filtered out from inside his delicate moustache. He had fallen asleep, not leaning left or right, but seraphically sunk into his centre of gravity, sublimely oblivious of us staring at him in silence. He had blissfully flown someplace else.

When my mother finally came in carrying coffee cups and pot on a tray, she stopped in midstep on seeing Signor Pasquale asleep. She looked at us as if she thought we had had something to do with it, and then placed the tray very carefully on the table without making a sound lest we should wake him. Then she undid the frilly apron she had put on, folded it loosely on her chair and motioned us to get up carefully and follow her. We tiptoed in a line out onto the landing, through the lobby, out of the big entrance door, into the black summer night. Only then did my mother speak. She said that we should wait outside until Signor Pasquale woke up, so as not to embarrass him. Besides, there was no question of us going to sleep in the apartment because my sister and I slept on the two couches in the room where we also ate.

We sat on the two slats left on the only bench the war had spared in the parkette in front of our house, in the dark, in view of our windows, waiting for Signor Pasquale to wake up. It must have been well past midnight because we heard the workers of the night shift, whistling and calling to each other. We didn't see them in the dark but we saw the flicker of their bicycle lights weaving around like fireflies. My sister and I were almost asleep, drunk with tiredness. But Signor Pasquale seemed to have settled in for the night. We kept looking at our window, but nothing appeared to be stirring. Finally, my mother lost her patience and sent me to ring our bell. I rang the bell many times until my mother saw something moving behind the curtains and called me back to our place. In a few minutes we saw the lights go out in our window and the stair lights go on one floor at a time, revealing the descent of Signor Pasquale to the level of the street. He emerged, staggering out of the door carrying his two suitcases, and disappeared into the night at the end of our street. We never saw him again.

We climbed the stairs to our apartment. I think that both my sister and I fell asleep even before we touched our beds, we hardly had the strength to undress.

It was towards dawn, just about when the church bells had begun to announce the first mass, that I woke up and saw my mother just finishing her restoration of the room to its usual neatness, barely half an hour before the first of her private students were to appear for their cramming sessions.

It was then that I vomited the whole of Signor Pasquale's dinner on the freshly washed floor. It must have been because of the baby eggs.

The Gift

Some friends in the United States have given me the address of some people in Ferrara. He is a professor of genetics at the local university, she is looking after a large extended family. I have telephoned from Bologna and was immediately and warmly invited to stay with them. I refused, as I always do. As long as I can afford it I prefer staying at a hotel. Staying in somebody's home is stressful both for the host and the guest. I have asked them to find me an inexpensive hotel not too far from where they live. They have obliged by cabling me the name and location of a small family-run establishment built against the city walls. When I arrive, the sun is beating hotly on a city built on the only piece of Italy left flat after the building of its mountains: the Po River valley.

Ferrara is famous for being the home city of Lucrezia

Borgia, who after allegedly having been the object of unwanted attention by both her father, the Pope, and her brother—the murderous prince on whom Machiavelli modelled his famous treatise on political manipulation—entered history, not as victim of her own beauty, but as a poisonous villainess. Justice is hard to find even in the history books. Ferrara must have been quite beautiful at one time: small, elegant, with canals instead of streets—like a miniature Venice. Then a piece of mountain, uphill from here, was shaken lose by an earthquake and diverted the river to another valley, leaving Ferrara with the problem of what to do with streets that had become ten feet deeper than their curbs, with barges and barques dangling vertically from their moorings.

The worthy citizens of Ferrara lost no time mourning the loss of their canals and their sewage system; they filled the moats with garbage and topped them with the pebbles from the river bed. The result is that the streets of Ferrara are paved with little upright pebbles of varying colours, giving the city the appearance of one of those garden follies built by gifted amateurs with lots of time on their hands. It's so hard to walk on these pebbles, I feel as if my feet are pummelled by a thousand little blows. The wheels of my suitcase resent the pebbles too; in fact, they look as if they are about to fall off.

When I finally arrive at my hotel, I almost laugh at my having been concerned about its being central. Ferrara has no more than ninety thousand people, and just about everything, from the cemetery to the city walls, is central. It's hard to understand why anybody would own a car. And, in fact most people are on bicycles. They must have developed bums of iron to be able to ride on these pebbly streets on a bicycle.

The hotel is facing the city walls, the top of which is used as a road. The appellation "family hotel" is quite right, since a toddler is running around in his polka-dot pyjamas, and an infant is gumming something in a pink cage. Meanwhile, the mother is on the phone taking bookings. She hands me a key without even asking my name, or for a deposit, while she continues talking on the phone. I take the key and walk through what appears to be a series of buildings connected by small, secluded yards, big enough for a fig tree and a few potted plants. My room is half submerged in a greenish light since it is almost below street level. It is immaculate, cool and spartan, I even have a telephone and a bedside lamp. Pretty good, no?

In the room next to mine two young female voices are having an argument. One of the two voices is louder and more aggressive than the other. Finally, a door gets slammed with such violence, the crucifix above my head swings on its nail as if on the brink of a miracle. I see the girl who just slammed the door sitting in the little yard, crying under the fig tree. She is in her underwear, curlers on her head, and in running shoes and heavy socks. Even so she manages to look quite cute. The one in the room is crying too, loudly talking to herself. I feel tempted to intervene, since in this country nobody would think it unseemly to interfere in other people's business. I would probably be quite welcome, but I decide instead to go and see the professor and his wife and leave the two Lolitas to their squabble.

With a talent that is one of my assets I manage to get lost for a while in a downtown area no bigger than a main square in a real European city. In fact I think that the whole of Ferrara could be contained within the Place de L'Etoile in Paris.

After half an hour I finally arrive at my destination. It is a small provincial palace of sort. The door is not a door but a portal equipped with an intercom, out of which, upon ringing, comes a voice asking me to come up. I shout back, asking if I should let a cat in the door and receive an order to let no cat in, under no circumstances. I enter the door feeling as if I am being filtered, undesirables out, desirables in. I leave the cat outside with a deft manoeuvre and enter a stairwell of a size fit for a Napoleonic army descending in lines of eight. In the immense spiral of ornate banisters the head of my host is like a lost dot of forlorn kindness.

I am received with open arms by the professor's wife and am escorted into one of those rickety, grand old mansions kept alive more by dint of benevolent neglect than by any effort at maintenance. The tiles on the foyer floor have long lost their mortar, so I walk on a seismic disaster about to occur at every step. The walls might once have been white, but now they are a crumbling lifeless grey. Up there, near heaven, is a large chandelier with many lights, but it is so high that its light has nowhere to bounce off. So, it remains in a self-contained pool of its own, shedding almost no illumination at the bottom where we are. The furniture consists of disparate items, representing the impulses, tastes and necessities of a couple of centuries of continuous occupancy.

I love the place instantly. It is so shabby and unpretentious I am almost sorry I didn't accept Signor Orlando's invitation to stay at his house. When I am shown the bathroom, I want to dive right in. It is the size of my living room, with a tiny discreet water closet in a corner and a bathtub in which, with a bit of goodwill, one could drown.

Signor Orlando rises from his chair when we enter the living room and kisses my hand. I feel stupidly flattered by such gallantry, even though I take it to be an ironic gesture. Later, when I know him better, after several conversations, I realize that this was not an empty gesture but a real expression of gentlemanly kindness. There are other people in the room, and I am introduced to them in English out of regard for an English lady who doesn't speak Italian. One of the ladies is the sister of Signor Orlando; she is also a geneticist who is visiting from Rome.

Signor Orlando asks me how can I live in such a selfish country as Canada. I am surprised by this question, since I am under the impression that none of the people in the room has ever been to Canada. When I question him, he answers: "But my dear, a country that large with so few inhabitants can only produce selfishness."

I don't know what to say to an opinion that is not based on experience and so, say nothing. He then takes my hand and says in an avuncular manner, "It's almost time to come home, isn't it?"

I feel in dangerously sentimental waters. I change the topic of conversation to an exhibition of Michelangelo's drawings that I have seen advertised on posters in town. I have the nerve to say that Michelangelo is not my favourite painter. Signor Orlando's sister becomes almost apoplectic with indignation. She is one of those people who believes that holding an opinion different from hers is a personal affront. Unfortunately, the old combative spirit is rekindled in me and I stick to my guns, proposing that Michelangelo, as a painter, is overrated. I know while I am saying it that it is very ungracious of me to insist in such an unpopular view, and I feel foolish and aggressive. Thank heaven the meal is announced and we all move into the dining room. I am careful after that to remain neutral on just about everything from the ravioli to the political situation.

Around the middle of the meal a tiny lady of great age is brought in and sits at the end of the large table, a little distance from the rest of us. The aunt of one of the hosts, she is ninety-four years old and still pretty. I am mesmerized by this ambassador from another era. Like the rest of the family, she speaks perfect English and apologizes for not being able to take me around Ferrara. She says that, had it been the previous year, she would have been able to do so. I ask the usual silly question that is posed to all people of great age, "What has allowed you to live so long?" She answers, with a simplicity that admits no doubts, "The love of my family."

When I think of all the dysfunctional families that I know, this sample of harmonious domesticity stands out like a beacon. I want to stay here for a time, basking in this warmth and unpretentiousness, but the sight of the old lady has rekindled a memory of another old lady I met in my childhood. I want to go to the hotel and write about it. After coffee and another kiss of my hand by the professor, I walk the dark, safe streets to my hotel.

My sister used to say that the rich were no different from the rest of us, they just use more marble, but I knew that wasn't true. I had seen the rich portrayed in American movies. I also knew my sister's friend Alexa and I knew that she and her family were a different species.

They had so many more things than we had. They had coats with little velvet collars, and in the summer Alexa's brothers wore shorts that were longer than those of the rest of the boys—more like those the English boys up the hill wore. The family's dogs had collars around their chests like miniature harnesses, instead of around their necks.

Everyone in the family even had nicknames. Alexa was known as Tata; her older brother Giangiacomo, was Gio; and the youngest, Marco, was called Momo.

I wanted a nickname too. So, for a while I told everybody that I was to be called Gigi. But when people called me Gigi, I forgot it was me and didn't answer. So I reverted to Giovanna.

Tata and her brothers also smelt differently. All one had to do was stand very close to them to realize that they smelt of soap and freshly laundered hair. Also, they could take off their shoes without worrying about whether their socks had holes in them.

The difference between us and them was particularly evident in the fact that at the time we lived in one of the unused classrooms in the school where my mother taught. Well into the war, my father had decided that Milan was a safer place than Florence because Milan had better sanatoria for him. After my father died, we came back to Florence only to find that our apartment had been confiscated by the landlord, furniture and all, after we left for Milan. When we found ourselves without a home, the municipality took pity on us giving my mother a teaching post in the local elementary school and putting us up in one of the classrooms. The room was not very large but had two great windows with a baroque metal grate curving onto the street below. During the day it was a room like any other, with a big table in the centre, at which my mother gave her private lessons, and a smaller table, where my sister was starting to give private math lessons of her own. My mother was nothing if not ingenious: she had erected a screen, artistically painted by me, to hide a small electric stove on a wooden ledge and, under the ledge, two pails of water, one for drinking and one for washing. Behind a cupboard, which acted as a divider, was a double bed where my sister and my mother slept. I couldn't sleep with them because of my bed-wetting, so every night I unfolded a camp bed and placed it under the table, the only space available. I loved to sleep there because it felt as if I didn't exist and was part of the furniture. It was a place to fly away in, giving me an upside-down perspective of the room, which, seen from above during the day, had a totally different feeling. My mother seemed to feel underprivileged and always talked nostalgically about the apartment we used to have, but I preferred this kind of camping. Sometimes wars came for a purpose.

Both my mother and Lieta were embarrassed by our circumstances and preferred that nobody come to our house, except, of course, their students. But, since it was my sister's opinion that they were stupid—otherwise they wouldn't need private lessons—they didn't count.

Even so, my sister had made friends with Tata. Lieta explained her friendship by the fact that they were both in the same grade at school, and also because they had both been struck by an attack of religious zeal. Because of this peculiar fixation they went to all parts of Florence to listen to particular preachers whose fame had reached their ears in order to compare the performance of one to another. For once my mother was on my side in thinking that it was all quite crazy.

Lieta would have denied it, of course, but I suspected that all this religious fervour was Tata's idea and that my sister went along with it because she liked being the friend of a very rich person. When Lieta was in Tata's presence, she even spoke differently. Although Lieta talked as if she knew everything about rich people, the first time we went to Tata's house I could tell she hadn't been to a rich person's house before.

Why, she could hardly speak and kept apologizing for things when there was no need to. But we thought we knew how to behave: when they gave us tea we both held our little fingers up in the air, as if we were a bit rich ourselves, and when the maid gave us biscuits we thanked her politely and ate all the biscuits to show appreciation.

I was a friend of Tata's too, much to my sister's annoyance. I felt very important in being Tata's friend, because not only was she rich, but she was also five years older than I was.

When I went with Lieta to see Tata, my mother always washed my face and hands, and tightened up my braids.

In Tata's house there was so much to look at I hardly knew where to begin. While Tata and Lieta were busy with their homework, I was allowed to wander in the rest of the house on my own. My exploration started with the washroom. Once there, I opened all the jars and tubes of great-smelling stuff, sniffed them, used them on me, only a little of course, tried on the bathrobes, weighed myself on the scale, sat on the bidet and looked at the back of my head in the ricocheting mirrors. There were never any dirty clothes in the hamper. I concluded that rich people didn't soil their clothes, not even their underwear.

There was never anybody in that immense house of theirs. The maids were as silent as ghosts and even the dogs were obedient and still in their bed made of fur.

If we arrived in the afternoon, we were served tea, but if we were there in the morning, we were given fruit and milk. Once, one of the maids came and brought us some peaches that had been peeled and cut in quarters. They rocked precariously on a little dish. I picked up a piece with my fingers, but it slipped and splatted on the floor. The maid tried to retrieve it, but I was quicker and picked it up and ate it before she could reach it. At first I couldn't understand why my sister was looking at me as if she were about to murder me. But then I saw that, on the tray, was a tiny fork, shaped like a miniature Devil's trident. I had failed to see it because the maid had taken the dish with the fruit and offered it to me neglecting to give me the fork. I understood then that I should have used the fork to retrieve the peach from the floor. Well, sometimes I would make a mistake.

The only place I was forbidden to go was Tata's parents' room. I couldn't think why because they were never there. They were always in some exotic and faraway place, from which they brought back the most extraordinary gifts for their children.

I used to sit in the music room sometimes, playing the piano or the spinet with one finger. Other times I would wander into the library where I would look at some of the books that had pictures in them. Once, Lieta mentioned that I was an artist and Tata brought me some coloured pencils and some paper, so that I could go into the library and draw. I sat at the immense table and drew a little mouse, with whiskers and a pink tummy. I painted the eyes black with a dot of white in them, to make them look alive and polished. Tata couldn't believe I could draw so well. She took the drawing and put it on the wall in her study, together with her collection of images of saints and photographs of Hollywood stars. I had drawn a mouse to be funny, but she said she really liked mice, even if she had never seen one. I reasoned that what's good once, must be better more times, so I drew her more mice. She always praised my drawings in ways that neither my mother nor my sister ever did. In the beginning, my sister was a bit bewildered by all the praise lavished on a few mice, but after a while she surrendered to the fact that Tata really liked mice. Rich people can like what they want. Lieta started to cut mice out of magazines and put them up beside my drawings on Tata's wall. When Tata and Lieta took a break from their studying, they talked mouse language—a silliness I failed to understand. Tata had started to put together a small collection of mice in porcelain, silver and wood. She had even got hold of one that played the violin when the tail was wound.

When I wasn't drawing, I would sometimes go downstairs into the kitchen. There the slightly funereal atmosphere of the rest of the rambling house relented, and became more normal, a place that in spite of its size I could identify with. First of all, there were the familiar odours of cooking, and Frumenzia, the cook, didn't mind asking me to help a bit with the peeling of vegetables. But I couldn't understand the need for such an immense kitchen, because, apart from us—and we were never invited for a meal—there were only the three children, and the boys were at boarding school during the week. I never saw anybody else.

But the kitchen was also like an Aladdin's cave of pots and gadgets. On one side, all the copper pots hung in decreasing sizes, so shiny you could see each pot mirrored in the other like fading echoes. The stove was always burning even when there was nothing cooking on it. It had so many doors one never knew where the fire was. There was also an electric range but I never saw it being used. Along the wall of one side of the kitchen was a series of shelves where dishes of every shape and dimension were arranged. One was so large a whole piglet could have crouched in it comfortably; it was propped all by itself on a brass bracket like a porcelain monument. Other kitchen monuments were an enormous water carrier in polished copper, which must have been used before the house had running water , and a perforated pan for roasting chestnuts sitting beside the fireplace, which, however was also no longer in use. It was now a black and silent cavity with no other function then a decorative one because of its marble carvings. The table in the centre of the kitchen was so large I never saw it fully occupied. When all the maids and the servants were eating together, they needed only one end of it.

One day while roaming as usual, I stumbled upon a

door I had never before seen open. I walked right in and saw a little garden of Eden, all under glass. I had never seen a greenhouse and had never imagined one could grow bushes, trees and flowers—even oranges and lemons—all in one's own little indoor farm. I could hardly wait to tell my mother, who loved flowers and plants but had to make do with a couple of aspidistras, and not very flourishing ones at that. A small path among the plants wound artistically up to a little fountain in which stood the statue of a naked man with goat's feet holding a naked girl in his arms. On each side of the walk were nothing but flowers. I only recognized the oleanders because they grew in the garden behind the school in which we lived. The rest of the flowers formed a magic carpet of exotic shapes such as I had never before seen, even in the florist's windows. I now understood why the the house was always full of fresh flowers.

The trees were not really trees, but tiny versions of the ones outdoors. Along the brick wall the pear trees hugging the wall were spread out in symmetrical shapes as if they had been crucified. The lemon trees, which were in big clay pots, looked like little ceramic sculptures. Only the fig trees were left to grow whichever way they wanted. A brown smell of earth and a heaviness of wet air made entering the room like stepping into another universe—one that was different from the rest of the house, a place with a different meaning. I felt I had to be silent here, as one would in a public library or chapel. If I stayed long enough, I imagined I would start to sprout. Walking around the fountain, I suddenly faced an even stranger sight.

Sitting on a high wheelchair, propped up with a thousand cushions was a scrawny, tiny old woman, sound asleep. She must have been close to a hundred years old because she appeared to have more skin than she could possibly use, and her hands were like small claws. On her lap was the smallest dog I had ever seen, all rolled up into a furry knot and looking at me out of bulging eyes. His tail was the only thing alive in the place.

I approached the woman gingerly with the intention of looking at the dog, but it suddenly barked at me, a tinny asthmatic little bark that wouldn't have scared one of my paper mice. Before I had time to withdraw, the old lady woke with a start and looked at me as if she were behind a foggy glass. It took time for her to come fully alive and when she did, her face splintered into an unexpected smile of new teeth that encouraged me to go nearer. She calmed the dog with one hand and beckoned me with the other. She took her glasses from her pocket and put them on. She looked at me with interest and kindness, all the while keeping her teeth in a fixed, smiling position.

"And who are you?" she said with voice as thin and high-pitched as her dog's bark.

"Giovanna," I said.

"Oh. I see," she said as if expecting me. "Take a chair and sit down." I went in the room from which I came, to look for something not too heavy, and found a stool. I took it to the greenhouse and placed it next to the lady. When I looked at her, she had fallen asleep again. I didn't know what to do, whether I should wake her up, wait for her to do so on her own, or leave.

One of the maids came in and saw me sitting there.

"Visiting Grandma, are we?" she said briskly.

"She asked me to sit by her," I said, thinking that maybe I had trespassed.

"Oh well," she said, "she doesn't really know what she is saying." And then she tapped the side of her head in a gesture that said the old woman was crazy. I was quite surprised, because the lady had spoken to me very gently and normally. I left the greenhouse and said nothing to Tata about my encounter. I still felt vaguely that I might have trespassed, and I didn't want to be forbidden to go back to the greenhouse.

In the days that followed, I would often look in the greenhouse but the old lady wasn't there. One day, I was in the kitchen shelling some peas when one of the maids called me to go with her. We climbed up to the second floor where most doors were locked—I knew this because I had tried them all—and entered a room at the end of one of the corridors. It was a bedroom in which everything was white and pale blue, with the lace curtains drawn, and the bedside lamp on, as if it was night. There was a smell of staleness, as if the windows had never been opened, plus a faint one of lavender. On a monument of a bed, which by virtue of a majestic canopy looked like a whole room of its own, sat the old lady with the dog at her feet, her teeth smiling at me from a glass jar on the night table. She beckoned me to go over to her, as she had done the first time I met her. I went over and stroked the dog—it didn't bark, this time—not knowing what else to do. She again asked me to pull a chair over and sit by her. I did so and waited for her to tell me something. She must have forgotten my name because she asked it again.

"My name is Miriam," she said. And then, after a while, she said in a conspiratorial tone, "I am dying, you know."

I wanted to say something, but nothing came out. I looked at her, waiting for more. She was dressed in a silk cloud of delicate lace, cut deep on her front. She had many rings on her contorted fingers, with stones of different colours. Her hair was no more than a wispy halo, giving her head the appearance of a ripe dandelion. She had lipstick on and a smudge of mascara on her

periwinkle eyes. Her fingernails were painted scarlet. I
was fascinated by her, for I had never seen anybody so
old. I sat there watching her weave in and out of consciousness, without even a semblance of conversation. All
I wanted was to look at her and her extraordinary room.
When her slumber became a deep sleep, I left.

In time, I began to go into her room without waiting
to be invited, since she seemed to appreciate my visits.
She was not always there with her head. Sometimes she
talked in a way that was understandable, sometimes in
riddles. Most of the time I got the riddles. She had
promised me that she was going to die, and I was wondering when she was going to do so. I was worried that I
might not know it if she did. When she was asleep, I was
always afraid that she might be dead. I waited by her side
and if I saw the lace on her chest tremble slightly, I knew
she was only momentarily away. During those times,
while I was waiting for her to wake up, I would look at
her intently, something I couldn't do while she was
awake. I was intrigued by the splotches time had sprinkled on her and blue veins like cords all over her arms
and hands. Once, out of curiosity, I pressed one of those
veins to see if her blood would stop and she would die a
little. But she must have had other veins hidden inside,
because she woke up instead.

It wasn't until the fig tree started to produce the first
figs (so tiny, they looked like Silvio's testicles, only green)
that she finally died. I didn't see her die, I heard one of
the maids telling another maid, that, on dying, the old
lady's teeth had fallen from her mouth and the little dog
had jumped down from her lap and bared his own teeth
at the false ones. The maids started to laugh together, but
I thought it was quite irreverent to laugh at someone who
was dead.

Neither I nor my sister were invited to the funeral,

although my mother had bought black ribbons for our braids, just in case. Tata never spoke of her, neither when she was alive nor when she was dead. I never told her of my encounters with her grandmother. When I went into the conservatory, it felt quite empty. I missed the old woman sitting there, like another potted plant. But the little dog was still there, a furry knot on his silk cushion. After only a month he died too; apparently he was also very old. His name was Jupiter. I learned that from a little tombstone they placed where his ashes were buried, in the greenhouse among the oleanders.

It was September and my mother was already thinking about Christmas. We couldn't afford to buy a present for Tata adequate to her social standing. We knew that, come Christmas, a season of extravagant present-giving in Italy, we would be given a gift, and we didn't want to be caught without an adequate present. My mother thought for a long time about what could we give Tata that she didn't already have. My sister was not much help because everything she suggested involved an outlay of money we didn't have. Finally, my mother decided to rely on one of her great talents: her ability to embroider. She bought some white muslin from a man she knew in the market and made Tata a long and frilly nightdress. She then started to embroider a border of little mice around the collar and all along the hem. She had me draw all the mice dancing in different positions, some on their hind legs, some somersaulting on their front feet. It looked like a little bouncing circus, all embroidered in pure white, to show refinement. I still remember my mother, bent every evening over the nightdress, trying to finish the labourious embroidery in time.

My sister and I watched the progress with great interest, offering encouragement and anticipating Tata's surprise when she saw what my mother could do.

Lieta and Tata, who had stopped the craziness about churches at the end of the summer, had now, at the approach of Christmas, renewed their fervour and went around looking at crèches to pick up ideas for Tata's crèche. About two weeks before Christmas, Tata's parents arrived from wherever they had been, with a trunk full of presents for their children.

But, much as I would have liked it, I never got to see what was in that trunk. Out of regard for our own poverty, neither Tata nor her brothers (now home from their boarding school for the holidays) showed us what they had received.

On the day before Christmas Eve my mother washed us more energetically than usual, put new ribbons in our hair, polished our shoes and trimmed our nails. When we looked perfect, my sister was given the parcel with the nightdress, washed and ironed with a little starch to show the embroidery at its best. I was given the mouse Christmas card, which I had been made to draw.

When we arrived at Tata's house, we were surprised to find her parents in the large living room. The lights were all on, sparkling in crystal droplets like stars. Numerous candles were burning, poised on window-sills and mantelpieces, as if for a funeral. The dogs had been given red ribbons, and all the maids, usually in plain black, now had little lace collars around their necks and white cockscombs on their heads. Walking in, we felt a little shy before all that light and the presence of the rest of Tata's family. But Tata's mother made us go near her by coming around and pulling us gently towards her. I was surprised to see that she wore no jewellery except for a wedding ring. Nor was she that well dressed: she wore a cardigan over a woollen dress and plain shoes on her rather large feet. I had always imagined that rich people dressed in a way that would not disappoint the rest of us. I thought that rich people ought to look rich. But she seemed warm and really interested in us, asking us questions about our lives, as if we mattered. The father stood at the window looking outside, showing no interest in any of us.

When we gave Tata our present, we almost held our breath in pride. She opened the package in front of us, inexplicably apologizing, as if she should not have been doing so. When she saw the present, she gave out a little cry, which she immediately muffled by bringing both hands to her mouth. She ran to Lieta and embraced her, and then turned to me and embraced me too. We could tell we had stunned them all. In the great surge of emotion we felt, I forgot to give her the card that I had made and which my mother had so carefully written. I noticed it in my hand when we were halfway home. Lieta wanted to murder me, as usual; she couldn't believe I could be so vulgar.

My mother was waiting, eager to know how the present had been received. We told her that they had almost burst into tears at the sight of such a beautiful present, had thanked us until we were embarrassed and said they could hardly believe that anybody could embroider so beautifully. My mother was positively glowing with pride. For a moment we felt we weren't so poor.

Meanwhile, we were left to speculate on what Tata's gift to Lieta would be. We expected something, but we didn't know how they could top what we had given them. The next day, Christmas Eve, our one room was kept spotlessly clean; my mother didn't even cook, because that would have meant taking the artistic screen that covered the makeshift kitchen away from the corner. Then it could be seen that we didn't even have running water. Only after the expected visit from Tata, would my mother have felt relaxed enough to prepare our Christmas dinner.

It was almost dark when we heard a knock on the door. My mother, all ready with the little liquor glasses and the biscuits, sent me to open the door. But it wasn't Tata. It was one of her maids with a parcel for us. We were so disappointed we didn't know what to say. We asked the maid to sit with us and have a drink but she politely declined and left.

The three of us gathered around the table to open the present. The wrapping was quite astonishing in itself. The paper was the yellow straw kind used to wrap groceries, and holding it together was the type of hemp string we used to tie common parcels. Tied to one end of the string was one of those labels used for the pricing of merchandise. On that label Tata had written a little poem in bright red ink. I don't recall the poem now, but it was something about her love for the two of us, her thanks for my mother, and a little blurb about mice that we didn't find funny. We took the wrapper and the string off, and inside we found a fairly large chunk of everyday, ordinary Parmesan cheese.

We were so stunned that for a few minutes nobody said a word. Even my sister and I knew this was an insult. We both looked at my mother. She could hardly contain her tears. She had worked so hard at making a nice present for Tata, with all those embroidered mice, white on white to show refinement, and all we got was a chunk of cheese. We were poor, true enough, but did it mean that we had to be given food—something one would give to a beggar? We never asked for anything from anybody. We never even expected to be fed when we went to Tata's house. I was told, under pain of death, never to say that I was hungry, and for once I never did. It was important to us that we not be seen as people without pride. But this, this had revealed a contempt for us that we didn't feel we deserved.

I still remember my mother preparing the Christmas dinner with tears running down her nose and falling into the chicken stuffing. For a moment the thought of sending it back crossed her mind, but then she didn't have it in her to be that unkind. The rich don't even notice when they have trespassed onto the poor's territory. As usual, the grating of the cheese became one of my chores; I didn't want to, but I was made to do it anyway.

The holiday came and went and my sister went back to school. According to her, Tata seemed as kind and as open as ever. Nobody mentioned anything. My sister didn't thank her for the so-called present, and Tata didn't ask about it. Lieta found it a little difficult, in the beginning, to go back to Tata's house, but after a while she relented and went back anyway. I also went back and resumed my explorations in her house. The incident seemed to be forgotten.

But not by my mother. My mother's dignity had been hurt. We, the children, could cope with poverty better than she could. My mother's poverty was of a different nature. It had the bitterness of the person who has done everything right; worked hard and been conscientious, parsimonious and self-denying. She taught us and her pupils the rewards of honest labour and strict morality, only to be rewarded with a lack of means as hard to shake and as sticky as some sort of economic leprosy. Dignity should surely have been the reward for so much self-denial. But correct behaviour hadn't been enough and that fact was just killing her. Every time she used the cheese she would make comments about the lack of consideration *those* people had shown.

Sometime near the end of February, I was grating the cheese to sprinkle over our pasta. As I was doing so, something fell from the centre of the cheese to the floor. I picked up the object and saw that whatever it was had broken in two pieces. Putting the pieces together I saw that it was a little mouse with a body of cut crystal, head and tail of silver, and eyes consisting of two little rubies. Even though the crystal body had broken right through the middle, it could still be seen that it was a thing of great beauty.

My sister and I fell silent and gave it to my mother. She held it with both hands as you hold something precious, and then she looked at us. Suddenly, we all understood the little poem on the price tag: it had had something in it about mice liking cheese. And we suddenly understood also that the hunk of cheese was nothing but a wrapper.

We felt even worse than before. We had failed to appreciate a delicacy, a subtle gift of great beauty.

My sister talked to Tata later, and thanked her as was proper. But my mother never quite recovered. Before she had felt insulted, now she felt ashamed. She was always a little distant towards Tata.

Because, like savages, we had eaten the wrapper and thrown away the gift.

The Birthday

I am on my way to Milan. This is the last leg of my trip and I know it will be painful. I have no good memories of Milan. Here the war raged on for years unrestrained, merciless and, ultimately, like all wars, futile. We spent two years here, the worst of my childhood. It was from a sanatorium here that my father was taken to die somewhere in Germany. Here we became squatters, intruding on other people's domains, and looked on by the locals as inferiors coming from an inferior place. Here I saw men killed by firing squads across from my window, as if human life was a matter of no concern to anybody. And here I saw children burned alive in a flaming school. No, that's not right. I didn't see them, I heard them.

I don't really want to go to Milan, but it is part of my

past. I would feel like a coward if I didn't go.

Milan is a busy city with no grace or elegance, its people a harried lot, its dialect incomprehensible, its prejudice towards the south unshakeable. It has the brash arrogance of the nouveau riche. There is, to be sure, a sort of vulgar energy attached to money, but the people from the south huddle in slums around its outskirts like desperate vultures waiting for morsels. The Nigerians are now taking the place of the southerners in a pecking order that leaves them vulnerable and derelict. But in the centre of the city, the famous Galleria and the great fashion shops surrounding it are full of Japanese and Hong Kong tourists trying out little nothings at astronomical prices. The size of the garments are inversely proportional to their cost. Nothing here is made for me. Shoes for the jet set feet are of incredibly small sizes and, as far as clothing, anybody over size 10 is a trespasser.

Never mind, I can't even afford the shoe laces. In fact, I can hardly afford the hotel in which I am staying. It's a tiny enterprise run by a husband, his wife and their three children. What it lacks in breadth it makes up for in height. I have to haul my suitcase up four Italian floors, which in essence are five because of that quaint habit of counting the floors from the second landing. By the time I arrive at my room I feel I am owed a view a little better than the one I have: that of a light-well over the back of a bar. This, of course, means there will be noise at night because bars don't close until well past one o'clock in the morning. But the modest room has a small vase with a real flower in it. A carnation. Every time a streetcar rumbles by, the flower shakes in its vase and so do the window panes, although the noise is muffled by the fact that the room is on the inside. On the wall hangs a painting of a saint, his body pierced by an array of weapons, the least lethal of which is a spear. I dislike all that piercing, but I resist the temptation of turning it towards the wall. The mirror in the bathroom must have been bought from a "seconds" dealer or in an amusement park, because depending on how I move in front of it, either I have a lot of head above my eyebrows or none at all. I can't decide which I prefer.

Milan is usually almost as hot as Florence, but more humid. I can't walk for any length of time without feeling exhausted. I am not yet ready to see the sights of my childhood, so I walk without a purpose towards the Sforza Castle. I pass Piazzale Loreto where my sister and I saw the corpses of Mussolini and his lover hanging upside down, in order that the populace could enjoy the spectacle of justice being done. I remember keeping close to the walls as I passed by because it frightened me to see dead people. My sister was braver, she pulled my hand past the bodies, while holding her other hand by the side of her head so she didn't have to look.

I used to think of Milan as a very large city; in fact we felt quite safe if the bombs fell on a part of the city we didn't know. We used to feel safety in distance. But now, I see that almost everything is within a long walk. I can go to where we lived, Via Giotto right now, and get it over with. Instead, I circle around looking for distractions. A little dark man sells pizza by the roll, literally. He has rolled the pizza and sells it in large sliced spirals. I buy a piece and eat it while I walk. It doesn't taste any better than when it is flat, but, what the hell, why not indulge in a new experience. I keep walking around window shopping—sometimes I go in a store and try on a pair of shoes. But I am starting to be a little tired of only looking at the life of the city unfolding around me. I am beginning to miss some routine activity, nothing more dramatic than just drawing a still life. Travelling has this peripheral quality, which in the long run becomes a bit alienating. I am starting to be tired of encounters, I long for relationships. In other words I am physically and mentally tired. I sit in a little park full of children and pigeons. I read the news from a newspaper left by somebody on one of the benches. When I finish, I fold the newspaper, return it to where I found it and start to walk towards the hotel.

Something has happened while I was reading. The streets are almost empty; there are a few people around but most have disappeared as if by magic. I look at my watch and see that it is only 7:30, definitely too early for Italians to retire; in fact, at about this hour is when they start to come out to talk and socialize until early morning, so I don't see the reason for this emptiness. The pizza man, the mothers with their strollers, and the ice cream vendors have all disappeared. I ask myself if I have gone mad and stepped into one of those De Chirico nightmares of empty perspectives. I can't bear this emptiness, and I walk fast to my hotel with an eerie sense of foreboding. I need to ask somebody what's going on. Once in the hotel I see that even the manager is not there. I could take my room key from the box behind the desk, but I don't want to go to my room without asking somebody if it is me or the rest of Italy that is walking through a mirage.

I go gingerly behind the manager's desk and peek into the back room. There they all are. The manager, his wife, all the maids, and most of the hotel's guests. They are all entranced in front of the television: Italy is playing soccer in America against Ireland.

I breathe more easily. I realize I am not crazy, they are. I join the group at their invitation and accept a soft drink on the house. I may as well. Every goal will bring shouts, so I can forget about sleeping. But I am so tired, I end up retiring to my room before I know the outcome of the match. While I am getting ready for a shower, I hear a deep noise like a distant hurricane rising from the surrounding streets and piazzas. I am tired of surrealistic experiences and hope nothing more than a garden-variety earthquake is approaching. I am surprised the dogs don't howl. But from the bar below comes the shouts of "Goal, goal!" So, the great rumbling must have erupted because we are winning. I go to bed with a feeling of satisfaction, bizarre because I don't understand anything about soccer. I don't really care who has managed to put a silly leather ball into whose net and believe that national pride, silly in itself, should be enlivened by something less trivial than a soccer match.

The next morning I find out we have lost. It serves me right. I shouldn't have had that tiny twinge of silly national pride the night before. To make up for the loss I go to a self-service restaurant on my way to the Sforza Castle and give myself a cappuccino, with a generous sprinkling of cocoa, and a croissant.

The castle is as massive and forbidding as I remember. Its towers are squat and graceless and its entrance significantly monumental. It is a great structure of relentless masculinity with no embellishment that would dilute its metaphor of war. I wonder how a multi-sexual person like Leonardo Da Vinci could have lent his services to people who lived in this upscale military barrack. Even more surprising is the fact that he was hired as a builder of war machinery and organizer of court masked balls, rather than as an artist or a great thinker. It goes with my theory that a great man is always a walking contradiction.

When I enter the vast hall, I am puzzled by the fact that great masked balls were held here, since nothing I see is conducive to amusement or intimacy. The effort to impress is so paramount that the everyday life of the former inhabitants becomes blurred in a great posture of power. In such places I always look for the kitchens; unfortunately, though, the kitchens were never deemed relevant enough to restore. Only the grand, sweeping gesture remains.

I walk through a gallery of titans, portraits of fierce, dominant males. Their suits of armour stand at attention, in long rows, like empty warriors. The whispers of women are nowhere to be heard. Yet I look at the stone seats carved in the thickness of the windows and know that centuries of women polished those seats—embroidering, sewing, nursing babies, listening to the minstrels paid to flatter them. Maybe they were the ones listening to an oddball like Leonardo, a man certainly not suitable for the company of ruffians endlessly preparing for war.

And then, deep in the bowels of the building, there are the prisons. A dungeon is a place of such fear and contempt for human dignity that it must have been enough to look at it to scare people away from crimes. I would prefer death any time to being forgotten in one of those holes.

But, despite this rampant egotism, in the remotest part of the castle, stands one of the most moving and intimate of Michelangelo's sculptures: the Pieta Rondanini. Although I don't think of Michelangelo as a great painter, I find his sculptures truly moving. The magnificence of this work is the reason I am here. It is the other side, the better side of masculinity. The same intensity that waged war and scattered mayhem about the land, is here put to use in a dialogue between an artist, now old but not entirely spent, and his Creator. The reverence and dignity of the work gives almost a voyeuristic feeling to the onlooker, who is witnessing the last mystical surrendering of a dying man. The sculpture is unfinished; it was while creating this sculpture that Michelangelo died, a solitary titan.

A group of French tourists is having a picnic in front of the statue, with pieces of pizza being passed out and jollities being bounced around the echoing, secluded place as if Michelangelo was of no consequence. It must be because the only bench available is in front of the statue. Even so, I am disturbed by the lack of regard for other visitors; so I put some distance between me and the French group. I amble along a walkway circling an internal courtyard, high above a mossy fountain, which gurgles discreetly twenty feet below me. The ivies around the fountain struggle up to the square of sky above, mutated by the deep darkness into vertical cords, until they reach the edge of the roof three floors above me and explode into a cascade of emerald leaves.

I am trying to reach the entrance to the ceramics gallery, which is situated on the floor above the one I am now. Renaissance Italian rooms being the height that they are, I am out of breath by the first landing, so I sit in a niche carved in the thickness of the wall. I sit there in the dark coolness looking both down the stairs I came up and up the stairs I have yet to negotiate to reach the floor above. I notice an official-looking lady at the top of those stairs and hope that it means that I have come the right way. The door above me, though, could very well be an exit. I'll wait here to catch my breath and then go up and ask for directions.

Before I do, a man comes up the stairs with the bouncing step of an athlete. Wearing a sleeveless top and a pair of shorts, he looks tanned and fit. He passes by me without seeing me sitting in my niche and continues his ascent to the door above. When he arrives there I see that the official-looking lady turns him back. I surmise that it must be an exit, but I want to know for sure. So, when the man is beside my niche, I ask him his reason for coming back.

He is a little stunned, not having noticed me in the shadow until I spoke, but he is kind and responsive and, without waiting for an invitation, sits right beside me. The niche is small and I feel quite invaded by his presence. He has smothered his body with a strong aftershave lotion but his armpits are still alive, and I feel that he is too close for me to be at ease. He has a strong aquiline profile, with a thick Pancho Villa moustache and a heroic shock of hair turning grey at the temples. I do not need to ask him what he does: he begins telling me his life story immediately. I am sure I'll know quite a lot about him before we part, whether I want to or not. He is a truck driver for a relief company that brings food and medical supplies to war-torn Yugoslavia. I don't believe him, of course, but I ask him to tell me about it anyway.

Instead he asks me what I do for a living.

"I teach at an art college," I say, feeling immediately classified.

"Well, a professor!" he says and takes my hand and kisses it lovingly with mock respect. I don't like his mocking tone, and even less his grabbing of my hand as if I have no say in it. Now he turns personal.

"Are you married?" he asks as if it had anything to do with anything.

"Yes," I say rather tersely, hoping to discourage him from taking that path.

"How is your husband in bed?" I am starting to feel quite annoyed at the level of intimacy he is assuming and at this sophomoric conversation.

"Horizontal," I reply, congratulating myself on my devastating wit. He looks at me slyly.

"Nothing vertical about him?" I ignore the lewdness of his remark, but secretly I admire the quickness of his response. Maybe he really does drive trucks to Yugoslavia. He is also not totally insensitive because he suddenly realizes that he has trespassed and goes on to lighter subjects, like the scatter of bodies he has seen in the streets of Sarajevo. Every time he needs to underline something, he pokes me gently in the ribs with his elbow. I make myself as little as I can but the space is small and becoming smaller by the minute.

But he has not lost hope: he says, "Do you think I am married?" Since we are into non sequiturs, I say, "How about seeing the rest of the castle?" He jumps to his feet.

"Sure, let's go."

"No thanks," I say, "I'll stay right here."

"But we have been here for half an hour," he says, as if we were already into a relationship and he was entitled to make reasonable demands.

"And that's where I want to be for another half-hour," I say.

He stands in front of me now, his feet apart, his hands in the pocket of his shorts.

"Do you know, Professor, what's wrong with you clever women?" I can hardly wait. "You are not very sexy." I feel a little piqued, so I answer.

"Is the reverse true?" He looks at me blankly, so I add. "Does it mean that if you are sexy you must be a bit dense?"

"What do you mean?" he asks.

"I mean you are really sexy," I say, feeling triumphant. I smile sweetly and say, "Ciao."

He doesn't even bother to answer, but turns and goes down the stairs without looking back.

He has managed to upset me, but not because he was mildly offensive and more than a little pushy. This is something I can easily dismiss. The reason is that deep inside I felt guilty for not being beautiful and young, the fulfilment of his fantasies. Something in me imagines that in the shadow of the niche he had miscalculated my age and that in the light of day he probably would have had to make an excuse in order to go away without being rude. Also, part of me knows that this might very well be not the case and it is my old painful obsessive shyness, my own physical insecurity, coming to the fore again. I thought that after so many years I had shaken that oppressive feeling of not being able to come up to expectations, as if I owed men beauty and youth, as if my own demands of them didn't matter.

And why would it still be so important that I not disappoint someone like this truck driver, whom I do not know, who was looking for a quick sexual fix on his way to Yugoslavia or wherever he was going? I feel vulnerable and stupid, I want to shake this dependency on the opinion of others, this feeling slightly guilty for not being enough of what I think I ought to be. I thought that by leaving Italy I would leave some of the old me behind, that I would create a new me out of the ashes of the old one. To a certain extent I did that. But now that I am here, in the old language and the old culture I find that this painfully insecure person still exists inside. I had been so sure she had died thirty years ago. I am mad at myself because I have just found out that I didn't really leave. I have been sitting in this dark niche for the past thirty years. I was a fish out of water then, and I am a fish out of water now, even though I don't live here anymore. Now I am a fish out of both waters.

"Damned men," I say to myself, "they are nothing but a waste of moisture." I find this funny. I think I should send it to a comedian who could use it. I walk in the warm sun for a while, looking left and right to make sure I don't meet the truck driver again. After a bit of walking in the smell of the jasmine climbing up the walls of the castle, I realize that it's me who could use the funny line. I can use a bit of a sense of humour about myself, lest the old wounds start to fester again.

I have walked nonstop since nine in the morning and it's five in the afternoon now. I go to the only place where I feel at ease having a meal by myself: the restaurant of a large department store. The restaurant is almost totally empty, nobody eats anything at this hour in Italy. The decor is soberly comfortable and I am a little intimidated, I don't feel particularly in tune with the designer's dream of glass and pale polished wood. One side of the restaurant is sloping glass with a stunning view of the gothic pinnacles of Milan's cathedral against a curtain of blue sky. The restaurant is a place of utter elegance and understated poise. I ask the waiter if it is possible to have something to eat, readying myself to leave if it is not possible, but he gives me the menu and asks me to order.

At first I think of having something upper class, like a tea and a few nibbles. But I am hot, tired and ravenously hungry, so I order the "special." I have by now sunk into a chair, which is as deep as a bathtub. As I sit, I soak up the coolness and the view, pitying smugly the poor pedestrians in the piazza below battling the heat and the traffic. I savour a moment of pure sensuality in anticipation of the meal to come. I expect the usual long wait for the meal I have ordered, but this time the waiter appears with my order surprisingly quickly. In silent dignity he places the dish in front of me and unfolds the damask napkin on my knees. I feel very aristocratic and let him pour the *acqua minerale* into my glass before I start the serious business of eating.

For the first time since arriving in Italy I have in front of me a meal so badly cooked I can hardly eat it. The pasta has obviously been cooked the day before and is so dry I can hardly stick a fork into it; when I chew on it, it crunches with the abandon of a pretzel. Next to it, all on the same plate, is a little green scoop of what I take to be mashed peas, slightly greener and curlier at the edges than in the centre. And then, all by itself—no other pieces accompany it—a chicken leg, the bone of which has turned an ominous black. It might have all been quite good in its heyday but now it is definitely a left-over left-over. The waiter has disappeared and I am so intimidated by the ambience that I nibble at the meal, thinking that as soon as the waiter shows up I'll send the order back. But before I know it, I have finished the meal, the *acqua minerale* and a piece of bread.

When the waiter finally appears, I have no choice but to ask for the bill. I hope for a lucky strike of moderation. No such luck. The bill is so steep I become enraged. I will pay, but, for a change, I am determined to let them know what I think of the meal. I go to the cashier, pay the bill and then, almost inaudibly, tell him that he should let the cook know that the meal was almost inedible. The cashier is as polite as I am and says that he will do so. While I am talking to the cashier, an older man approaches us and asks me what seems to be the matter. I repeat the same subdued complaint to him. He asks me to follow him and navigates me through a closed door into the kitchen. Here is a sparkling stainless steel space station of a kitchen that is totally empty. The man closes the door carefully, then turns to me and explodes into such a rage that he becomes scarlet, his eyes sticking out frog-like, the veins in his neck a map of his blood circulation. He accuses me of being a liar, a demented hysterical woman with nothing to do but go around creating trouble and trying not to pay my bills. I obviously do not deserve to eat in an establishment such as his, since I do not understand good food when I am given it. I am so stunned I cannot find the words to defend myself, and even if I could I wouldn't be able to make myself heard above his shouting.

I feel enveloped in a white impotent rage at being treated like vermin, when both he and I know that the meal must have been cooked at least a couple of days ago and was waiting for a sucker like me to eat it and shut up. To my horror I feel the sting of tears in my eyes, so I turn my back at him and leave. I hear his voice still screaming at me while I descend the stairs. I never managed to tell him that I had already paid the bill.

Outside I walk fast, pushed along by adrenaline. I enter the cathedral and, sitting down in one of the pews, I let my breathing subside to normal while the lights from the candles slowly come into focus. A function of some kind is taking place. The organ is enriching the senses with a cascade of coloured notes and a choir of children in white robes sing an earthly angels' cantata. The immense church absorbs the organ's music, the voices of the children and my feeling of helplessness, like a calming sponge. I slowly start to look around the beautiful structure and feel composed and assuaged. I go where the candles are burning and take one to light. I do it automatically, expecting no thanks from any gods.

I have a story about candles. I stole some once from a church, here in Milan.

It had turned cold overnight, and very still. The few trees that had survived the bonfires the people had made to keep themselves warm did not even shiver. It felt like the calm before an earthquake or an eclipse, or my mother's wrath.

Tomorrow, Christmas Eve, would be my eighth birthday, and my mother had promised me a present. Not the usual pair of shoes, which I needed anyway, or an embroidered something. She had said it would be a real present.

Not that she always kept her promises. Last year she promised to take me to the zoo, the day before my birthday, to see a new baby giraffe named Greta Garbo on account of her long eyelashes. But then a bomb killed a tiger and sent Annibale, the elephant, charging in a panic all over Milan. Nobody knew how to stop an elephant, particularly a hysterical one. The biggest animals around where those wine horses used to haul cartfuls of wine caskets. Not that we still had any of those running around; the few that hadn't been taken by the retreating Germans had been eaten long ago. So, an elephant rampaging along the streets was a problem. However Annibale, had had the good sense to solve the problem by getting himself electrocuted. Having touched the streetcar wires with his trunk, he had fallen in a great heap in the middle of Piazza Stracca.

It must have been quite a sight, the elephant in a dead heap while all around people were trying to carve it to take a piece home to eat. The butchers had appeared, all in white aprons with knives and sharpeners, and carved it on the spot.

When we heard about it, my mother and I headed for the Piazza with me running by her side holding the string bag and the food coupons. When we arrived, my mother quickly covered my eyes with her hand, for I would likely faint at the sight of so much blood.

I managed, though, to have a quick look, but by then the elephant didn't look like Annibale anymore; just a great rib cage and an obscene piece of meat. People were running away with chunks of it. We hadn't seen so much meat since the beginning of the war. Some were laughing and saying, "Come and have some elephant tetrazzini!" But my mother wasn't able to get any. We were too late.

Although it had all been exciting, and even a little scary, I still felt I was owed my present. But no matter

how much I pleaded with my mother, she remained adamant.

"Public places in times of war are too dangerous."

She had spoken, and that was that. I did not talk to
her again until Christmas Eve when she presented me
with a couple of handkerchiefs with my initial embroidered on the sides. Just what I always wanted.

Well, this year she could not renege on her promise
because the present was already in my bedroom, leaning
against the wall. A small bicycle, which she had rented for
seven hours. It was just the right size for me, and had a
bell on the handle, a pump attached to the main shaft, a
little purse under the seat for the house keys and a red
net over the back wheel to stop one's skirt from getting
caught in the spikes.

It smelled of rubber.

My mother had had quite an argument with the
bicycle man. He didn't want her to take the bicycle the
night before unless she was willing to pay for at least half
the night. My mother was definitely not willing. She
accused him of being insensitive to the danger a bicycle
represented for a young child who, without the extra time
needed to practise, could easily have an accident. I knew
how to ride a small bicycle, though shakily for lack of
practice, but my mother had become accustomed to
pulling all the righteous strings, the safety of children
being one of the most effective. And, anyway, to whom
did he think he would rent the bicycle during the night?
She won, as usual, and as I carefully pedalled home
hoping for somebody I knew to come by and see me, she
held onto the back of the seat.

The morning after, my mother left at dawn to go to
work. At eight, my sister Lieta left in a hurry as usual, to
meet some friends.

I was left alone with my bicycle. I got dressed, gulped

my *caffe latte* and put my tent on. I could see that the tent would be a problem. My mother had made two cloaks, one for Lieta and one for me out of two blankets she had been given by the Ladies of Mercy, on our arrival from Florence. I hated the cloak and still referred to it as the tent. My mother had embroidered two little yellow ducks on each side of the collar to make it look more like a cloak and had stitched around the two small slits for my hands in the same colours. I liked the slits. I fantasized that people thought I was without hands. When I felt they had almost made up their mind that I was handicapped, I surprised them by producing my hands out of the slits. My life was not without pleasures.

I had to admit that the cloak didn't look like a blanket anymore, but I still didn't like it much. The problem today was the slits were too small to allow my arms to go through and reach the handlebars. So I opened the tent in the front and fixed the sides of the opening to my arms with elastic bands. This made me look like a bat, but I had no choice. I knew I was going to be cold because this arrangement left the front of my body completely uncovered.

So, I decided to steal our neighbour's newspaper. I put a couple of the printed sheets between my vest and my dress. My mother had taught me to do that; she maintained that it gave the body shelter against the wind. The first time I did it, I put the newspaper right next to my skin. When I undressed, I found that I had "Murder in Padua" printed in reverse across my chest, with the picture of the murderer just above my navel. My sister just about killed herself laughing. She suggested that next time I put the front page on my back so that I could have the picture of Mussolini coming out of my arse. Lieta could be so crude at times. She got away with it because she was four years older.

I pumped up the tires a little and checked the brakes, as I had seen my friend Ovidio do, and hauled the bicycle on my shoulder down the five floors to the entrance hall. Then I put it down and opened the heavy bronze door.

A great whiteness almost blinded me.

A blanket of snow at least half a metre thick covered the curb, the trees, the statue of Anita, the wife of Garibaldi dying in the pinewood of Ravenna, with the bronze pines looking like cauliflowers.

I didn't know whether to laugh or cry. I had seen snow before, but never in such quantity. It had snowed back in Florence, but it was never more than a dusting that melted as soon as it touched the ground. But here in Milan it sometimes snowed quite heavily, and this time it broke all records.

I tried to ride the bicycle, but I slithered all over the curb and couldn't keep my balance. It wasn't until I gave up climbing back on the bicycle and stopped to think what to do next, that I noticed the silence. It was as if the city had stopped breathing. The snow covered the half-destroyed houses, the mounds of debris, and the bomb craters. The blackened, naked trees looked as if they had bloomed overnight, and the wires had puffed up until they looked like white cords. The shapes of the buildings and some of the biggest bomb craters could still be seen, only they looked a bit erased.

People walked carefully, minding their steps, laughing and shrieking, and generally behaving as if they were my age. When I looked at the sky, I saw a greyness out of which little cold feathers came to touch my lips or got trapped in my eyelashes.

I was impatient to join the playing in the snow, but first I had to get rid of the bicycle. I thought of taking it back to the apartment, but in the excitement I had forgotten the keys inside. I decided to take it back to the bicycle man. While I was walking holding it by the handle, I thought that maybe I could ask for a refund. It seemed quite logical since I had not been able to use it at all. The more logical it seemed, the more I knew the man would never give me the money back. He had been awful to my mother. He would laugh at me. "Money back?" he would ask. And to whom did I think he could rent the bicycle in that snow?

I was so convinced that he wouldn't give me the money that by the time I arrived at the store, I was already crying. He was bewildered and looked at me as if he didn't know who I was. I sobbed my request for a refund and without a word he went to a little drawer beside the counter and gave me back my money. I was so surprised that I went on crying for a while longer not knowing how to stop. Then I walked quickly out of the store before he had time to change his mind.

Now, here I was, with money and time and snow all around me. The thought of giving back the money to my mother never entered my mind. She would never find out. For the first time in my life, I had money to spend any way I wanted. I felt dizzy with choices. I could have my hair cut shorter, wear ribbons at the sides of my head and have a little fringe over my forehead down to my eyebrows. But my mother would ask me where I had got the money for that. And I would have to explain. Besides, she refused to have my hair cut. "No need for it," she would explain.

What about a dog? A little whippet like the one Ovidio had. A female who would produce little puppies all pink and blind with little voices. She would roll over for me and show me a row of buttons like the ones on the municipal guard's uniform, only pink. I would call her Gorgonzola and she would bite my mother and my sister if they as much as touched me. I could tell my mother that I had found her in a bombed house, shivering and dying of starvation. Even my mother would relent after a while. But where could I find a whippet in bombed-out Milan, a few days before Christmas?

I was still embroidering about the dog when I saw the cake. Small, with coloured layers and sugar icing all along the top edge. It stood all alone in the middle of the baker's window, displayed on a raised crystal tray covered by a frilly paper doily.

I stood in front of it for only a few seconds. If I had enough money, I would buy it. I entered the bakery with a certain amount of trepidation. After all, I was doing something quite unusual and forbidden. The lady in the shop looked at me blankly as if buying a cake were an every-day thing. I asked her how much the cake cost. I showed all my money, I was a few lire short. But the lady must have been in a compassionate mood because she sold it to me anyway.

"But without the box," she said. She handed it to me on a little piece of cardboard that she tore out of a packing box. I took the elastic bands off my wrists, held out both hands to hold the cake and let my tent fall around me like a parachute. I walked away gingerly, careful not to let the tent touch my cake.

I knew where to go. It had been a rich person's house at one time, but a bomb had left it charred and gutted, the upper-store rooms were left open in mid-air, looking as if they had been cut in half by a giant knife, with the crystal chandeliers tingling in the breeze. The kitchen still had all its pots on the stove ready for the family meal. Except, of course, there was no family. Everybody had died except the dog. After the bodies had been removed, the animal hung around for days, crying out his loneliness, and then disappeared. But the garden had been left almost untouched except for some scattered debris. The magnolias were singed to death but the wisteria looked as if it would probably flower again in the spring. A small fountain was silent, but a stone boy clutching a dolphin remained. Apart from me, nobody went near the place, not even Lieta. It was considered spooky because of all those exposed echoes of its former life. It was a bit like a cemetery. But I liked the place and went there often precisely because nobody else did. I felt it belonged to me. I would go there, sit inside the fountain and eat my cake.

I was walking along, careful to avoid the people coming towards me, lest they bump into my outstretched arms bearing the cake, when I saw the church. Actually, I smelled it even before I saw it: incense, candle wax and the musty odour of holy things. I knew the church well. When my mother came home at night and found my sister and me still alive after a bombing, she used to take us to the little church to light candles.

"Two candles," she used to say, "for two miracles. The lives of my children."

From the open portal, I saw the candles shimmering in the gloom.

I was quite happy with my cake, but the candles would have made it perfect. Not that we ever used candles for our birthdays. This was a peculiar foreign habit. But my friend Ovidio had had candles on his cake when he turned ten, and I thought it would be a nice touch to have candles for my birthday.

I had no intention of stealing them, I would just borrow them for a while and then take them back. I went inside. It was dark and deserted as usual, except for the permanent group of widows in the front row. The candles were in the back, at the side altar to the Virgin Mary, so nobody would see me. I put the cake carefully on the steps in front of the altar, looked around to make sure no one was looking, took eight candles and held them under my arms, while holding the cake with my hands. Although I had not been seen, I was perspiring so much that, by the time I reached the door, the newspaper inside my vest was starting to get soaked. When I arrived at my secret place the circulation in my arms had almost stopped.

My secret place was as I expected it to be. Solitary, silent, its snow untouched. I stepped over the rim of the fountain, flattened the snow in the middle with my feet, let the candles fall by opening my arms slightly and placed the cake carefully on the flattened snow. I took the candles and put them on the cake. They were large candles, but I kept them from toppling by sticking them all the way down to the bottom of the cake.

Now I had to light the candles, but I had no matches. For a few moments I was torn between eating the cake without lighting the candles and leaving the cake un-guarded to go into the street to ask somebody for a match. To leave the cake was dangerous, for there were pigeons and cats prowling around. But I decided to make a very quick attempt. I put my tent over the candles and the cake and rushed in the street. People looked at me, without a coat in the snow and must have thought I was begging for money, so nobody stopped. Finally, a man with a ciga-rette in his mouth stopped to light it and heard me asking for a match. He gave me one. I waited for him to disap-pear around the corner, because I didn't want to run the risk of his following me, discovering my secret place, and eating my cake. Then I ran to the fountain and took the tent off the candles and the cake. I was finally ready to light the candles. But then I realized there was nowhere to strike the match; everything was wet, even the under-side of the dolphin. I took one of the candles, went into the house, lit the match and then the candle, covered myself and the lit candle with the tent and walked backwards to the fountain, almost stepping on the cake. At last, I lit all the candles and sat on the folded tent, in front of the cake.

All around me the snow became orange and glittering. The heat from the candles melted the snow on the stone boy, making the statue drip as if the water had come back. There was no wind, and the snow flakes made little frying noises as they touched the flames.

It was the most beautiful thing I had ever seen.

I had no knife to cut the cake, so I took out one candle at a time, licked the cake off the base of each candle, ate the rest of the cake with my hands and stuck the candles one by one in the snow around me. In between mouthfuls of cake, I scooped up handfuls of snow and let them dissolve in my mouth. It tickled cold all the way down to my stomach.

So many happinesses in one day.

When I had finished eating the cake, I sat for a while among the lit candles before I blew them out, slowly, one by one. Then I picked up the doily on which the cake had been, to keep as a souvenir, hid all the candles under my tent and went back to the church. I put the candles back in front of the altar, turned to the Virgin Mary, crossed myself and left.

At home, I found my sister mad at me for not being around to help her build a snowman in front of the monument to Anita Garibaldi. I didn't say anything. I sat there like a python with my cake in my stomach, secretly happy.

When my mother came home, she asked me if I had been able to use my bicycle in the snow.

"No," I said. "I took the bicycle back to the rental shop and asked for a refund, but the man wouldn't give it to me. He was horrible; he even threw a candle at me."

"A candle?" asked my mother.

"Yes, a candle. He probably stole it," I said, "from a church."

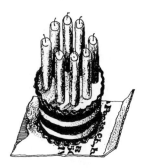

Via Giotto

I am in Via Giotto, the street we lived on during the war. Nothing reminds me of the place I knew. Gone is the large expanse of vacant lots in front of our windows. It was an abandoned and sinister area of weeds and dunes. There was only a short wall of bricks in the middle of nowhere. It was used, sometimes by the fascists, sometimes by the partisans, as an execution area. They used to bring the condemned on a truck, or in a car, put him against the wall, blindfold him and, at the harsh command of one of the soldiers, shoot him. I remember the person executed falling as if crumbling from the inside, the life gone out of him before he touched the ground. There was a Franciscan friar who would witness the operation from the side and run to bless the body before it got cold. I used to watch this two or three times a week, and at night I got convulsions and was unable to go anywhere without being accompanied.

The vacant lots are now covered with luxury high-rise apartment buildings. If it wasn't for the monument to Anita Garibaldi, I wouldn't know this was the area where we lived. I enter some of the buildings trying to find the one where I spent two years of my life, but I can't recognize the one I am looking for. I look up at the windows trying to remember which one was ours, but I see nothing but closed Venetian blinds. Looking up, I remember one bitterly cold winter morning, when I looked out one of those windows, down at two boys—they must have been no more than fourteen years old—who were trying to exchange their shoes for some civilian clothes. They were dressed in fascist uniforms and were afraid of being killed by the partisans who were starting to come into the city more openly now that the American army was nearby. They looked up at all of us at the windows, pointing at the good quality of their shoes, desperate for help. The fact was that nobody had any male civilian clothes, or if we had they had been swapped for food long ago, since the men were all away, busy losing a war somewhere else. Finally somebody threw down a bedsheet. One of the boys tore it in half, and both took off their uniforms in front of our eyes. They were not wearing underwear, so they smiled up at us, a bit shyly—their penises, purple with cold, eliciting a maternal rather than a sexual reaction. They draped the half-sheets around themselves, left their shoes by the monument for us to pick up and disappeared at the end of the street, looking like impersonators of ancient Romans. All day long, nobody picked up the shoes, but by morning, they were gone.

And this is where we lived when we received the news that my father had been taken by the Germans to an undisclosed location in Germany. When my mother went to the sanatorium, with the little pot of prepared food that he demanded, she found his bedding rolled up and the window open, for a change of air. She asked where he was and was told that some soldiers had come and taken him away. She went to anybody who would listen to her to find out where my father had been taken. Nobody knew.

Slowly, some news started to percolate down, but it was always so vague we hardly knew what to make of it. Some said that the Germans had taken him to Mauthausen, but the name had no meaning for us, we didn't know what it was or where. Some people who lived through the deportation to German Camps said that he had been seen in one of those wagons heading north, past the Brenner Pass. Some said he had been shot while trying to escape.

For years I have tried to imagine the death of my father. Unlike the rest of us, he had never feared the Germans, and in fact, he still considered himself one of them. To him, the war was nothing but a sorry accident of history. Besides, it was us crazy Italians, who, realizing halfway through the war that we were going to lose, had turned coats and gone with the Americans. The Germans were too honourable to do something like that. And he always maintained that he could speak a better German than that of those uneducated foot soldiers from Bavaria. He believed that his superior education would save his life. He never wanted to believe that the Germans—those disciplined, correct and accurate people—would behave inhumanly. My father despised the Italians so much that he must have been happy to see German soldiers coming to the sanatorium. He must have thought that he would be able to talk to people he understood better, people who would appreciate his sense of duty and his profes-sionalism as an engineer. He might even have thought that he was going to his beloved Rhineland. But then, I might be wrong. I really didn't know him.

He never came back. He was thirty-seven years old.

What I remember with a pang of clarity about my life in Via Giotto is the hunger. We had a bowl of boiled rice in the morning. By three in the afternoon I would pass out. It seems that I couldn't go for so long without eating. At night we had more boiled rice and some beans, sometimes an orange. A good day was when we had a few eggs. It wasn't as if the food did not exist—partly it had been hoarded—the problem was the difficulty in transporting it to the city. Anything that moved, like a cart or a truck, was machine-gunned from the air. So, big cities like Milan or Turin remained virtually without food. Once we tried to eat a cat. I think we had eaten cats before, sold as rabbits, but they were already dead. The problem had been the killing of the cat. It took all of my mother's strength to smother the beast. My mother cooked it, but in the end we couldn't eat it. The reason might have been that it had had a name.

When I read what I write, it sounds as if our life consisted of nothing but misery. Amazingly, it was not so. Even in the midst of so much death and deprivation, there were small areas of untouched and untouchable happiness. It certainly wasn't an everyday thing, but then happiness never is. Sometimes Lieta and I took things into our own hands, and life felt pretty good.

Like the time I wrote a poem and my sister Lieta got it into her head that I was a genius and deserved to be known. She wrapped me up well against the cold and took me door to door for the purpose of letting the world know about me. When people opened the door, she would give her name very politely, and then recite her little spiel.

"This is my little sister, she is only eight years old and she is already a genius. This is a poem that she has written." Then she stepped aside and pushed me forward, and I would read the poem. On the surface I was very shy, but inside I felt such an immense pride I almost peed.

I have no idea what the world thought of my poem, but sometime people gave us something. One day we brought home three eggs. It became a little industry; I wrote poems and people gave us some food. Sometimes, very rarely, somebody slammed their door in our faces and I would cry a little. But my sister told me that geniuses were always misunderstood, and that that would be my lot in life, and off we would go to the next door. I don't have any of the poems.

Suddenly, I don't want to be here. The place is indifferent and anonymous, people are going about their business in a purposeful manner, and the buildings are alien, impersonal and banal. Nothing here speaks of what has been; the balloon vendor over there could well be sitting where the young soldiers died. Time has covered all that futile pain. But why shouldn't the balloon vendor sit on the bones of young soldiers? Even I don't really want to remember all that pain. Pain doesn't make people stronger, the result of pain is hurt. I am almost ready to close the book on my past. It's time for me to move on.

Tomorrow my husband is arriving from Canada. Tonight is the last night I have to myself. I have already changed rooms from a single to a double, and plan to look around for a little gift to welcome him. I find absolutely nothing I can afford. This city is expensive and arrogant in its luxury. I decide to take Adrian to the city of Bergamo instead. A better idea, I think, than buying him something he doesn't need. Meanwhile, while I am still alone and can walk anywhere I want, I feel the need to see the wealthy part of Milan, where the moneyed live for a tiny part of the year. When you are that rich you live in a city only when you must; the rest of the time you spend in villas on the Lombardy lakes or in Switzerland, which is a mere hour away. I take a yellow streetcar to an area of grand boulevards, with immense trees guarding apartment buildings that manage to appear both monumental and introverted. There are uniformed guards at the doors and minions taking care of the cars when they pull up at the entrance. I am aware of looking definitely like I don't belong, the looks the doorman darts at me are a mixture of superciliousness and commiseration. Sometimes I'm looked at almost conspiratorially. I am glad I have my camera around my neck, which puts me in the category of tourist gone astray, not exactly one of them but at least not one of the undesirables. I sit on a comfortable bench under a plane tree and think of my beautiful house in Canada. I survey with smug satisfaction the long road that brought me to where I am now. I was the weakest, the most vulnerable, the youngest in my family. I am the only survivor. One after the other they all died. The latest was Lieta who lost her life when the car she was driving went out of control and slammed into a tree. She was forty-two years old.

I am able to sit here under this plane tree, for no other reason than a bit of stray luck, looking at the Ferraris of the wealthy, who seemed so remote once. I remember how I looked at rich people when I was a child, when they looked as if they belonged to another species; they had things my family could never aspire to have in the course of a life time. I wonder if I will ever learn to buy something without looking at the price. I am certainly not wealthy but I am comfortable. But never comfortable enough. I have been on the other side of the tracks too long.

The following day, I go to the Malpensa Airport and wait for my husband to arrive. A stream of travellers, their eyes searching the waiting crowd, passes by me, while I scan the unknown faces one by one. Suddenly, I see Adrian among the crowd. He is as always shy and gentle, and I am elated by his presence. I feel an irrepressible urge to cry. I try to stop myself, because I feel a little embarrassed about it; I hardly ever cry, but the tears keep swelling up in my eyes. I realize then how hard and difficult this journey has been for me. I thought I would look at my past as one looks at a movie, some funny bits, some painful, but with an awareness that it's all water under the bridge. I know now that it's not that simple. I look for a place to hide my emotions. I hate to look sentimental, but I know I will have to explore what I'm feeling some time later, in safer surroundings. Right now we are on our way back to Milan and then from there we will go to Bergamo.

I ask for news about Canada and I feel as if I have been away for years; the events here and the memories have transported me to a place where I hadn't been before, a place I don't even know the name of. Perhaps, like the hotel in Bologna, it has no name and it should remain so. I am afraid that if I name it, it might lose its inchoate emotional essence.

I am quite happy to travel with Adrian, to see the sights and eat at leisure in restaurants that no longer intimidate me, now that I am no longer alone. But I also know that my journey is over. Being with my two companions was a way of reacquainting myself in an oblique, often stressful way with the country where I spent the first twenty-seven years of my life. But being with Adrian is like being in a closed emotional ecology that excludes raw experiences, which can only be had when one is alone. Yes, for all intents and purposes my journey is over.

We drive to the upper part of Bergamo. The city is on a steep hill; the road with brilliant green sides is large and turning gently, like a slow dance. At the city walls we must leave the car since the small medieval street can hardly accommodate large groups of people, let alone a car. We find a hotel for the night that is so rambling we get lost twice. Once settled, we wander around that tiny and almost perfect jewel of a city. It still amazes me how citified these little towns are. In casual company, are the municipal palace, the civic museum, and the oversized cathedral. There is always a focal point where everyone meets. Evident also is an awareness of local history and a sense of civic pride.

All the roads converge in the main piazza where the cathedral is. We enter the church. In it a full orchestra is playing Vivaldi, Bach and Haydn, while a crucifix looks on, somewhat marginalized in his own house. Bergamo is too small a city to be able to afford a concert hall, so the main church fulfils the function. I sit in one of the pews and wonder if the spectators will applaud when the music is over. After all, this is a church. But they do. They applaud with abandon and even shout for an encore. I am thrilled by this mixture of the Sacred and the Artistic. I am told that sometimes lectures on secular topics are also given in this cathedral. Well, why not? The acoustics are perfect, and the interior is serene and solemn, with a slant of coloured light coming in from a stained-glass window. I am pleased by this intellectual promiscuity.

We drive along the lakes, first Maggiore, then Como, and finally Garda, the largest of the three. The traffic on our drive to the lake is intense, as it is everywhere in Italy, and I am a nervous passenger. After a long drive, Adrian tires of being behind a truck on a two-way road and drives onto a side road that climbs up the Alps. The road is so steep it doubles up on itself, through ravines so profound and secret, that when the car enters into these blue shadows it feels like we are entering a momentary winter. We keep going, driving with great care because the road is narrow and winding, the view alternating between that of the lake and that of the approaching mountains. When the road becomes horizontal again, we know we have arrived. But after a road that cannot have been easy to wrestle from the side of the mountain, we are surprised to see no village at the top. The hamlets are sprinkled all over the high plateau in miniature clusters, separated by alpine meadows and shallow valleys.

Tired of driving and, since it's almost evening, we try our luck at a little restaurant almost tucked away by the side of the road in the hope that, as is customary in villages, they also have a few rooms to let for the night. We are lucky. After a bit of negotiations we are ushered into a super-clean room embellished with photographs of the owner's family. We almost feel we are among relatives. I ask the lady at the counter where we are. It seems we have arrived in Tremosine, an area that includes seventeen villages. I have never heard of it and can't think why. It has certainly been discovered by the Germans, though: all the signs indicating the bathroom location and how to use the electric water heater are in both Italian and German.

From inside the room I open a door and step out onto a triangular balcony suspended above infinity. A thousand feet below me is Lake Garda and all around me as far as I can see are curtains of mountains in ever paler shades of indigo. The sun still touches the mountaintops on one side while the moon rises from a crag in the Alps on the other. Adrian has gone for a walk and I sit for while in front of this bravura performance of nature outside my bedroom door. I feel as if I have wings above this azure void. I want to shut off all thought, to let the silent iridescence of the moment make its way into me.

But I am not trained in silence. I have come here to find the new and the past, and both have crowded my mind with impressions, stories, images—an overall noise that I can't silence. Going back is almost always finding a stranger, a person that I no longer am, and a country that doesn't exist, and maybe never did. Most of our lives, particularly when we are young, we live in mirrors, looking at others looking at us. Growing up is to turn the mirrors to the wall and start to look around. It's astonishing what one can see then. But I wanted to give a last look in the mirror. I am surprised by how Italian I still am, and I am equally surprised at how much of a foreigner I have become.

Tonight, on this ledge above the void, I am happy, and now I think I always was. I think I was born with a talent for happiness, the way others are born with an artistic talent. I don't feel I want to change anything. No regrets, no guilt.

Or maybe only one.

My high school final exam marks were the best I had ever received. In fact, I think I was the best in the class. With my mother dying, I had very little time to prepare myself for these exams, but I had found it in me, not in spite of, but because of her illness, to apply myself enough to come out a winner. It had been a sort of gift to her. Not that I was conscious of it; if somebody had suggested it, I would have vehemently denied it. The announcement that she had terminal cancer had been too sudden, too unexpected for me to have called an armistice via a set of brilliantly executed exams. I liked to think that I was still at war with my mother; the thought that she had already been defeated was maybe too painful for me to contemplate. I was more comfortable with the habit of war.

When I came home with the results and rang the bell from the ground floor, my sister Lieta asked me from the landing above how had I done. I yelled back my results and then took my bicycle over my shoulder and stomped up the stairs to the fifth floor. By the time I walked into my mother's room, my sister had already told her, thus taking away some of my glory. My mother asked me to come to her so that she could kiss me.

I refused. It was perhaps too little, too late. Except for when I was very young, my mother and I had been fighting a long, sustained battle that had embittered both of us. I was relentlessly punished, she was relentlessly disappointed. It's not that I wanted to be cruel in refusing to kiss her, I just didn't know how to deal with this unexpected new thing: approval. So, to cover my embarrassment, I had to look as if I was mad about something. I am sure I found some cause for it, but now I don't remember what it was. Later that evening, when the time came to say goodnight I became afraid she would become sentimental on me again, so I went on looking mad and went to bed without talking.

The next day she slipped into a coma, and after few days she was dead.

I don't want to sound too emotional now. I am shy about feelings.

Even in this little Paradise above the lake, after so many years, I don't have an unbearable urge for a great opera-like scene of reconciliation between me and my mother. I came here to visit, not to cry. Neither is there any use in wishing that I had behaved in a more acceptable manner. One is who one is, my lot was to rebel.

I just wish that, that last time, I had said good night.

🍏

About the Author

Giovanna Peel was born in Florence, Italy, where she graduated from the Academia di Belle Arti. Immigrating to Canada in the 1960's she attended the School of Architecture, Faculty of Environmental Design in Winnipeg, Manitoba. She is an award winning designer, an artist of considerable talent, and has been a popular lecturer at the Ontario College of Art and Design for fifteen years. From 1972 her articles and poetry have been published in English and Italian. Starting with Tuscany is her first full length book. She travels regularly to Italy, and lives in Toronto with her husband and son.